Understanding Poetry

EEG-06

For

Bachelor of Arts [BA]

By

Pratibha Thakur

MA (English)

Useful For

IGNOU, KSOU (Karnataka), Bihar University (Muzaffarpur), Nalanda University, Jamia Millia Islamia, Vardhman Mahaveer Open University (Kota), Uttarakhand Open University, Kurukshetra University, Seva Sadan's College of Education (Maharashtra), Lalit Narayan Mithila University, Andhra University, Pt. Sunderlal Sharma (Open) University (Bilaspur), Annamalai University, Bangalore University, Bharathiar University, Bharathidasan University, HP University, Centre for distance and open learning, Kakatiya University (Andhra Pradesh), KOU (Rajasthan), MPBOU (MP), MDU (Haryana), Punjab University, Tamilnadu Open University, Sri Padmavati Mahila Visvavidyalayam (Andhra Pradesh), Sri Venkateswara University (Andhra Pradesh), UCSDE (Kerala), University of Jammu, YCMOU, Rajasthan University, UPRTOU, Kalyani University, Banaras Hindu University (BHU) and all other Indian Universities.

Closer to Nature  We use Recycled Paper

GULLYBABA PUBLISHING HOUSE PVT. LTD.

ISO 9001 & ISO 14001 CERTIFIED CO.

Published by:

GullyBaba Publishing House Pvt. Ltd.

Regd. Office:
2525/193, 1st Floor, Onkar Nagar-A,
Tri Nagar, Delhi-110035
(From Kanhaiya Nagar Metro Station Towards Old Bus Stand)
011-27387998, 27384836, 27385249
+919350849407

Branch Office:
1A/2A, 20, Hari Sadan,
Ansari Road, Daryaganj,
New Delhi-110002
Ph. 011-45794768

E-mail: hello@gullybaba.com, **Website**:GullyBaba.com, GPHbook.com

New Edition

Price:

ISBN: 978-93-81638-82-8
Author: Gullybaba.com Panel

Preface

This book is mainly targeted for the exam of Understanding Poetry for all Universities. It has been introduced in market after seeing the huge demand of ready to grasp material for exams with high level of quality, and its un-availability in market. We the GullyBaba Publishing House took a step ahead to publish the quality material focusing on exams at the same time giving you indepth knowledge about the subject.

GPH Book is the pioneer effort that provides a unique methodology so as to perform better in exams. If your goal is to attain higher grade use this powerful study tool independently or along with your text.

On the Web : ***www.gullybaba.com*** *is the vital resource for your exams acting as catalyst to boost up your preparation. Now you can access us on the net through* ***www.doeacconline.com, www.ignouonline.com, and www.astrologyeverywhere.com.***

Feedback about the book can be sent at **eeg06writers@gullybaba.com.**

New Delhi

Constructive criticism is always welcome as it will add to our knowledge. You can email at eeg06@gullybaba.com.

TOPICS COVERED

Contents

Question Papers

Chapter – 1

Shakespeare and Milton

Q1. Distinguish between Poetry and Prose?

Ans. Poetry : Poetry is something written in verse. It is not straight forward. In poetry a lot of things are left over reader to imagine. The language of poetry is mostly figurative. A poet may use to deep figure of speech or he may talk in few figures only. A French critic Paul Valery has compared poetry to dance. Like a dance, the objective of poetry is enjoyment as well as information and instruction. The poetry is enthusiastic while sad too.

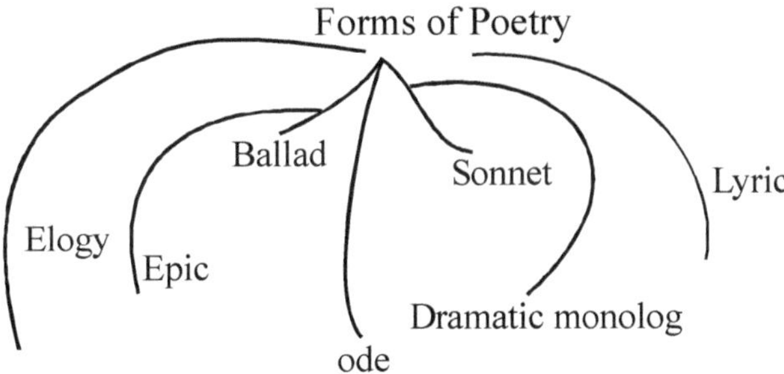

Prose : The prose is taken from the Latin word "prosus" which means direct or straight. In short prose is direct writing. The main aim is to communicate one's thought and feeling. It has various style and different topics too.

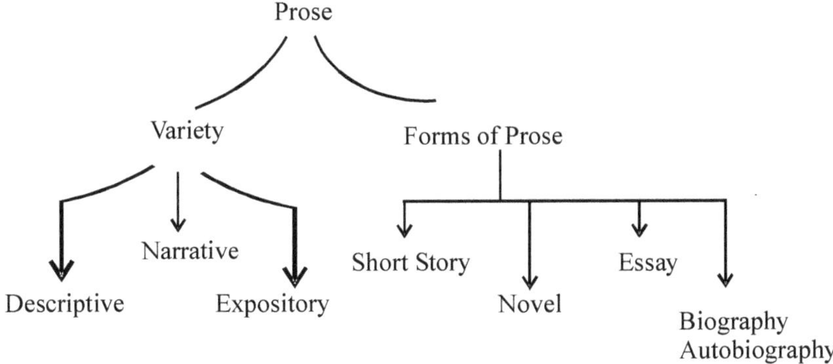

The main different between Prose and Poetry is that Prose is direct or straight word writing. The writer communicates his/her thoughts or feeling clearly and preciously as possible on the other hand poetry which is generally written in verse leaves a lot of reader. Prose is like walking that is, it is functional and provides information. Poetry is like dancing and aims to delight only. A prose piece can be paraphrase or summarized but not a poem.

Q2. What is an organized form of poetry?

Or

Write down various specialities of poetry?

Ans. Poetry has a highly organised form, which is determined by exigencies of metre and rhyme. In a verse, it is recognise at once that verse with its line ending has regular form while Poetry uses words in an organised arrangement or pattern to express feelings, sensations, broad mental impressions and visions which are intellectually difficult to express various specialities of poetry are:

(a) Metre: Metre is important for poetry. It is the arrangement of words into patterns based on strong and weak beats in line of poetry. In the poetry we can listen to sentence in English, we can hear the prominent syllables recurring at regular intervals. A syllable is a word or a part of word which contains a vowel sound the unstressed syllables occurring according to a pattern is called metre.

The group consisting of a strong and one or more weak syllables is usually called a foot. There are two types of foot (i) strong weak and (ii) strong weak-weak. A foot can be defined as a unit consisting of one strong and one or more weak syllables. Metre is poetry consists of one or more feet in line and the pattern can be described on basis of number of feet in line.

The strong weak pattern is called trochaic metre ad weak-weak strong is called anapaest.

A poet uses various feet for the variations when one kind of foot is usually dominant and this pattern, usually established at the beginning of stanza, we reassert itself later. Hence, it is metre which determines the rhythm and distinguishes verse from prose.

(b) Rhyme: Rhyme is the repetition of identical sounds at the end of lines. Poets use rhyme for three major purposes:

(i) The recurrence of the same sequence of sounds has a pleasing effect.

(ii) It also marks the end of line.

(iii) It binds the lines together and achieves unity.

(c) Alliteration: Repetition of identical consonant sounds at the beginning of stressed syllables.

(d) Assonance: Identical vowels in stressed syllables preceded or followed by differing consonants sounds in words in proximity.

(e) Stanza: The stanza is a group of lines repetitive pattern, forming a division of poem.

(f) Figures speech: It referred to as non logical language – comprises words used in new unliteral sense. The most common figures of speech are:

(i) Smile: It is comparison made between different classes with the help of connectives such as like, as, or then.

(ii) Metaphor: Metaphor is an implied comparison.

(iii) Metonymy: A figure of speech that substitute a word that relates to or suggests an idea or a person or place or thing.

(iv) Synecdoche: The word referring to a part of something is used in place of word for whole vice versa.

(v) Personification: It gives the characteristics of a human being to abstract ideas or things or animals in short to non-human beings.

(vi) Symbol: A symbol derives its sustenance through the suppression of direct metaphor. The symbol evokes unseen worlds.

(vii) Myth: Myth is modern literature is looked upon as a system of signs which helps the poet to express complex thoughts that do not easily lend themselves in direct language.

(viii) Onomatopeia: It is a device in which the meaning of a word is suggested by its sound.

(ix) Apostrophe: It is an address to a person or thing who is not listening.

So, all this specialies makes the poetry concrete, condensed and interesting and also provides fresh collocations.

Q3. Write down the various forms of poetry?

Ans. Poetry is something written in verse. The various forms of poetry are:

(1) The Ballad: A ballad is a simple, straightforward poem set to tune. There are two distinct kinds of ballads – the traditional ballad and the literary ballad. The traditional ballad is popular in England and in Scotland in the 15th century was a specific form of narrative poem which has become a part of the world of folk-song. By the end of the 17th century, the emphasis shifted from narration to music as the prime constituent of the ballad. The traditional ballads deal with episodes from well-known stories rendered impersonally. The literary ballad which came into vogue at the end of the 18th century and continued to be popular in the 19th century was not set to music.

The main characteristics of a ballad are:

(a) The ballad is full of refrains. This is known as the **incremental repetition** (a device which repeats what has been said before, sometimes lines, sometimes words) Stock epithets are also often repeated.

(b) The ballad is remarkable for its straightforward narration and it concentrates on striking details. It is compressed and tends towards the dramatic with a good deal of action and dialogue in the course of narration.

(c) The ballad is a poem in short stanzas usually of four lines, having eight and six syllables alternately. You will read an extract from Coleridge's ballad *THE RIME OF THE ANCIENT MARINER*..

(2) The Sonnet: The sonnet is a verse form of fourteen lines, usually of iambic pentameter with an elaborate rhyme scheme. There are two distinct kinds – the English or the Shakespearean sonnet and the Italian or the Petrarchan sonnet. A third kind is the Spenserian sonnet, which is a variation of the English sonnet.

(a) The English or the Shakespearean Sonnet : The sonnet is organised either into twelve lines and a couplet to make it 12 + 2 (14) or into three quatrains (3 x 4) and a couplet (12 + 2 = 14) with a correspondingly organised rhyme scheme such as a-b-a-b-c-d-c-d-e-f-e-f-g-g-.

(b) The Italian or the Petrarchan Sonnet : The Sonnet is n iambic pentameter, divided into two parts – the octave (8 lines) and the sestet (6 lines). The Octave has the rhyming pattern abba-abba while the sestet has cde-cde. The octave expresses in figurative language what is restated in direct language in the sestet.

(c) The Spenserian Sonnet : It is a variation of the English sonnet with a different rhyme scheme abab-bcbc-cdcd-ee. The Sonnet as a verse form is characterised by the tightness of rhyme in iambic pentameter and includes in its themes love, time, friendship, honour, duty, art, nature.

(3) The Epic: The epic is long, narrative poem on an exalted theme or action involving heroic characters and supernatural agencies and rendered in a grand style. Epics are also sometimes based on myths and legends. The main function of an epic simile is to focus the details of an action or event or a person by linking it with something familiar or something in the present state of affairs. These similes draw on ordinary life and the natural world we know and they relate to human interests.

(4) The Dramatic Monologue: Dramatic Monologue is a poem in which a single speaker – not the poet – speaks at a critical moment or situation in which he finds himself and he is seen addressing one or more persons who do not speak but whose presence we strongly feel. This form makes the reader follow the story from the point of view of the speaker who is involved in the action and it also throws light on his character. Dramatic poems are short and compressed and the reader is called upon to draw a good deal of inference about the character and situation.

(5) The Lyric: The Lyric is a short poem that expresses emotion and is meant to be sung. But lyrics written after the 15th century though not meant to be sung, nevertheless tend to retain their mellifluous quality and rhythm. The lyric lends itself to the expression of the intense personal joy or pain or offers a contemplative mood. The lyric expresses the poet's emotional response to an event or scene or to the recollection of an emotion. Thus, the lyric is essentially "en emotional or reflective soliloquy".

(6) The Elegy: As the lyric is a composition spontaneously written at the white heat of passion, it is not limited to expressions of joy or elation. Intense sorrow or pain or mournful contemplation can also give rise to poems of lyrical kind which are known as elegies. The Elegy is classical in its origin and is a composition in verse. But in its treatment of the subject matter, it is tied to a limited range of plaintive musing. In this form heightened emotional tension is restrained by the use of pastoral convention and the employment of pastoral characters like the **shepherds, nymphs,** and **satyrs** gives the poem an impersonal touch.

(7) The Ode: The ode is the most elevated and complex variety of the lyric, written to celebrate a public occasion or some high and serious theme. The ode originating from Greece and Rome influenced the English poets of the 17th century. The ode has two kinds – the **Pindaric** (Greek) and the **Horatian** (Latin). The Pindaric odes were composed to be chanted to music for dance and this resulted in its developing an elaborate stanzaic structure. The Horatian ode was often personal and reflective and had a greater degree of solemnity and dignity.

Q4. What is the poetic device by Shakespeare's sonnet?

Ans. Shakespeare's works are far from easy to understand chiefly because of changes in the meanings of particular words. A Sonnet in the English form or Shakespearean form consists of three quatrains and a couplet. Hence a full understanding of a Shakespearean sonnet will involve:

(i) an awareness of the relationship between the quatrain and the couplet;

(ii) the pace of its movement; and

(iii) a sense of the development of its imagery.

The Sonnet made a late appearance in English literature. It was in the 16th century that the English sonnet came to be written. The English sonnet (sometimes 'Shakespearean') is different in form from the earlier Italian or Petrarchan sonnet. The essential difference lies (i) in the rhyme schemes and (ii) in the arrangement of the fourteen lines that constitute a sonnet. In the Italian sonnet, the rhyme scheme is abba, abba/cde, cde and correspondingly the fourteen lines of a sonnet are divided into two parts – the octave (first 8 lines) and the sestet (the later 6 lines).

The English sonnet, on the other hand has three quatrains (12 lines) and a couplet (2 lines) with a rhyme scheme abab, cdcd, efef, gg. In the English sonnet, the turn comes at the end of the twelfth line. There is also a greater flexibility in rhyming with 7 rhymes (abcdefg) as against five (abcde) in the Italian sonnet. The twelve to two proportion in the English sonnet, unlike the eight to six in the Italian, makes the couplet (the last 2 lines) seem particularly **epigrammatic**. In the Italian sonnet, the turn is at line 9 (at the end of the octave) and the resolution that takes place in the last six marks the turn, and **encapsulates** the thought content of the entire sonnet.

Another interesting observation relates to the use of personal pronouns. Sonnet 18 refers to the friend (or the beloved) as "thou" and "thee" as against Sonnet 55 which uses the informal "you" in its address. Sonnet 65 makes no use of personal pronoun except for "my love" in the last line of the poem. Sonnet 18 is the first of Shakespeare's Sonnets to immortalise poetry, and hence the employment of formal address. There is certain hesitation to claim such a status for poetry (art) which in turn will acquire the power to confer immortality on his friend. By the time he writes his fifty-fifty Sonnet, Shakespeare's self-confidence asserts itself to claim this distinction for poetry. Hence the tone in 55 changes to a personal, intimate tone with the use of "you" in place of "thou". Since sonnet 65 pitches 'beauty' against the ravages of time, the sonnet keeps clear of personal address except to identify 'beauty' with "my love" in the last line.

The first quatrain is an attempt to compare his friend with nature: here represented by the beautiful English Summer. "Darling buds of May" refers to the spring of early flowers. The adjective "darling" carries with it the association of tenderness, love and beauty that relates to his tender, charming young mind. "Summer's lease" (4) is of a short duration. 'Summer' is personified as a tenant whose tenancy is for a brief time. Time has given a very short lease for summer, at the end of which, it has to yield its place to Autumn. Thus you can observe the figure of speech – "personification" – in this reference to "summer". You will see the same figure of speech in operation which he describes the 'sun' with its 'gold complexion' (6) and 'hot eye' (5) and later when he refers to Death as boasting and bragging about its power (4). All the images in this sonnet are derived from Summer season only to establish that his friend is "more lovely" and "more temperate" than summer and shall remain eternal in the lines of his poetry.

Q5. Attempt an analysis of Shakespeare's Sonnet "Shall I compare thee to A Summer's Day". [June 2006, Q3]

Ans. Sonnet 18 "Shall I compare thee to summer's day in the fist full scale fame of poetry and through art. The fame of his friend or beloved in this poem steps up the power of time and then introduces the power of his verse as a defence against time.

The poet suggests a comparison of the youth's beauty with that of summer and than appears to reject it by claiming permanence for the youth as against the inevitable transience of summer's glory. Poem's focus is hot on the apparent comparison and constrast between the order of youth and order of nature but shifts through these last two lines to affirm the eternity of time and art.

It is eternal. It never comes to a stop. It rolls on through days, months and years bringing in its cyclical motion the different seasons in organised succession. The eternal movements of time through birth- death and regeneration gives summer its immortality. In a similar manner poetry can encapsulate beauty, youth, and love within its lines and thereby confer immortality on them. So long as life continues, neither Time nor Art shall cease to exit, whereby both the order of nature and the order of youth shall gain permanence. The essential comparison is not between his young friend and beautiful summer but between the immortality of Time and the immortality of Art which together will bestows eternity on summer and his friend.

The first quatrain introduces a comparison between youth and summer in terms of shortness of duration. Both do not last forever. The second quatrain institutes a comparison in the terms of mutability or change which is to be seen in the decline or in the transience of beauty. In the third quatrain, the comparison seems to end with the three lines. But thy eternal summer shall not fade….in his shade. The poet makes the claim that the summer of his young friend will not fade nor will he lose his beauty nor decline the decay.

The keywords are "eternal lines" where lines refer to lines of poetry. It is evident that the word line suggests the powder of poetry to encapsulate and immortalise his young friend within its lines. But taken in conjunction with the preceding adjective eternal summer will regain its last glory as Time moves in cyclical progression through Autumn, Winter and Summer. This is rationale behind the rise and decline of natural order. This poem shows the power of time, everything changes according to time.

Q6. Analyse the Sonnet 55. "Not marble, nor the Gilded monuments" by Shakespeare?

Ans. This is one of the four or five greatest of Shakespeare's sonnet. It is also considered as one of the greatest immortalisation poems in English language. This sonnet reflects a supremely self- confident poet who claims for his poetry the power to confer immortality on his friend. This sonnet also talks a good deal about the power of poetry to triumph over decay, destruction and other ravages of war and time. The poet says that his sonnet, "the living record of your (his friend's) memory is built on a powerful rhyme which can withstand the onslaught of war and fire, death and oblivion. This monument in verse shall outlive all other erected memorials and monuments in marble and gold and thereby preserve his friend within its lines for posterity till the world draws to its 'ending doom'.

The first quatrain compares the verse monuments and the gilded monuments to establish the time-proof quality of strength, superiority and richness of the former. There is the poet's defiance of time and the assertive boast that his verse can confer immortality on his friend. These four lines claim not only eternity for the verse, but through it they seek to perpetuate the memory of his friend.

The second quatrain speaks about the ravages of war resulting in the destruction of all monuments other than his verse. Neither war nor fire can obliterate the living record of your memory. So both the quatrains have a similar refrain to affirm the permanence of verse monuments set-off against stone and gilded erections. 'Living Record' relates to the voice of the poet in the verse which shall remain a permanent record. All the hostile forces of time, such as war and death cannot reduce either the verse or the friend embodied therein to oblivion.

The day of judgement marks the end of the world. So long as life lasts, his verse will last and so long as the verse lasts, his friend will last. But the emphasis shifts at this point in the couplet when the poet asserts the immortality of his friend not just through the lines of poetry but in his own right as a symbol of love.

The three quatrains logically develop the concept of permanence of art (or poetry) whereby art bestows immortality on its contents. This sonnet confers immortality on his beloved friend. The first quatrain describes the ravages of time on ancient monuments; the second speaks of the ravages of war while the third states the onslaught of death and consequent oblivion. Against all these, stands the verse monument. The couplet at the end makes a swift and sudden departure by shifting the emphasis from the world of art to the sphere of Love. Love has the power to resist the passage of time and the poet's proper mode of love is poetry.

This sonnet as it exists is s living record of his friend's memory. It is in itself a strong monument which recognises not only its own power, but also recognises the existence of the friend and other lovers throughout the history of mankind. The sonnet which represents art seeks its inspiration from the friend who in turn gains immortality through its lines. The friend, who embodies love is the inspirer of the immortal verse.

Sonnet 55 is Art and Love that have the power to retain within and to bestow immortality on their creations.

Q7. What is the central theme of the poem "Since Brass Nor Stone, Nor Earth, Nor Boundless Sea" by Shakespeare

Ans. Beauty is so frail that it can neither escape mortality nor arrest the ravages of time. There is no strong force that can prevent the destruction of beauty that takes place with the inexorable march of time. The first twelve lines (the three quatrains) thus present a strong case for the inescapability of mortality that spares neither the animate nor the inanimate creations on earth. Beauty pleads in vain against the awesome power of the twin forces of time and mortality. But the couplet at the end reverses this gloomy trend of the quatrains and with one deft stroke holds out of the miraculous possibility of preserving beauty by confining it within the lines of poetry.

The power of beauty is no match for the ravages of time. The second quatrain continues the "fearful meditation" of the first quatrain on the defenselessness of beauty. From the visual imagery of the earlier lines which saw beauty in the likeness of a flower, the poet moves to the **olfactory** imagery when he describes beauty in terms of summer's sweet fragrance. The diffusive and pervasive nature of beauty is seen all the more fragile when it is placed in continuity with the solid rocks and gates of steel which are shown equally vulnerable to the battering of time.

The third quatrain reiterates the argument that nothing can stand against time. Here the image is that of a jewel. Beauty is the most precious gift of time which we are anxious to hide from time who will take it back and lock it in his treasure chest.

The **incipient** personification of time in line 8 as a fearsome opponent is enhanced here with the employment of the capital letter 'T'. It points to the timelessness of the operation of time. Beauty, which in the last line 14 is made synonymous with "my love" is not just a physical attribute, but it includes all that is lovely and inspires loveliness in others. Beauty thus acquires a timeless quality and thereby gains immortality. Time which does not take away from beauty its eternal distinction can still keep it hidden from mortal beings. The poet wonders which mortal, has the power to unlock Time's treasure chest and release it for mortal eyes to see. Who can prevent Time from enjoying the booty of its precious jewel? On this note of human powerlessness against Time, the quatrain ends and prepares us for the magnificent couplet on a different conceptual plane.

The gloom of the previous twelve lines can be removed possibly by the miracle – the miracle of his verse in black in. Nothing is asserted here except a possibility. This miracle – this verse may have the might to obliterate Time's concealed activity.

The end of the sonnet is tentative, suggesting a possibility (reference 'may') and there is nothing of unreal optimism in the statement. It is this that gives weightage to the couplet. The "fearful meditation" on the widespread ruin that occurs with time and which will make even "Time's best jewel" almost hidden from sight give way to its possible recovery through the means of poetry. So, its faith in the art of poetry by the judicious introduction of the word "miracle".

Q8. Write down the personal element in LYCIDAS by Milton?

[Dec 2006, Q3]

Ans. Lycidas is the name of a shepherd in the songs of Theocritus, the ancient Greek poet and Virgil, the Latin poet Milton reflects on the tragic possibilities of death overtaking creative attempts to resolve these fears culminating in state of calmness and quietness. The poet is able to build on this note helplessness to digress about validity of dedicating oneself to the vacation of a poet. In the context of the immutable fact of death, the poem leads to the second part of the digression, where he says that fame is what one receives in heaven and not on earth. Milton, the humanist valued the aspiration of human mind that sought after high values and ideals. He himself cherished great literary ambitions and relied upon great classics to nurture human achievement, he never forgot that true glory consisted in earning the approval of God. Milton is in search of fame and the Christian poet who recognises that true fame cannot be had on earth but only humanism. The concept of true fame conferred by God is common to Christian and classical thinking.

The first consolation is common to both Christian and classical. It is Phoebus who offers there words of consolation and it is Jove who shall be the all powerful judge of men's deep.

The second is purely Christian, while the consolation given in backdrop of pastoral scene suggested the idea, pastoral world of the shepherds where such calmness can exist. Lycidas is dead but he (poet) is still living. There is no need to despair and he can proceed with great determination and comfort towards further poetic achievements with the arrival of the new dawn. The idyllic, calm beauty of the postral world affirms the calm bliss that Christian redemption offers on a note of despair at the start of his clergy uses the Dorick lay to sing again a song of promise and expectation. Lycidas shall be resurrected. So, the poem ends on a vision of a hope and promise. Christian religion does not accommodate despair. It nurtured on faith in a grace of God. Man has to continue with life in a spirit of humanity, faith and do his duty to earn heavenly reward.

Q9. Give the poetic devices in Lycidas?

Ans. Lycidas is the rich synthesis of the classical, Christian and Humanist elements in the poem. It is evident that Milton has employed both **classical** and **Christian allusions** and effectively blended them to suit his twin purposes of an elegy on a learned friend and of a scathing attack on the corrupt clergy of his times.

The opening lines provide a good deal of examples such as "myrtles dear", "season due". These adjectives coming at the end intensify the poet's poignancy at being compelled to write the elegy on his learned friend who had met with an untimely death at a very young age.

Another significant feature of the poem is its use of **repetition.** The opening line strikes the note of repetition with "yet once more….and once more" and a little later we have the heightening of tension in "For Lycidas is dead, dead are his prime, Young Lycidas….."

Milton employs **alliteration** that helps him to slow down the tempo and at times to gallop and flow without a pause. For example, in the opening stanza, when he is disturbed at the thought of writing an elegy on his friend who had died prematurely, he speaks of "forced fingers rude" and later when he invokes the "sisters of the Sacred well" he says "Begin, and somewhat loudly sweep the string".

Milton has employed **synecdoche, apostrophe** and antithesis in this poem.

Apart from the rich classical and Biblical allusions, Milton's imagery is striking.

Q10. Attempt a critical appreciation of Milton's sonnet on "Oh his Blindness"? [June 2006, Q3]

Ans. The sonnet On His Blindness, the poet's near-despair in the opening lines gives way to faith in Providence at the close. The poet with his "soul bent to serve the Lord" is reconciled at the end to 'stand and wait' and thereby serve him. The sonnet moves from point to point to meditate upon the active and the passive ways of service to God. When the poet despairs that he can no longer serve his lord actively (due to blindness), the Sonnet takes a turn to give him the strength to accept his physical weakness with a consoling thought that "they also serve who stand and wait".

Milton's appropriate selections of the Biblical phrases to reinforce the theme of Christian virtues of Patience and Faith.

Milton's Sonnet begins with "I" and ends with "They" (14). This gives a clue to the change that occurs in the sonnet from a single, self-centered man, desiring to illuminate the wide world to thousands of God-centered angels who move through this world "over Land and Ocean", spreading the message of God. Yet another point to note is the completion of his adverbial clause in line 1, "when I consider…..". The main clause that marks the completion occurs when Milton raises his query "I fondly ask" as to whether God exacts "day-labour" even when he denies light.

In truly Christian terms, Milton acknowledges the operations of Diving grace in human affairs. There is a perceptible change in his tone – from nervous despair to an admission that God is both the giver and the withholder of gifts to man. Milton's disturbed state of mind, with its concomitant feelings of despair and anxiety is set to rest by the revival of his faith in God's actions. He recognises that whatever suffering or affliction he has to undergo is part of God's plans. He who accepts his burden without a murmur, serves him in the best way. There is no one-to-one equation between labour and wages as illustrated in the Biblical parable. Milton realises that God does not exact day-labour, but he desires that a patient bearing of one's suffering is in itself a form of superior service.

Some critics are of the opinion that Milton regarded the order of angles who left God's presence to move over land and ocean to spread the message as secondary in comparison with those who never left his presence and waited attendance on Him. But the main distinction does not concern the different orders of angels. Milton is only asserting the virtues of services within one's capability. If he is denied light – both the power of vision and the power of creation – then he will have to patiently wait – to stay in expectation of the unfolding of God's will and commands. His service to God is likely to be hampered on both counts. If his poetic inspiration fails him, he may feel the emptiness within and may not be able to sing his Lord's praises. But on both planes of existence on the physical and the inspirational the recovery is possible if one submits himself to God's will and waits for his grace to recover the lost power and render service to Him in accordance with God's bidding.

Q11. Give Bibalic References used in Milton's sonnet?

[June 2007, Q3]

Ans. The Bible is the sacred book of Christians. It is the Gospel of Jesus Christ. In a simple and elegant style, it narrates the life and teachings of Christ with the help of a number of parables. The Bible, often referred to as the New Testament of our Lord and Saviour, Jesus Christ, also includes Psalms and proverbs that direct men through the right path to attain the kingdom of heaven. There are four versions of the Gospel by St. Mathew, St. John, St. Luke and St. Mark. Milton in his sonnet XIX 'On His Blindness' has employed the Biblical phrases to restate the task of the Christian – to stand and wait, in acceptance and acknowledgement of God's gifts, in abiding faith in his providence with no concession to despair even in one's darkest moments.

Service to God's through the usage of God-given talent is the essential focus of this sonnet. This theme can be traced to Christ's parable of the talents in Matthew XXV.

Milton is distressed that his blindness may hamper him in the discharge of his service to the Lord and he may not put to use the talent – in his case, the literary talent to sing his Lord's praise. The unprofitable, slothful servant in Christ's parable suffers spiritual death in losing the kingdom of Heaven. Milton expresses anxiety that he may also be forced to hide his talent on account of the impending blindness. "To hide it" is "death". A Poet can gain immortality through the use of his literary talent. To keep it unused will amount to spiritual death.

The second Biblical reference is related to line 6, where Milton speaks of presenting "my true account". The word "account" is possible from Mathew XVIII.23 :

"Account" means reckon with service. Milton uses the term "account" in the sense of an account of his services. Milton in many of his writings has acknowledged gratefully the gifts of God, but there has also been an undercurrent of anxiety lest he should account for fewer of the gifts and thereby incur God's displeasure for not utilising all that had been given to him.

The third reference is from Matthew XXV 1 ff, where the allusion is to the parable of labourers in the Vineyard. It tells the story of a man who hired labourers to work in the Vineyard for a penny a day. While some worked for a full day, other were appointed at different times even as late as the eleventh hour. Yet when the evening came, everyone was paid the same wage of a penny irrespective of the number of hours they had worked – To those who protested against this equality in the distribution of the wages disproportionate to the longer duration of work put in by a few of them, the man replied that he did no wrong for he paid as per the promise he had given to each one of them, at the rate of a penny a day.

The word 'Patience' in line 9 refers to Christian Patience or faith in Providence. The source can be traced to the Book of Revelations XIV. 12 and Psalm XXXVII. The Revelations interpret 'Patience' as faith as Jesus. The Psalms state "Rest in the Lord, and *wait* patiently for him" and a little later, "those that wait upon the Lord, they shall inherit the earth".

Yoak in line 11 is yet another Biblical term taken from Matthew XI (29-30) where the Lord says "Take my yoke upon you, and learn of me.....for my yoke is easy and my burden is light". God's demands are not exacting nor does he overburden those who serve him. God expects everyone to accept His dispensations. Those who carry God's Yoke lightly serve him in the best manner. The biblical word 'Yoke' thus underlines the importance of faith in God that gives no room for despair.

"Wait on the Lord" is from the Psalms XXVII. 14 and is a phrase frequently present in the Bible.

Milton uses 'wait' as the concluding word of his sonnet, to equate it with passive service to God. In the context of this sonnet that begins on a note of pessimism, the poet needs courage to accept his blindness and to sustain himself in the midst of physical darkness. In the **Second Defence** written in 1654, he says, "not blindness" but the inability to endure blindness is a source of misery. The suffering which his blindness imposes on him itself a service for it implies an acceptance of Lord's dispensation and a willingness to serve Him passively through standing attendance on the Lord and waiting for his commands.

Q12. Give introduction to pastoral Elegy of the Lycidas?

[June 2008, Q4]

Ans. Pastoral elegy, as the name indicates, combines the two forms of poetry – the elegy and the pastoral verse. An elegy is a poem or song which mourns the death of a person. It also includes the poet's reflections on certain aspects of life. The mood of an elegy is thus serious and pensive.

Pastoral elegy incorporates these two forms of poetry and the poet, in the grab of a shepherd mourns the loss of his friend, a fellow-shepherd and the poem is set in the background of a rustic countryside. Personal elegy has its origin in ancient Greece and three of the major Greek influences in Milton's **Lycidas** are those of Bion, Theocritus and Moschus. Milton calls his poem a **Monday**, which is a variant of the elegy, but rendered by a single voice or a single mourner.

Milton follows the fixed conventions of Pastoral elegy where both the poet and the deceased are in the guise of shepherds livings in the midst of nature. The poem begins with an invocation to the Muses (goddesses of poetry). This is followed by a reproach of the guardian Nymphs for their failure to protect the dead shepherd. There is a list of a procession of mourners which includes nature with her flora and fauna. Yet another convention of the pastoral elegy is to include a list of flowers that are strewn on the shepherd's grave. The poem, which begins with a querulous tone of despair ends on a calm note of reconciliation and the poem celebrates the immortality of the dead shepherd – his reunion with God or Nature. In keeping with the character of an elegy, there are a few digressions in the course of the poem which help the poet to present his reflections and views on society and life. The three great pastoral elegies in English are Milton's **Lycidas,** Shelley's **Adonais** and Matthew Arnold's **Thyrsis.**

Chapter – 2

Donne, Pope and Gray

Q1. Describe the Metaphysical poetry? **[Dec 2006, Q3]**

Ans. Donne belongs to the late 16th and early 17th century, his love-lyrics are unlike the Elizabethan love lyrics of Shakespeare, Spenser and Sidney, which employed courtly form of address and expressed the values of the Courtly world. Donne employs a simple style and a colloquial diction and presents love in a context other than that o the court.

Donne and his contemporaries – Marvell, Crashaw, Vaughan and Herbert are known as metaphysical poets. The term "metaphysical" in a general sense is applied to anything abstruse or abstract or philosophical, but when applied to this school of poetry, it signifies in essence the employment of learning as the stuff of poetry. Donne presses into the service both of his love poetry and religious poetry diverse experiences, thoughts, and imagery from various fields such as Law, Alchemy, Philosophy, Astronomy etc. Hence metaphysical imagery unlike pastoral or mythical imagery (as you studied in Milton) or natural imagery (as in Shakespeare) is full of learned imagery seemingly far-fetched, but apt.

Another feature of metaphysical poetry is its blending of passion and thoughts. There has always been the misconception that passion and reason are irreconcilable opposites. The Elizabethan passionate lyrics were expressions of pure feelings. But you will notice that Donne's poetry is at once passionate and cerebral. The best definition of a metaphysical poet is that he thinks with his heart and feels with his mind. The unique blending of passion and thought accounts for the presence of Wit, a characteristic quality in metaphysical poetry.

Summing up, metaphysical poetry is characterised by its intellectual content, passionate feeling, learned but startling imagery (known as conceits) and it uses a direct form of address, spoken voice and dramatic tone.

Q2. Analyse The Sunne Rising by Donne?

Ans. The poet and his beloved are still in bed as the morning. The poet playfully chides the sun not to disturb him and his mistress and to attend to other matters. The poet mocks at the sun for imagining itself to be all powerful for the poet can shut out its beams by closing his eyes but he says he shall not do so, lest he loses sight to his beloved even for an instant. Continuing his impertinent tone, he tells the sun that he and his beloved constitute the whole world and therefore, if the sun needs a little rest from his labour, it can do its duty of warming the world by sampling circling round the two of them – for they are the whole world.

In the course of first five lines, the poet shifts attention from the sun to himself and to his mistress and then back to sun. The tone varies from derision and scorn to lazy contentment and back to protest and gentle mockery. The sonnet "Sunne Rising" is typical example of humorous bravado "the exultant brag" of a lover which conceals the intense passion underneath. Donne does not accept the new philosophy. He intentionally claims a central position for him and his mistress in the face of all contrary scientific evidence. According to him sun does not posses the dignified Copernican centre and deliberately strips it of all is majesty to reduce it to foolish busy-body making his rounds to mark time. He dismisses as impertinence on the part of sun to impose time on the lovers – its arbitrary division of time into days, hours, month.

The expression focus the attention on the experience of love, rather than on physical beauty of his mistress. This is achievement of Donne. In other words, a lover may be mistaken in his judgement of his mistress's beauty but the experience he undergoes as he thinks of her cannot be false.

Thus the end of the poem the majestic sun has been relegated to the role of an ancient tired workman compelled to do his daily duties of walking and warming the world. The lover suggests that sun can minimise its movements by remaining static in his room and shining on him and his mistress who constitute the whole world. The poet has established the lovers superiority and he is no longer irascible as at the beginning. On the contrary, he welcomes the intrusion of the sun by extending his permission to shine on them and thereby save its labour.

The poem thus amalgamates diverse experience, diverse tones and diverse imagery which gives it the specific metaphysical poetry as "heterogeneous ideas yoked by violence together and nature and are the ransacked for illustration, comparisons, and illusions. Metaphysical poetry is full of conceits or far fetched imagery. There are three modes of conceits in this poem, the dialectic, the rhetoric and the witty modes.

Q3. Give contrast between the poetry of Shakespeare and Donne and Milton with Donne.

Ans. The sharp contrast between Donne's poem and Shakespeare s' sonnet is:

(a) Shakespeare's love poems are in the majority sonnets, while Donne's are not.

(b) In Shakespeare's sonnets, the poet speaks of his love for his mistress. It expresses his passion and his constancy in love, while Donne's poems express him firm confidence in their **mutual** love.

(c) There is a remarkable variety of tone in Donne's love poems. For example, you notice his opening invectives hurled at the sun, calling him **"a busy old fool", "saucy pedantic wretch", "unruly"** etc. But as the poem ends, you recognise the happy mood of fulfilled love. But in Shakespeare's sonnets, one notices the idealisation of love throughout the lines.

(d) Donne makes use of geographical images. There is also a suggestion of the new scientific theory of Copernicus that posited a heliocentric world (Sun as the Centre of the world). This was against the medieval belief in a homocentric (man centered world. By asking the sun to circle round them, he reduces the status of the sun and goes counter to the newly discovered Copernican theory. Donne's poems are full of imagery related to contemporary scientific and astronomical discoveries in place of the earlier natural, pastoral and mythological imagery.

(e) The language of Donne is rhetorical. There are no fanciful images nor any explicit reference to feeling. Yet the poem conveys a heightened emotional experience underlying the words.

The contrast between the Milton's poem and Donne's poem is:

Contrast: Unlike Milton's sonnet which employs Biblical imagery. Donne's sonnet uses metaphors from everyday world. In place of the high degree of solemnity of Milton's sonnet, Donne's poem has a touch of humour, almost bordering on specious logic and frivolity.

The tone in Donne's poem is one of scorn and raillery at the beginning and of mock compassion towards the close.

Milton, the following the Petrarchan tradition employs the technique of question and answer in his octave and sestet respectively. Donne writes the Shakespearean variety where he builds up the arguments in the three quatrains to dismiss them in the couplet. He begins with Death's claims to power and tyranny and then shifts the tone in the couplet to affirm immortality for man vis-à-vis mortality for Death. The incongruity of Death dying makes the couplet strikingly witty, so characteristic of metaphysical poetry. Those whom death intends to overthrow do not die, but it is death which shall ultimately die.

Q4. What are the poetic devices used by Donne in his poetry?

Ans. The poetic device used by Donne in his poetry are given below :

(a) A swift glance at the two poems will suggest to you the archaic spellings that Donne employs. For example, you have **Sunne, Sawcie Pedantique** ("The Sunen Rising"), **Sleepe, bee, mee (**'Holy Sonnet X') to cite a few. Similarly, there are archaic constructions as in line 18 "Be where thou left'st them…." Line 12 "Why should'st thou."

(b) You also notice L.11-12 of "The Sunne Rising" where the poet has employed the technique of inversion.

(c) Metaphysical poetry is characterised by conceits or far-fetched imagery. Donne's use of geographical imagery and the scientific imagery.

(d) There is the tone of playful irony as seen in "Holy Sonnet X" when he speaks of death & Death. "And death shall be no more; Death thou shalt die". In *The Sunne Rising,* he playfully tells the sun that he can eclipse it and his beloved's beauty can blind the effulgent sun.

(e) There is also Donne's use of hyperbole. Hyperbole is an exaggerated statement made for effect and not intended to be taken literally.

Q5. Comment on the Alexander Pope's use of the heroic couplet?

[June 2008, Q5]

Or

What do you mean by Neo Classical Poetry and Mock Heroic Poetry?

Ans. Pope is the epitome of neo-classicism poetry. 18th century poetry is termed as neo-classicism poetry because the poetry of 18th century modeled itself on the classical literature of ancient Greece and Rome and imitated many of its characteristics. The epic form was highly valued during the 18th century for it exalted theme and grand style and 18th century had skillfully adopted for satirical purpose.

Use of Heroic Couplet

The metre of the *The Rape of the Lock is the heroic couplet.* It consists of two consecutive lines of *iambic pentameter* verse whose end-words rhyme.

The term may come from the extensive use of this form in 'heroic' plays of the 17th and 18th centuries. The form subdivides into the 'closed couplet' whose meaning is complete within the two lines without reference to what precedes or follows and the 'open' or 'run-on couplet' which is not self-contained and the meaning is carried over to the next line. Examples of the 'closed' and Lines 1-4 of the 'open' couplet. Try to select examples of both types of couplets from the extract you have just studied. The closed couplet achieved great popularity after its use by Dryden and became the dominant form of English verse under the influence of Pope. It is particularly suited to the expression of thought with balance, repetition and antithesis often creating a witty, epigrammatic or humorous effect. This made it the recognised metre for satire. Pope achieves a tremendous range and variety of tone within the compass of the couplet form.

E.g. Snuff, or the fan, supply each pause of chat,

With singing, laughing, ogling, and all that

This couplet catches the casual tone of gossip in fashionable society.

But when to mischief mortal bend their will,

How soon they find fit instruments of ill.

This couplet is used here for serious comment

Swift to the Lock a thousand spirites repair

A thousand wings, by turns, blow back the Hair,

And thrice they twitch'd the Diamond in her Ear,

Thrice she look'd back, and thrice the Foe drew near.

The use of repetition creates the effect of suspense and excitement

Note also the use of inversion or a change in the normal word order to give variety, as in

Here, Britain's Statesmen oft the Fall foredoom (1 5)

Or

Hither the Heroes and the Nymphs resort (1 9)

Or

In various talk th' instructive hours they past (11)

Mock Heroic Poetry

The Rape of the Lock had its origin in an actual quarrel that occurred in

1711 between the two aristocratic London families – Petres and the Fermors. The young Lord Petre cut a lock of hair from the head of his distant relative, Arabella Fermor, a young lady renowned for her beauty. This incident caused great embarrassment to the lady and deeply offended her. It caused considerable ill-feeling between the two families. It was suggested to Pope by a common acquaintance and well-wisher. John Caryll, that he should write a poem about the incident "to make a jest of it, and laugh them together again."

An epic is a narrative poem describing heroic events on a vast scale and is therefore referred to as heroic poetry. Such as poem celebrates the achievements in war of great heroes who are remarkable for their courage and resourcefulness. Their actions affect the lives of the entire community they belong to and they come to represent the ideals and values of that group. An epic becomes a poem of celebration glorifying the deeds of individual heroes and also the civilization to which they belong. The theme of an epic is lofty one and the style used is deliberately grand. The epic makes his style 'grand' by using certain literary devices.

(i) Some of the words he uses are poly-syllabic and not native English words but those of Latin or Greek origin.

(ii) He generally avoids direct and simple descriptions preferring to use elaborate phrases which present the idea or thing in a roundabout way (this is called periphrasis)

(iii) There are often passages of general comment on human nature or life expressed in an abstract way. This is part of the moral intention of the poet but it also serves to elevate the style.

(iv) Certain words and phrases which are simple and familiar in themselves are repeatedly used by epic poets and have come to be associated with it. These are called 'stock-phrases'. 'Poetic diction' or the use of deliberately 'poetic' words is also a feature of the epic style.

(v) The epic or extended simile is an important literary device. The poet frequently compares characters and objects to remote and noble things. The comparison is developed until it becomes a distinct picture by itself with only a slight connection to the context.

The epic has an ancient tradition. The earliest Western epics were *The Iliad and the Odyssey* written by the Greek poet. Homer more than 2,500 years ago.

The epics of Homer and Virgil provide the basic characteristic of an epic. The protagonist of an epic is a man endowed with extraordinary physical strength and skilled in warfare. The epic deals with this heroic struggle in the world against forces or opponents of an equally formidable kind. The narrative should cover vast stretches of time and space and should convey a sense of poet's sincere dedication to the task of writing a lofty poem.

Pope was asked to write a poem concerning a petty quarrel. He had the added task of bringing about reconciliation between the two parties, by showing the folly of blowing up a trivial incident to magnified proportion. He makes the petty quarrel assume epic dimensions and thereby ridicules the folly of inflating a trivial incident to serious proportions. The genre perfectly suited Pope's intention and helped to defuse a petty quarrel and place it in its right perspective. It also had the additional benefit of combining the two forms of epic and satire that wer popular in the 18th century. The immediate examples of the mock-heroic before Pope were the *Le Lutrin of* Boileau, Dryden's MacFlecknow.

The function of a mock-epic is two fold :

(i) a literary satire and

(ii) a moral satire

The Rape of Lock is brilliant in its adoption and modification of the epic form. Pope has studied the great epics closely and used their features to highlight the triviality of his subject. The poem provides a humorous parallel to all the principal features of the epic and affords the reader the pleasure of recognising parallels in Homer and Virgil. A mock-epic uses the devices of an epic altered to a lighter mood. It demands from the poet a comprehensive knowledge of the classical epics and satirical skill.

In a mock-epic the reader is constantly made conscious of the disparity between the trivial subject and the grand style of an epic that is employed to describe it. This incongruity produces amusement which is used by the poet to make his satirical comment. We are made aware of the element of bathos (anti-climax) brought about by the constant descent from the sublime to the ridiculous.

The satire in *The Rape of the Lock* is good-natured unlike his other satires because there is an underlying admiration for the charm of the fashionable society. Pope specially emphasizes the importance of 'good humor', 'good sense' and 'virtue' as protection against the petty irritants of social life. Pope suggests that a sensibly detached attitude will enable men and women to view life with equanimity.

Q6. Give brief sketch of the poem The Rape of the Lock?

Ans. The Rape of the Lock appeared in 1712 and consisted of 2 cantos. The poem was success but Pope recognised the potential for further elaboration. Chiefly by addition of race of fairy spirits called 'Sylphs'. Pope got the idea for the sylphs from 17th and 18th century 'Rosicrucian' doctrine of supernatural beings as explained by the Comte de Gabalais. In the poem these supernatural creatures act as the guardians of young heroine in imitation of the gods who protect their favourite mortal heroes in an epic form. The poem is consists of five Cantos. The setting for the poem is beau-monde or fashionable world of 18th century London Society.

Canto 1- The heroine of the poem is Belinda is a society lady. She has an early morning dream sent by her guardian sylph. Ariel to warn her of an impending disaster. The elaborate ritual performed before the dressing table prepares Belinda for her day.

Canto 2 opens with the description of Belinda's journey across the River Thames to Hampton Court. The poet describes Belinda's locks and the Baron's (Lord Petre in real life) desire to possess them. The Canto ends on an ominous note with Ariel assigning positions to the sylphs around Belinda to protect her from harm. This parallels similar actions of the gods to protect the hero at crucial stages of action in an epic.

Canto 3 describes the elaborate social pastimes at Hampton Court. A game of cards and the ceremony of serving coffee are described in the same way that an epic poet describes scenes of battle, individual combats between heroes and elaborate feasts after epic deeds or funerals. The Canto ends on a climatic note with the Baron cutting off the lock of Belinda's hair.

In a Canto 4 a wicked spirit, Umbriel open a bag full of 'spleen' (anger and melancholy) which throws Belinda into deep depression. In Homer's *Odyssey* we have a parallel when Aeolus, the god of winds opens a bag of furious winds to drive the hero's ship away from its destination. Belinda visualizes the terrible implications of this public disgrace and bewails the loss of her hair.

Canto 5 contains the moral of the poem where good humour and good sense of recommended. The advice, however, is ignored and a battle between the 'beaux and belles' (fashionable young men and women) ensues. The poet concludes the poem with the fanciful suggestion that the lock has been converted into a star which will immortalize Belinda's name.

Q7. Analyse the Rape of the Lock? **[June 2007, Q3]**

Ans. This is only a description of Canto 3. Pope begins with Canto 3 and gives the description of Hampton Court which is the scene of the climatic action in the poem. The description of a grand building in a minor epic feature. There is a deliberate mingling of serious and trivial matters to suggest this fashionable society lack of perspective. Politicians discuss with equal seriousness the full from power of despotic foreign ruler and the loss of female chastity and honour. The gossips are important for social life beside that how casually reputations may be lost. The high society talk are scandalous. Poet expresses the concern for women in such a society where irresponsible comments against them may bring them into disrepute. Pope reproduces the exact rhythm and tone of casual but superficial conversation clevernessly. The excessive use of snuff and female affectations is the use of fans were often satisfied in contemporary writtings.

Poet use elevated language and dignified tone because these are to heighten the mock epic irony hinting at the disproportionate seriousness with which success or failure at cards is treated by Belinda. Belinda's successive eagerness to triumph in the game of cards, her fear lose and exultation at ultimate victory are highlighted as these suggest a complex lack for perspective and the inability to distinguish the significant of trival. This attracts Pope as the main flow in Belinda's society and in her character. This gives contrast between situation and dignity of language. Pope also used some magical significance attached to nine cards dealt to each player and the sylphs fulfil their duty of protecting Belinda.

There is also an ironic reference to women who are over conscious of their position in Society. An accurate description of playing cards give Pope's powers of observation and careful attention to detail. Beside that much of humour and irony in mock epic lies in finding similarities between entirely different situations. Pope imitates the epic devices of periphrasis. Pope has explained in his dedicatory letter to his poem that the Sylphs would guard any woman condition that she does not earthly lover and remains in chaste. The repetition of emphasises that the hair, unlifee the sylphs cannot be rejoined. The effective use of anti climax to make moral comment. The Pope comment on the fashionable society with its confused values. There is lack of discrimination between serious and trivial is stressed again. Thus Pope seems to feel through Belinda over react to loss of her hair there is some justification for the dismay.

Q8. It is also remarkable for blending landscape poetry with funenal elegy. Comment.

Ans. Gray's **Elegy** can be related to two of the distinct poetic traditions of the first half of the 18th century, namely the Elegy and Landscape Poetry.

Gray was influenced by *Lycidas* and he introduces ethical and philosophical discussions in the poem. The poem also partakes of certain features of Landscape poetry that include the use of a scene of the countryside (churchyard) to embody the poet's philosophic reflections. Gray's *Elegy* alternates between description and reflection and this sets a pattern and contributes to the basic structure of the poem. Frank H. Ellis in his essay on Gray's Elegy has given the following analysis of the poem:

(a) Description of the churchyard.

(b) Reflections on the scene

(c) The rural life which the dead no longer enjoy

(d) Admonition to the 'proud' not to mock the poor people's graves

(e) Opportunities for good as well as possibilities for evil are denied to the poor

(f) Description of the gravestones in the country churchyard

(g) Reflections on the psychology of dying

(h) Description of the stone cutter – his life and death.

(i) Reflections on the stone cutter – Epitaph

Q9. What are the Poetic Devices used in Thomas Gray's written in the country Churchyard?

Ans. The Poetic Devices used by Gray are:

(1) Gray uses the four-lined stanza or the **quatrain** in his poem. Gray prefers the quatrains to the pentameter couplets that Pope used.

The couplets essentially give a poem a quicker pace or measure which does not suit the **Elegy.** The quatrains on the other hand, give the **Elegy** a slow and languid measure that is essential to produce the desired effect.

(2) Pope uses Caesura to serve the purposes of antithesis.

Gray avoids all antithesis. So most of his lines are without a middle punctuation. Whenever he introduces any punctuation, there is no hint of antithesis. On the contrary it serves to suggest the parallel between the two halves of the line. For example:

> The board of heraldry, the pomp of power,
>
> And all that beauty, all that wealth e'er gave. (33-34)

(3) The Elegy is a **carefully patterned** poem. The commonest line pattern follows the general sequence adjective-noun-adjective-noun as for example, "The breezy **call** of incense-breathing **Morn"** (17) or "The boast of **heraldry,** the pomp of **power,"** (33) or "Some **village – Hampden,** that with dauntless **breast"** (57). Such a patter is often seen in the first line of a quatrain. There is a different pattern to be observed in the fourth line of a quatrain: verb-noun-adjective-noun.

"To scatter plenty o'er a smiling land" (63)

(v) (n) (adj) (n)

"And read this history in a nation's eyes" (64)

(v) (n) (adj) (n)

(4) The poem abounds in adjectival and adverbial epithets which lend sonority and dignity to the poem. For example.

Parting day, **lowing** herd, **wearily** plods, **winds** slowly (1-3)

(5) Diction – Gray uses a considerable number of archaic words like "jocund", "oft", "yonder", "glebe" etc. Most of the nouns and verbs are everyday words and usually monosyllabic. The language of the **Elegy,** unlike that of the language of 18th century poetry consists of "words as they are used and not as separate and independent entities". There is hardly a word that is not used in conversation, but the way these words are made to work is not the prose way.

(6) Gray uses personifications not to bring them to life, but to gain weight and conciseness.

But knowledge to their eyes her ample page

Rich with the spoils of time did n'er unroll

Knowledge is not described here in terms of a human being involved in the activity of unrolling the pages, but personification is here employed as "abstract personification" where the abstract concept of Knowledge is presented in a non-pictorial way.

(a) Onomatopoeia used in poem:

"beetle wheels his dronin'g flight" (7)

"And drowsy tinklings lull the distant folds (8)

"The Swallow **ittering "** (4)

"The Cock's **shrill clarion** or the **echoing horn"** (19)

(b) Alliteration found in poem:

"The **lowing** herd wind slowly o'er the **lea" (**2)

"The ploughman homeward plods his weary way"

(c) Vowel sounds of poem:

"And leaves the world to darkness and to me" (3)

"The **breezy** call of incense-breathing morn," (17)

(7) The **elegy** is also remarkable for its striking **images and metaphors.** The gem and flower metaphor has been analysed in the section on interpretation.

(8) The poem uses the figure of speech, metonymy as in "mute inglorious **Milton"**.

(9) The syntax is notable for its inversion, where the verbs are often used at the end of a line.

(10) The poem is full of ironic contrast as is evidenced in the contrast between the Cathedral tombs and the churchyard graves. But the contrast serves to balance the rich and the poor and to equate them on a fundamental common ground despite the apparent contrast. There is balance even in speaking of poor when the poet says that they were not only denied opportunity to do good, but also to do evil. They were denied not only "glory" but also "ignoble strife".

Q10. Give the difference between Neo classicism and Romanticism in terms of the poem?

Ans. The difference between Neo classicism and Romanticism is:

	Neo-Classicism	**Romanticism**
	Turning from	
1)	Reason	to senses, feelings, imagination and intuition
2)	the civilized, modern and sophisticated society	to the primitive, medieval and natural life
3)	urban society	to rural solitude
4)	preoccupation with human nature	to preoccupation with the aesthetic and spiritual values of Nature
5)	Mundane activities	to the visions of the mysterious, the ideal and the Infinite
6)	Satire	to myth

7)	the expression of accepted moral truth	to the discovery of "Beauty That is Truth"
8)	Belief in God and evil	to belief in Man and Goodness
9)	Established religious and philosophical creeds	to individual speculation and revelations
10)	Objectivity	to subjectivism
11)	Public	to private themes
12)	Formal Correctness	to individual expressiveness
13)	The ideal of order	to the ideal of intensity
14)	The poetry of prose statement	to the poetry of images and symbol
15)	Poetic diction	to common familiar Language – "the lan--guage of man"
16)	Self-conscious traditionalism	to conscious originality
17)	Rational sobriety of Latin Literature	to Romantic Hellenism

Q11. Comment on the poem written in a country churchyard?

Ans. In the description of the churchyard the poet does not give a pictorial representation of the place, but by apt images, he evokes a sense of weariness, darkness, gloom and parting and thereby sets the scene of the poem.

In poem the announcement is about the parting day. The image of the curfew bell tolling contributes to the solemnness and gravity of the scene that is evoked. The philosophic reflections that are made in the course of the poem are occasioned by the scene evoked in the opening lines. The next 15 lines (after the opening line) intensify the atmosphere and build a sensation of a world closing in. The oxen wind their way slowly home to be followed by the weary ploughman plodding homeward and the world grows dark with the approach of the late evening.

In continuation of the preceding four stanzas present the supremacy of death against which honour, heraldry, power, wealth and glory prove no match to sustain the living. The poet is not contrasting the rich against the poor, but the introduction of the rich at this point is part of a larger statement of the poem that death is common to both the rich and the poor. At no stage in the poem does the poet romanticise about the virtues of the poor not attempt to eulogise these underprivileged classes, but he makes it explicit that mortality is a common fact of existence that spares neither the lowly nor the great.

The poet thus balances the two classes – the rich and the poor – and thereby admonishes the rich not to scorn "the short and simple annals of the poor." He addresses the rich with unflattering epithets such as "Ambition", "Grandeur", "boast", "pomp", "proud", "Flattery" and states that their story painted on the urns or their images carved in animated bust cannot save them from death or bring them back to life.

The poet makes the observation that man fears oblivion and seeks posthumous remembrance through some frail or resplendent memorial.

Human desire to be remembered even after death is so strong that it is imagined to smoulder in the ashes of the dead. Men are pretty much alike in their fundamental fears and desires and their difference in rank and status in society is only a matter of chance.

Without being sentimental about the poor, the poet says that our rustic forefathers would have ended as cruel, vain sycophants had they "learn'd to stray from the "cool sequester'd life" of "noiseless tenor" (quiet and uneventful life). The portrayal of the villagers has been realistic and not sentimental.

According to him, the poor and the rich share alike the essential destiny of mankind – namely, the graves. The essential and fundamental ambition of mankind is the desire for self-perpetuation after death. The short-simple annals of the poor are inscribed on the tombs – not in artful rhymes, but in artless tales. But who erected the rhymes on the graves? It is illiterate village poet who scribbled these lines often quoting not too assuredly from the Holy Bible and thereby paying his tribute to the dead.

Introduces the stone-cutter Poet, "Thee" is a reference to this stone-cutter who has inscribed the uncouth rhymes as memorial to the dead fellow rustics. The poet observer has created the stone-cutter in his imagination. In the same way "the kindred spirit" is the projection of the poet spokesman. The poet-spokesman speaks of the stone-cutter as one who mindful of the dead "*dost* in these lines their artless tale relate."

In a similar fashion, he imagines the "hoary-headed swain" – an illiterate old man to speak of the stone-cutter's life. Hence the swain's reply is in pastoral language and thus the imaginary swain leads the imaginary kindred spirit to an imaginary epitaph.

The Epitah: Here lies a young man, who had known neither fortune nor fame. He was of humble birth bit fair science (native wisdom) did not frown upon his humble birth. He was apart from the rest of the villagers as he possessed both intelligence and melancholic sensitivity. It is this that made him respond to their suffering with generosity and compassion." He gave to Misery all he had, a tear" – in the form of uncouth rhymes. The lack of earthly riches was amply compensated by heaven's bounty that gave him a generous heart and a genial soul. At the end he received heavenly blessings. This epitaph praises one of the literate poor who was rich in the possession of Heaven's blessings. No one need know further his merits and faults for the (with his merits and faults) has earned his repose in the bosom of the lord. The poem is thus an elegy for the poor and of the poor.

It is difficult to concur with such a view. In the context of the opening quatrain of the poem that places the poet in the country churchyard at a late hour in the evening. It is difficult to explain the poet's address – to himself. The rest of the lines relating to the daily activities of the "Kindred spirit" as told by the "hoary headed swain" seem to be true of a rustic semi-literate poet than of the educated poet who writes this **elegy.** The last but one line before the epitaph that says "thou cans't read" can only be a reference to a kindred spirit like the poet who sings this elegy.

The Elegy is a unique poem fusing neo-classical objectivity with romantic subjectivity. The objectivity is seen in the analysis of the poor which is not sentimental nor a glorification of the poor in ideal terms. The subjectivity is seen in the Poet's intense empathic response to the humble and unexciting life of the poor and his hightened feeling of kinship with them.

Chapter – 3

The Romantic Poets

Q1. Write an introduction to Tintern Abbey **[Dec 2006, Q4]**

Or

Write outline of the poem 'Tintern Abbey' **[June 2006, Q4]**

Ans. Introduction: Tintern Abbey is the abridged title of the poem. Lines composed A few miles above Tintern Abbey on revisiting The Banks of The Why During A Tour. This poem was composed and published in 1798 and stands as testimony to the two basic creeds that Wordsworth enunciated in his preface to The Lyrical Ballads in 1800. Wordsworth stated that poetry has its origin in "emotion recollected in tranquility" and that poetry is "the spontaneous overflow of powerful feelings". Wordsworth's emphasis is on the word "revisiting". This poem was composed on his revisiting. Tintern Abbey that stands on the bank of rivier Wye after a lapse of 5 years. Hence poem is a recapitulation of the emotions that Wordsworth had experienced on his earlier visit to the place. The poem in short, is an expression of Wordsworth's thoughts & feelings in the presence of remembered scene. Tintern Abbey is a spiritual autobiography. Wordsworth's recollection of pleasures enjoyed during an earlier visit interlaced with harmony experienced in his present visit holds out to him. The prospect of a similar joyous experience in the future and thus knits the poem into an autobiographical framework. The poet traces his spiritual growth and development in the poem and therefore it is referred to as a spiritual autobiography. The poem also falls in the category of meditative poetry, which is philosophical in intent and circular in structure Tintern Abbey begins and ends with an invocation to Nature.

The outline of the Poem: The poem can be summarized along its five movements. In the first movement, the poet describes nature with a special emphasis on its essential quality of harmony & order.

In second movement, he speaks of the gifts of nature to him. Harmony in nature brings about harmony in the poet – in his senses, heart, mind, soul. As a result, the poet enters into a state of mystical trance when all his external sensations are laid asleep and only his soul his awake, which with the help of his power of imagination sees "into life of things". Nature's gift is to transport him to a sublime state greatest where he can get a glimpse of the infinite.

In the third movement he wakes up from his state of trance only to be tormented by doubts as to the validity of these gifts of nature.

In the fourth movement, the poet surveys the scene before him – the sense that had given him so much pleasure and reassurance in the past.

In the fifth and final movement Wordsworth addresses nature with gratitude and renewed paper. He seeks nature's blessing on his sister, Dorothy Wordsworth, who is in second and youthful stage of her approach to nature. He prays that she like him, shall be led from joy to joy and shall also experience the intimations of immortality in the presence of nature.

Q2. Write down the poetic devices in Tintern Abbey and The Daffodils?

Ans. In his preface to the *Lyrical Ballads,* Wordsworth presented a set of propositions about the nature and criteria of poetry. We have dealt with Wordsworth's basic definitions of poetry as "a spontaneous overflow of powerful feelings" and as "emotion recollected in tranquillity". Besides these, he had also commented on *Poetic diction* and *figurative speech.* Wordsworth believed that poetry is the instinctive utterance of feeling and passion and so the language of poetry is the language of passion and emotion and therefore, it is natural. In other words, he said that there is no need in poetry to deviate from ordinary language – (i.e.) the language spoken by men under the stress of genuine feeling. He describes natural language as "the simple and unelaborated expressions of essential passions by men living close to nature". As for the figures of speech employed in poetry, Wordsworth rejected the concept of figures as the ornaments of language. He said that the figures of speech instead of being "supposed ornaments" should be naturally suggested by passion. Both dichin and imagery in these two poems *Tintern Abbey and Daffodils* are consistent with Wordsworth's pronouncements. For example the imagery is *Tintern Abbey* expresses its quietness and harmony. Wordsworth speaks of harmony in sights and sounds. The progression to the quiet phase of nature is seen in the progression in the imagery from the "din to cities" to "the *soft* inland murmur" to "the still, sad music of humanity". Note the harmony in colour in the opening lines of the poem. Similarly in *Daffodils,* we notice the poet's creative imagination that turns "a crowd" of yellow flowers into "a host" of "golden" daffodils.

Wordsworth's use of similes in *Daffodils* is illustrative of his use of figures as suggested by his emotion and feelings. He begins the poem by instituting a comparison between himself and the cloud - suggestive of his drifting aimlessly in a mood of desolation and despondency. Try to explain the other comparison in the poem between the daffodils and the stars on the milly way.

Identify the use of alliterations in the two poems.

(Hints: "*Sensations Sweet*", "*Secluded scene*", "*Sent up in silence*" (Tintern Abbey), "*Stars that Shine*", "*Beside the lake, beneath the trees*" (Daffodils) "*Ten thousand...Tossing*".

Wordsworth's insistence upon language as primitive utterancc of passions is seen in the archaisms in the poems. For example we have the expression "beauteous forms" (TA), the "jocund company" (Daffodils) that suggest the impassioned utterances of the poet.

Q3. Discuss 'Tintern Abbey' as an autobiographical poem?

[June 2008, Q6]

Ans. Tintern Abbey is a spiritual autobiography. Wordsworth's recollection of pleasures enjoyed during an earlier visit interlaced with harmony experienced in his present visit holds out to him the prospect of a similar joyous experience in the future and thus knits the poem into an autobiographical framework. The poet traces his spiritual growth and development in the poem and therefore it is referred to as a spiritual autobiography.

The poem also falls in the category of meditative poetry, which is philosophical in intent and circular in structure. Tintern Abbey begins and ends with an invocation to Nature. The last stanza with a reference to woods, cliffs and the green pastoral farms is an echo of the opening stanza and thus the poem gains a circular frame.

Q4. Write down outline of poem "The Daffodils". [Dec 2006, Q4]

Ans. The poem records an ancedote of Wordsworth's life history when he came upon a bunch of daffodils while walking in Lake District. Daffodils are yellow flowers that are found in plenty in Lake District, a picturesque mountainous region in England. Wordsworth says that Daffodils is not just a poem of simple human sentiments of pleasure and delight on his seeing a bunch of daffodils, but this tender and delicate poem has much to offer to the reader in terms of "knowledge". By "knowledge" Wordsworth means knowledge of the process of poetic creation. The poem is remarkable for its accuracy of description, and it also offers an account of the way poetry is created. It illustrates the working of Wordsworth's imagination as it acts on the picture of daffodils given by the senses and turns it into a rich, perennial source of joy and inspiration. He can recall these images at times of stress and strain or during periods of loneliness and experience joy and tranquility. Daffodils is yet another instance of the overflow of emotion recollected in tranquility.

Q5. Write down outline of poem "The Ancient Mariner".

Ans. Part I : An old sailor (the Ancient Mariner) detains as guest at a wedding to tell him the story of his strange voyage. The guest eager to join the festivities protests but the Mariner with the force of his personality compels him to sit and listen. The voyage begins normally and the ship sails southwards till it reaches the Equator. It is then driven by a storm to the regions of perpetual ice. There is no sign of life there till a large sea bird, the albatross appears. This coincides with the coming of a favourable wind and the ship returns northwards. The bird is welcomed by the ship's crew who feed it and enjoy a company. It follows the ship for nine days when all of a sudden without any apparent cause the Mariner shoots the bird.

Part II: The ship moves northwards but the foggy conditions of the polar regions persist. The Mariner's shipmates blame him for killing the bird of good omen that made the breeze to blow. When, however, they approach the equatorial regions and the fog clears and the sun shines brightly, they applaud the Mariner's deed of killing the bird as though it had brought the fog. They thus become accomplices in the Mariner's crime. At the equator the ship is stranded without a breeze and the crew suffer terribly from heat and thirst. The marks the beginning of the punishment for the killing of the albatross. The shipmates now blame the Mariner for their suffering and they hang the dead bird around the Mariner's neck as a sign of his guilt.

Part III: The ship remains stationary and the torture of the crew continues. They are visited by a horrifying skeleton ship manned by two fearsome figures. One is identified as Death and the other as Life-in-Death. They gamble for the lives of the crew. Death wins all of them except the Mariner whom Life-in-Death takes possession of. Part III ends with the death of all the crew members while the Mariner remains alive to be left alone with his torment.

Part IV-VII: The Mariner suffers total isolation and he is plagued by a sense of guilt. The only living things visible are the sea-creatures which took ugly to him as they crawl about. He is surrounded by the bodies of his shipmates whose eyes seem to curse him even in their death. This agony continues for 7 days when under the light of the moon the Mariner observes a Hermit and asks him to listen to his confessional story. As he begins to narrate his experiences he is wrenched by a terrible agony which leaves him only when his story is finished. This compulsion to roam from land to land and narrate his story (and relive his experience) is the penance that he must do all through his life.

Sounds from the wedding celebration are heard and as the wedding guest gets ready to leave, the Mariner tells him that his greatest joy in life is to be a part of the human community once again. The Mariner teaches by his own example that as part of God's creation we must love and revere all things that God has made. The poem ends with the departure of the Mariner and the wedding guest finds himself 'a sadder and a wiser man' after this strange encounter with the Mariner.

Q6. Write down about the background of poem "Roll on the thou deep and dark blue ocean"

Ans. The poem Childe Harold's Pilgrimage describes the journey of Childe Harold, whose experiences correspond to Byron's Own. On 2 July 1809 Byron left England along with a Cambridge friend John Cam Hobhouse, his servant Fletcher and his 'little page', Robert Rushton. On 6 July they reached Lisbon.

In April 1816 Byron left England, never again to return to it. He went to Geneva in Switzerland where he met Shelley and completed the third canto of Childe Harold, which was published in the same year. It describes the pilgrim's travels to Belgium, the Rhine, the Alps and Jura. Childe Harold also reflects on the Spanish War, and the Battle of Waterloo (1815) at which, Napoleon suffered his final defeat against the United Kingdom.

In October 1816, Byron left Geneva for Venice with Hobhouse. In the fourth canto he speaks directly about his experiences in Italy, his meditations on time and history, on Venice and Petrarch, Ferrara and Tasso, Florence and Boccaccio, Rome and her great men ending with the symbol of the sea. Byron has an abiding interest in the mountains and the sea.

Q7. Write few lines about background of the poem "George the Third"

Ans. In Southey's poem, the poet in a trance sees George III rise from his tomb and reach the gates of Heaven where the Devil and Wilkes the democrat leader come to charge him with crimes he committed on earth. However, they retire in discomfiture when Washington eulogises him and he is greeted by the previous English monarchs, the eminent English and finally his own family.

In the preface to his poem Southey made a direct attack on Byron's works and referred to him as the leader of the 'satanic school' of poetry. In response Byron wrote the parody in which Southey is swept up by one of the devils from the Lake District where he offers to write Satan's Biography and on being declined the favour, Michael's.

Byron praises George's domestic virtues. His family life was free from the characteristic vice of his predecessors. However he wanted to re-establish his personal rule prevalent during the reigns of the later stuarts. He opposed Catholic emancipation, the American War of Independence and the French Revolution. He suffered from recurring fits of insanity and finally became insane in 1811. His eldest son was appointed regent until his father's death in 1820.

Q8. What do you conclude from the poem "To a Skylark"

Ans. It was written in the spring of 1820 and is representative of Shelley's thought and style in his major poetry. Shelley seeks "in this natural world" for analogies by which he wants to assure himself that regeneration follows destruction [as in West Wind]. The bird's joyous spirit – symbolizes the divine essence, the aspiration of the soul and the fore of inspiration. The possibility of world's salvation is through the power of human thought when it is given memorable expression in poetry. The musical quality of Shelley's poetry comes out striking in this poem.

Q9. Discuss development of thought in "Ode to Autumn"

Ans. The Ode was inspired by the song of a nightingale that had built its nest close to the house of a friend of Keats. The poet experiences perfect happiness in the bird's song and want to fade away unseen from the world into the dim forest. At first he want to take refuge in wine, but on second thoughts he understands, wine is not potent enough to transport him into the ideal region. Poetry alone shall transport him. The poet describes the romantic forest into which he has flown on the viewless wings of poetry. He compares the transitionness of the individual human life with the permanence of the song of the bird. The voice that the poet hears was heard in ancient times by emperors and clown. The illusion is then broken; the poet returns to his daily existence and is regretful that imagination cannot beguile him for a long time.

Q10. Write down the summary of Keat's "Ode to a Nightingale"

Ans. Ode To A Nightingale is a poem in eight stanzas.

Stanza 1 describes the poet's excitement as he listens to the song of the nightingale.

Stanza II & III express the poet's wish to enter into the world of the nightingale and thereby remain oblivious of the weariness and fretful stir of human existence. He asks for a draught of wine that can induce in him a state of druggednees so that he can fly far away into the blissful world of the bird.

Stanza IV records the poet's recourse to poetic fancy as an alternative to aid him in his flight into the realm of the nightingale.

Stanza V shows the poet's separateness from the bird. This appeal to poetic fancy has not liberated him from the human world of pain and misery, but has helped him to respond with delight to the naturalistic world, full of colourful flowers.

Stanza VI expresses Keats morbid impulse to die at that very moment of experiencing an intense joy and empathy with nature so that he can cease to experience pain hereafter. The poet says that it is rich to die in his present state of heightened ecstasy.

Stanza VII affirms the permanence of the bird's song in this world. It is not that the bird is immortal, but its song is. It had thrilled successive generations in the past and shall continue to thrill successive generations in the future.

Stanza VIII shows the poet waking up from his fancy and becoming aware that the nightingale has fled and he can no longer listen to it. The poem concludes with an unanswered question whether he had experienced genuinely a heightening of experience or whether it was all just a vision and a dream.

The movement of the poem is related to the poet's movement

(i) from the ideal happy world of the nightingale to the dull everyday world of pain, misery and suffering and

(ii) from a state of ecstasy to a state of forlornness (desolation)

The turn of these two movements comes at the end of the fourth stanza. The first four stanzas assert the poet's identification with the bird and its song and the latter four stanzas lay emphasis upon the poet's separateness from the bird. The bird is present only in the first section and it is absent in the rest of the poem.

Q11. In "Ode To Autumn" pictorial power finds it fullest expression. Comment. Also comment on Keats "Negative Capability"

Ans. Keats is known as a poet painter in words. He has been able to represent nature with the help of imagery which is sensuous and comprehensive as also pictorial. In the first stanza the ripeness of fruit is suggested by "mellow fruitfulness", "to swell", "plump the hazel shell", "sweet kernel", "budding", and nature's bounty in "clammy cells", "maturing sun", "to load and bless".

Keat's distinction lies in his ability to let sense impressions flow upon him and the rich store of sense impressions is absorbed and transmuted into an act of calm, meditative wisdom. The poet is himself completely absent. There is no "I", no suggestion of the discursive language. The power of self absorption, identification with things, he called "negative capability" which he saw as essential to creation of poetry.

Q12. Write a critical appreciation of Shalley's "Ode To The West Wind". [June 2006, Q4]

Ans. The Ode is charged with speed, force and energy like the tempestuous wind itself. The powerful movements of the verse is carried on by use of a series of images thrown us in rapid succession. The movement is not just confined to the elemental forces of nature: It is also to be seen in the emotions roused in the poet's mind by his contemplation of the wind. The movement shows down in Section 3 and then gains rapidity in line with the poet's impetuous spirit, as he drives to the close.

There is, in this poem, a blend of natural and spiritual forces, the West Wind is a force of nature, but it also symbolizes the freespirit of man untamed and proud. Shelley's great passion for the regeneration of mankind and rebirth of a new world find a fitting symbol in the West Wind which destroys and preserves, sweeps away the old and obsolete ideas and fosters fresh and new ones.

The West Wind is a force of Nature, but it also symbolizes the free spirit of man, untamed, free and proud. It also symbolises the inspiration of the poet and becomes the message of the prophet. Shelley was interested in happiness, in reforming the world, so that happiness to all could be secured. Shelley firmly believed that man was by nature good and capable of perfection, but social and political institutions corrupted him. Evil lay not in man's heart, but outside in the State, in Society and, in Religion. Shelly had been deeply influenced by the ideals of the French Revolution: "Liberty, Equality, Fraternity".

Q13. Write an essay on Shelley as romantic poet with special reference to poems you have studied? [Dec 2006, Q4]

Ans. Good qualities in Shelley's poetry are described in terms of music, bright colours, light, air, sky, water, wind, fire and natural growth such as plant, flowers, etc. Shelley's poetry is full of images and symbols. We find a succession of images. His difficulty at all times seem to be to get a line or a stanza completed before successive images came crowding in. However, the rhythmical case is marked out as the musical quality of Shelley's poetry comes out striking in poem "To a skylark"

The romance in the poem can be seen in every line. He has mentioned 'rainbow clouds' in this poem in stanza – 7. It happens towards the end of rainy season as in month of 'Bhadon' in India that when sun is stuning, some clouds burst forth.

We can also notice archaic words such as: wert, purest, though springest, wengest, art, thy and so on. It is difficult for a reader to identify with Shelley's use of archaic words. It seems to have constituted some kind of fashion among the Romantics – to draw on the diction that is archaic. Shelley's both poem placed a high value on joy as it is the symbol of Romantics. Shelly has deliberately and painfully explored a state of depression. The Romantic placed a high value on joy, a number of their finest poems, deal with negative states of mind, with the failure to achieve joy or to sustain it, and with fluctuation of their moods.

Q14. Write down the critical view on "George the Third"

Ans. The first stanza sets the background of the poem. It announces the event - the demise of George III – and sets the comico-satirical tone of the poem. 1820 was the year in which the struggle for Greek independence began in which Byron also took some interest. George died in the same year. Byron thus makes use of periphrasis. He tells us about some of George's good qualities - that he was no tyrant and was a good farmer - and some bad ones - that he shielded tyrants. A satirist attempts to rectify the vices of the society in which he lives. While Byron, apparently ridicules the king alone, at times he hints at the shortcomings in the British people also. He points out that George left his subjects, 'One half as mad – and t'other no less blind.'

The second and the third stanza describe the melodrama that the funeral was.

From the fourth through the seventh stanzas are the words of the Devil who has come to claim George from Michael at the Heaven Gate. Hence you find the king subjected to caustic satire. The 'I' of the first line of the fourth stanza refers to the Devil. His chief attack is on George's attempt to establish personal rule in England. During his reign Britain's American colonies became independent. Britain both in trying to suppress the American colonies and Napoleon who was in the popular imagination a symbol of liberty, became the butt of Byron's satire. Besides being a foe to liberty George had an insatiable thurst for gold. The sovereign besides was a tool in the hands of other people.

The last two lines of the seventh stanza make a transition to the main subject of the eighth, recounting, George's virtues – 'his household abstinence', faithfulness to his wife, qualities as a father, etc.

The last stanza shifts the focus of our attention from a dead British monarch to the monarchs of Europe who either as drones sleep on their thrones unmindful of their country's plights or are despots who have refused to learn from the mistakes of the deceased monarch.

Byron's satire thus has a nobler intention, that is, of rectifying the sources of politico-administrative power of their ills. The sovereigns on the European thrones are George's heirs, metaphorically speaking and Byron's satire is directed at them also.

Chapter – 4

Victorian Poetry

Q1. Explain with reference to the context the following lines

Only reapers....................The fairy Lady of Shalott

These lines have been extracted from the Poem "The Lady of Shalott" (Part-1) composed by Tennyson, the poem is divided in two parts and is about a mysterious lady Shalott. In part-1 we are told that the castle is situated on an island in the middle of the river, where they lady lives. There is a strange curse on her so she is forbidden to look out of the world directly. But one day she broke the rule and the dreadened curse befall her. In these lines we are told that no one had seen this lady. Her existence is only confirmed by her songs that sometimes be heard by reapers late at night. The busy road and the boats playing in the river suggest a normal life which is direct contrast to the loneliness of the island. The poem has a musical quality and rich details of descriptions. The poet is successful in setting the stage for the intriguing story of the mysterious Lady of Shalott and arose the feeling of curiousity in us through his in pressing technique of writing.

(1) Describe the Theme of the passage from 'The Lotos Eaters' in about 50-60 words.

The poem is perfect fusion of sound and sense. The theme of the poem is that human life is useless if and if in the end of all tiles is to be the grave. We are given option one should chose life of rest and peace rather that duty and hardships. This is exemplified in the mariners debate about whether to return home as to stay on the enchanted lotus island and live a life of idyllic peace and restfulness.The debate is resolved in the final line when the mariners decide to stay on that paradise.

(2) Write a short note on the verbal music in the poem?

Tennyson has once again implied his technique of using the musical beauty. This beauty is created from his sensitive use of an arrangement of words. It is a perfect fusion of sound and sense. With alliteration and assonance combined with rhyme the verbal music perfectly adapted to the poet's tone and the exotic scene. The smooth flow of words heightens the feeling of imagined peace and languor. On reading opening lines of the poem we can appreciate its onomatepoeic excel once. His aims to evake, by the sounds of words, the feeling of sensuous life.

(3) Characterize Ulysses. What kind of person is he?

Ulysses desirer to travel does not simply represent a desire of adventure. Ulysses represents the human desire for striving beyond human limits to achieve something noble and great. Human beings must not simply live and die a mundane life but must try to achieve something great before life. Ulysses as The Legendry Great hero was the King o Ithaca. After the war of Tray, he set sail for home. He faced may storms and obstacles and he wandered for 10 years before he reached home. But he was so brave and adventurous that he desired to travel again to follow virtue and knowledge.

(4) Find evidence in the poem to show that Ulysses desire for travel represents more than a desire for adventure (100 words).

Clearly Ulysses desire to travel does not simply represent a desire for adventure. Tennyson say that 'it gives the' feeling about the need of going forward and braving the struggle of life. Ulysses represents the human desire for striving beyond human limits to achieve something noble and great. Human beings must not simply live and die a mundane life but must try to achieve something great before death.

"How dull it is to pause to make an end, To rush unburnish'd not to shine in use, And this grey spirit yearning in desire, To follow knowledge, like a sinking star, Beyond the utmost bound of human thought, Odage hath yet his honour and his toil, Death closes all but something ere the end, Some war of noble note, may yet be done___ for my purpose hold.

To bail beyond the sunset_____

To strive, to seek to find and not to yield.

(5) Explain with reference to context

"And the stately......................voice that is still"

Above stanza has been taken from the short lyric the poem 'Break, Break, Break written by Tennyson. This is simple poem expressing a deep sense of loss. In the above stanza, the poet watches the impressive e ships sailing towards their harbour below the hill. This rinse of journey safely completed only induces the poet to acutely miss the soothing touch of the hand of his dead friend – a touch that ends passage of time. The pleasant days spent in the loving company of his friend are gone forever and will never return. Poet is able to highlight his own grief and desolation. Through the poem, Poet contrast the joy of the scene around him. The poem is an personal expression of the poet's grief over the death of his friend Arthur.

(6) Explain the following lines with.................. to the context.

"For sudden...........with the rest"

These lines have been quoted from the poem "Prospice" of Robert Browning. The poet compares imminent death with a journey up a steep mountain. The poet speculates on the stages that one must pass thorough before one's death. Just like a climber reaches the summit after difficulties, similarly the poet will overcome all hardships and face death bravely. All must die eventually. In the above stanza Browning says that the brave person is always able to turn even the worst situation to his own advantage. The moment of despair will soon end. And even though the storm may flow in all its fury and strange wild voices may be heard, all will gradually subside. Worst calamities die down if faced bravely. The poet will be restored to his beloved whom he addresses as 'The soul of my soul'. He will embrace het and forget all else which he leaves unto the care of God. The poet moves from images of darkness to light, from despair to hope, from the pain of loss to the ecstasy of reunion with beloved. Death is considered powerless and ineffective.

(7) In a few lines write down a critical appreciation of "Meeting at night"

Narrator's boat is rowing in the grey sea. The long line of the shore looks dark in the night. The golden half moon seeks suspended low in the sky. The reflection of the moonlight on the waves give them the appereance of the tousled golden curld of someone who has suddenly woken up from sleep. Narrator then continues his journey on foot, walking along for about a mile on the warm beach that smells of salt water and fish. He reaches a farer after crossing three fields. He taps a window and hears his beloved's voice. The voice is full of joy and fear-joy at his arrival but fear of being discovered. The journey concludes happily as the two lovers join in a passionate embrace.

(8) Write short note on Browning's poetic device?

The first feature of the poem is its brevity and intensity. The lady is not described. The meeting is barely mentioned. The rhyme scheme of the two stanzas is ab cc ba; de ff ed. The lines are in pentameter and often irregular. The musical quality of his poem is ensured by extensive use of alliteration. For ex. 'long black land', 'yellow half moon large and low,' The reflection of the moonlight on the waves is conveyed in the effective image of a head of curly golden hair awaken with a start. The poem is reckly reassures an effect that is suited to its romantic mood.

(9) Pick out the words and phrases that convey the dukes arrogance. Does he refer to his dead wife body? Is he aware of his crime? What is your attitude towards him? Does he evoke sympathy, respect, hatred?

The Duke's arrogance can be seen in following words : "She thanked men-good, but thanked

Somehow - I knew and how – as if she ranked

My gift of a nine hundred-years-old name

With anybody's gift

'I______I choose

Never to stoop'

'I gave command's

The all shall smiles stopped together____'

The duke does not refer to his wife's beauty but only to its representation commenting on painter's expertise. The duke is totally unaware of his crime or else he would not refer to his wifes murder as'I gave command'. Then all smiles stopped together___________ His cold bolded attitude can hardly fail to evoke a feeling of disgust in the reader.

(10) Do you think that the duke's speech is an indirect to his next wife? If so give reasons to support your answers.

The duke's monologue certainly lays down the code of behaviour that he expects from any woman that he condescends to marry. A veil threat lurks under his words. For He says he has no sympathy with or understanding the young duchess' innocence. He complains that she liked all that she saw. He is shocked at her of discrimination. He could not get over the fact that since she thanked all equally she probably held his ancient family name in equal esteem with them. Duke did not like it at all and did not expect such thing from his next wife. He could not tolerate that his wife smiled at others as well.

(11) Briefly describe the characters of the Duke and Duchess from your heading of 'My Last Duchess'

Duke was extremely arrogant. He did not even like his duchess should speak to anyone or smile at anyone. He had a cold-blooded in his nature, he had no guilt for killing his wife. He was lover of art, in the very opening lines he appreciated the painter and the painting both. He hated politeness and friendly nature of duchess.

Duchess seems to be an innocent girl. She was pleased and impressed even at small things of common people. She enjoyed every bit of life with full fun. She was unaware of her husband's brand nature. She did not even think that her husband would kill her for her nature.

(12) Explain with reference to the context. The following lines:

For the loftiest................mortality

These lines have been extracted from the poem "Shakespeare" written by Mathew Arlond. Poet has given to tribute to the outstanding genius of Shakespeare. Shakespeare is the literary colossus who towers above other poets. Shakespeare is like the highest maintain whose magestic peaks are only visible to the stars in the sky. The mountain has a firm base in the depths of the sea and from these depths it rises to the highest heavens. The base of the mountain is submerged in the sea and it summit touches the zenith of the sky. Neither its height nor depths are visible to human being. Only the lower slopes, covered in clouds can be seen by them. Shakespeare's genius is highlighted by the use of antithesis. The continued contrast with lesser poets.

(13) In about 50-60 words, give central idea of the poem "To Marguerite"

The poem is not about any personal crisis as the title suggests but this personal loss inspired by separation from Marguerite has triggered off a more general feeling of the prevailing alienation besieging of one with its attendant isolation and separation of one individual of another. Te problem of isolation and alienation of the individual is not just personal; it is universal. There is a sense of spiritual decline and collapse that goes with this sense of loss.

(14) In your words write down the theme of Dover Beach.

Dover Beach is a small poem. Poet ruminates on the loss of religious faith and the subsequent vulnerability of human beings to the sufferings and pains of life. It is only through a satisfying love-relationship that one can wrest a meaningful existence in an otherwise meaningless and hostile universe. Arnold explains that at one time religious faith supported and helped mankind and was at its strongest. The religious faith was like a beautiful garment that engirdled the earth. The faith was universal. But now people have lost faith in religion which has withdrawn from everywhere like the outgoing tited. The spiritual decline has left human beings vulnerable and exposed to sorrows of life. People can have no peace and continue to suffer pain.

(15) Explain with reference to context:

"all down his..................from the sun's eye"

This stanza has been quoted from the poem Sohrab and Rustum. The poem is based on Persion mythology, the scene of Rustum's death is depicted here. Sohrab pierced Rustum's body with his spear unknowingly. Later when truth was revealed to him, he removed appear from his body. The blood flowed from the wound and gradually life ebbed with this flew. The stream of red blood flaved fro down his white body which looked dull and soiled like the bruised petals of white violets. The flowers were plucked by the children from the bank where they grew. As the children had been called away indoors by their nurses out of the feet of the sun, they left the flowers to witt outside.

(16) How would you describe the mood of the first verse? Pick out details that you find are most effective in establishing this mood.

The mood of the poet is sad and glooming in the first verse. The gloom is heightened by the bleak winter weather and the dark evening. The surrounding as very gloomy. The landscape looked as bleak and desolate that in the dark it looked like the corpse of the bygone century laid at rest. The poet sounds menlancholy. He is alone – everything around him looks bleak and dreary. The whole atmosphere looks desolate, bleak and gloomy to the poet.

(17) What does the image of 'Century's corpse' add to the poem?

The image of the 'Century's corpse' makes the idea of an abstract concept like the passage of time more concrete. It also makes us visualize the bleak landscape effectively.

(18) Why do you think Hardy describes the thrush as 'aged....frail gaunt and small?' Does this phrase lead you to expect the phrase 'to fling his soul upon the growing gloom?'

By describing the weak old thrush, Hardy is able to further highlights its fortitude and resilience in the face of the 'blast'. One is also startled by the sudden outburst of song from his frail creature. Hardy, by the use of contrast is able to express his own sad lack of the spirit that is seen in the little bird.

(19) Some reader fact that in the last two lines Hardy is admitting that the thrush is wiser and more courageous than he is. Others have felt that hw is being ironic. How do you read these lines?

Poet says The Thrush is the only cheerful creature around him but even the bird's songs frails to inspire cheer in him. The thin aged bird braves the water blasts and still continues to sing. The bird provide the poet with a ray of hope and a fresh incentive to face the new year with more courage and fortitude. The joyous spirit is infectious and can also joy among those who feel dejected and depressed. The small frail appears more courageous to the poet. It looks as it source of inspiration for him.

(20) Explain the following lines with reference

Alone, aloud in the ....welcome the dawn.

These lines are extracted from the poem "Nightingales" written by Robert Bridges. Here the poet addresses Nightingales as human beings. The poet wants to wander in the woods, among the flowers that bloom the whole year is divine atmosphere. The Nightingales then respond that the mountains where they hail from are barren and the streams dry. The Nightingales tell that their song is song of sorrow. They continue their tale of woe. They pair their hidden secret into the ears of human beings through their song. As the nights fades from the meadows and branches on a May morning, they sleep and dream while numerous other birds welcome the day break with their song. Bridges has personifies the Nightingales. The song evoked the image of the ethernal valleys of flowers that bloom. The Nightingales sang in the night song of their unfulfilled hopes and desires.

Long Answers

Q1. Write a short note on "The Victorian Age".

Ans. The reign of Queen Victoria which extended from 1837 to 1901 is referred to as the Victorian Age. However, it would not be far from the truth to term the Victorian Age as a **period of peace** and prosperity. Seventeenth century England was rife with Civil War and revolutions and the eighteenth century witnessed recurrent wars against France. However, during the nineteenth century the only wars were the Crimean War (1853-54) against imperial Russia and Boer War (1899-1902) in South Africa which only served to enhance Britain's power and prestige which reached its zenith in the mid-nineteenth century. It was a period of **imperial expansion**. It was also a **period of economic prosperity** marked by a strong ethic of self-help. Hard work was regarded as they key to success. There was an intense feeling on national unity and optimism. The familiar image of Queen Victoria with her husband Prince Albert and their children only served to emphasize the importance of the **family as a key social unit**. The Victorian age as also rather **moralistic** and the Queen's soberly clad figure only stressed the propriety and decorum that marked nineteenth century English society.

The Victorian age is often referred to as **'an age of giants'.** The writers of the period were confident and extremely prolific. The Elizabethan age can be seen as the age of drama, the Romantic age as the age of poetry, while the Victorian age can boast of the best English novels ever written.

The poetry of the age I a continuation of the Romantic tradition at one level, while on another, it is also an expression of the spirit of its age. In general terms, one might well say that while Romantic poetry emerged as a product of the poet's individual mind and experience, Victorian poetry seem to evolve out oa more general spirit of the age. For example, Romantic poetry comes straight from the heart, while Victorian poetry gives the impression that a poet is always aware of his/her own exalted status and this dictates the tone and the manner in which she/he addresses the reader. This does not mean that the Victorians did not express their emotions.

Q2. What do you conclude from the poem "The Lotos Eater"?

Ans. In this poem, the reader is greatly impressed with the musical beauty that Tennyson has created from his sensitive use of an arrangement of words. It is a perfect fusion of sound and sense.

By skilful use of contrast, the poet is able to evoke both the present serene location of the mariners and their turbulent past. At the very outset, we are told of the lotus flower that blooms everywhere on the island, the yellow lotus dust that is blown in the breeze has a magical soporific effect on the sailors. The mariners then contrast this with their earlier life of toil on board ship when through calm and storm all they did was work. Remembering their earlier hardships, the mariners exhort each other to swear unanimously to stay on in this enchanted island.

The *theme* of the poem is that human life is futile and if the end of all til is to be the grave, then given the option one should choose a life of rest and peace rather than duty and hardships. This is exemplified in the mariners' debate about whether to return home or whether to stay on the enchanted lotus island and live a life of idyllic peace and restfulness. The debate is resolved in the final line when the mariners decide to stay on the paradise.

This poem is a masterpiece of sheer poetry that results from a flexible and free handling, of the metre. It is written in iambic lines of varied length-of between three to seven feet.

He adopts the rhythm to suit the sense of what he is saying in that particular line. For example, when he talks about the mariner's life of toil, the lines become quick-paced but when reference is made 5to th3 indolent life of the island, the pace slackens, becoming more serene.

If we look at the opening lines of this Section, we can at once appreciate its onomatepoeic excellence. He aims to evoke, mainly by the sounds of the words, the feeling of the sensuous life. The words flow effortlessly.

The Lotus blooms below the barren peak;

The Lotus blows by every winding creek:

With alliteration and assonance combined with rhyme the verbal music is perfectly adapted to the poet's tone and the exotic scene.

Q3. Who is Ulysses? [June 2007, Q4]

Ans. Ulysses, the legendary Greek hero was the king of Ithaca who after the siege of Troy, set sail for home. On his way home he was subjected to many storms and obstacles because of the wrath of the sea-god (Poseidon). He was forced to wander for another 10 years before he reached Ithaca, his wife Penelpe and son Telemachus. But a sedentary, lie was not what he wanted and desired to travel again 'to follow virtue and knowledge' (ante). In this poem, Ulysses is about to set and sail on a final voyage from which he will not return.

Having a wandered on many adventures, Ulysses returns to his island home of Ithaca to resume his life as a ruler. But he finds himself bored with the commonplace activities of daily life and longs to 'sail beyond the sunset' in search of a more fulfilling life.

Ulysses wishes to 'sail beyond the sunset'. This means that his route would lie west. He says that much of life is over but still plenty of it remains. And thought they do not have the strength of youth which they once had when they could achieve the impossible, he says their spirit is still indomitable though they may have declined in physical strength. All of them heroically inclined and their motto would be 'To strive, to seek, to find and not to yield'.

Clearly Ulysses' desire to travel does not simply represent a desire for adventure. Tennyson used to say that it gives the 'feeling about the need of going forward and braving the struggle of life....' (RB Martin, 267). Ulysses represents the human desire for striving beyond human limits to achieve something noble and great. Human beings must not simply live and die a mundane life but must try to achieve something great before death.

Q4. Write down the critical summary of poem "Prospice"

Ans. The poem begins with a rhetorical question. 'Fear death? – clearly the poet does not. What does the poet suggest in the next eight lines? He compares imminent death with a journey up a steep mountain. A climber must experience a feeling of suffocation and shortness of breath as he climbs through the mists. As he goes higher up the mountain, the snowfall and the stormy blasts of wind seems to signify that the summit is approaching. In the same way, a man passes through several trials and tribulations before he comes face to face with death. The poet continues with the image of the climber toiling up a mountain. All turn dark, the storm rages fiercely as he approaches the position of the enemy. And who is this 'foe' that the poet refers to? This foe is none other then the 'Arch Fear' death. Death is the enemy that all human beings fear. Just as the journey ends when the climber reaches the summit after surmounting all difficulties, similarly the poet will overcome all hardships and face death bravely. All must eventually die.

In the next eight lines, the poet ponders over how life's battles are won after great struggle. Even in life one achieves the highest point at the end of a difficult journey which one must face and overcome many obstacles. The reward can only be had after a fierce struggle.

Browning believes that the brave person is able to turn even the worst situation to is won advantage. The moment of despair will soon end. And even though the storm may blow in all its fury and strange wild voices may be heard, all will gradually subside. What does he wish to say? He simply means that the worst calamities die down if faced bravely. This then shall be his attitude to death. After the tumult, there will be peace and clam. It seems as if the poet will then emerge from darkness and despair to light and hope. The poet will then be restored to his beloved whom he addresses as 'thou soul of my soul!' He will embrace her and forget all else which he leaves unto the care of God.

Q5. Write poetic devices of "Prospice"

Ans. Death is an abstract concept. Browning has *personified* it giving it a 'visible form' that inspires fear. Death is thus a dreaded enemy who inhabits a stormy pitch dark place. The process of dying is likened to a journey through the cold, dark and dreary slopes of a steep mountain. The personification is sustained throughout the poem. The images of mists, storms and darkness capture the fearful aspect of death. These word pictures serve to make an abstract concept like death into a concrete fact that can be easily visualized. The *metaphor* of the journey is extended to stand for the struggles of life as well. In the lines 'For sudden the worst turns the best to the brave. The lack minute's at end' you will notice that 'sudden' means 'suddenly'. Also notice the *economy* of the sentence 'The black minute's at end'. As we pointed out in the introduction, this tendency to pack a lot into a few words is a specific trait of Browning's art.

The lines rhyme alternately and the rhyme scheme is abab cdcd efef and so on. The metre is more difficult to determine. The pentameter lines alternate with trimester lines thus crating an impression of quick forward movement that ties up with the journey metaphor. As you can notice, Browning makes extensive use of *alliteration.* Read these lines aloud and savour the sheer music of the s and p sounds. 'Shall dwindle, shall blend, Shall change, shall become first a piece out of pain.....'

Q6. Write features of dramatic monologue in the context of 'My Last Duchess'

Ans. Like many of Browning's best poems, 'My Last Duchess' is inspired in Italy. The poem is probably a dramatization of an account of Alfonso II, the fifth Duke of Ferrara that Browning had read around 1842. He married Lucrezia de'Medici the young daughter of the duke of Florence. They were a fairly new family compared with the count. Lucrezia died at the age of 17-she was poisoned. Three years later Alfonso contracted a marriage with Barbara, neice of the Count of Tyrol. The poem is set in Renaissance Italy (sixteenth century).

As we have pointed out earlier, this poem is a dramatic monologue. In a dramatic monologue:

(a) the narrative is related by one person;

(b) we can get an idea of the situation in which the person speaks;

(c) we can also infer what happened before this particular circumstance is described:

(d) the motives and character of the speaker are revealed. For example, the speaker may praise himself but from the context of the poem, we can infer whether this is justified or otherwise.

(e) the poet makes use of colloquial speech that is appropriate to the speaker (Michael Manson):

(f) the treatment is serious (Manson):

(g) the exotic nature of the speaker and the remoteness of the scene distances the dramatic monologue from both the author and the reader (Manson)

Q7. Write poetic devices of "My Last Duchess"

Ans. The versification of the poem is marked by freedom of flow. The lines are arranged in rhyming couplets such as aa bb cc and so on. But these are not closed couplets which carry a complete thought or feeling. On the other hand, one line continues into the next line. This is thus an open couplet and the technique is called **enjambment.** This is more appropriate because the monologue form demands an unbroken flow of thoughts processes. It also caters to the digression that are a necessary feature of thinking aloud.

Another element that recurs in Browning's poetry, as we have noticed, is alliteration. For exmapl,e 'Oh sir, she smiled, no doubt. When'er I passed her; but who passed without much the same smile?' are not only musical but also stress the frequency of the offending smiles and the concomitant irritation that they caused. The voice of the duke almost turns to a venomous hiss that leads to his sinister commands.

Also notice the diction in this poem. By using words such as countenance, munificence, forsooth and durst, the poet has created an atmosphere of bygone age, Renaissance Italy in this case. The duke speaks in an ironical tone whenever he refers to his last duchess. '…she smiled, no doubt. Whene'er I passed her, but who passed without much the same smile? His exclusive breeding and social finesse are evident in his reference to her death as 'Then all smiles stopped together'. The speech is terse – not a single word can be removed without affecting the whole poem. There are sudden transitions, changes of mood and shifts in argument induced by the silent envoy. These not only help to generate an impression of realistic portrayal, but they also reveal the character not only of the duke but also of the duchess whom he wishes to denigrate.

Q8. Write various aspects of poem "Shakespeare"

Ans. The sonnet, as we have seen is a tribute to the outstanding genius of Shakespeare. Shakespeare is the literary colossus who towers above other poets and writers who can be understood but it is difficult to unravel the mysterious and multi-dimensional achievement of Shakespeare.

Arnold begins the poem by making a simple statement. He says that other writers and poets still provide some answers to our questions. In short, we know a lot about them. Shakespeare, on the other hand, is free from such simple comprehension. That is, his life is shrouded in mystery. Shakespeare continues to smile enigmatically and calmly like the incomprehensible expression on the face of the sphinx that sits eternally on Egyptian sands or the elusive smile of Mona Lisa that generations of critics have not been able to decode. In short, Shakespeare goes beyond the limits of our understanding.

For the next 6 lines, a 'lofty hill' is the metaphor that Arnold uses for explaining this idea further. Shakespeare is like the highest mountain whose majestic peaks are only visible to the stars in the sky. The mountain has a firm base in the depths of the sea and from these depths it rises to the highest heavens. As the base of the mountain is submerged in the sea and its summit touches the zenith of the sky, neither its height nor depths are visible to human beings.

Once Arnold has established the incomprehensible and inscrutable nature of Shakespeare's achievement, he extends his tribute by referring to his unique vision that was able to penetrate the mysteries of nature. Shakespeare did not have extensive schooling but taught himself in the school of life. He himself was the assessor of his own work, confident and secure of its enduring greatness. His contemporaries could not fathom or recognize his lofty achievement but he understood and honoured it himself. Arnold does not regret this fact. On the contrary he thinks it was perhaps better this way. Arnold is probably making an oblique reference to the fact that those who are acknowledged 'great' in their own lifetimes are usually besieged by biographers who take detailed notes on their lives as Boswell did in the case of Johnson or Mrs. Gaskell in the case of Charlotte Bronte in the eighteenth and nineteenth centuries respectively. Shakespeare had no biographer and as such details of his life are somewhat hazy.

Q9. Write a critical comment on "To Marguerite"

Ans. Arnold, as we know, was aware of the difficulties of the loss of faith and the complete isolation of the individual. This poem is not about any personal crisis as the title suggests but this personal loss inspired by separation from Marguerite has triggered off a more general feeling of the prevailing alienation besieging humankind with its attendant isolation and separation of one individual from another. This kind of feeling is well-known to people living in large metropolises like Bombay, Delhi or Calcutta where most people are aware of the complete breakdown of community that one can still find in the villages and small towns even today.

Arnold begins with an emphatic 'Yes!'. It is a revelation that has dawned upon him, as insight that he is convince is true. He says that all of us are like islands interspersed in the sea of life. Between us the waters roar keeping us separate and apart so that each of us, the millions who constitute humanity, is alone. Note that Arnold has emphasized 'alone' by italicizing it. The islands are aware of surrounding flow of the waters and they know that these flowing waves will continue to separate them from other islands and that these gulfs are insurmountable.

This stanza suggests a mood of enchantment as experienced in romantic love. This feeling of complete isolation is somewhat alleviated when the moon lights up the other islands and soft spring breezes blow across them and when the heavenly song of the nightingale is carried across the separating gulfs to other islands.

In the last stanza, Arnold wants to know who is responsible for this state of affairs. Once the fire of longing and desire has been kindled in the human heart, who is responsible for seeing to it that it soon dies down? Who is it that frustrates their deep desires? The answer is that it is God who has decreed that human beings remain separated from each other.

Q10. What do you conclude from the poem "Dover Beach"

Ans. As J.D.Jump has said Dover Beach 'is a short poem, but it embraces a great range and depth of significance.

Arnold observes that the sea is calm, the tide is high and the moon is shining on the English Channel. On the distant French coast he can see a slight flicker of light which shines briefly and then disappears. The white cliffs of Dover can be seen large and shining in the curve of the shore. The poet tenderly beckons his wife to the widow where she too can enjoy the pleasant breeze. Upto this point nature is calm beautiful and soothing. But from here on the poet discerns the underlying grating sound which he describes at some length till the end of the first stanza. The poet draws his wife's attention to the moonlit beach and to the point where the waves lap the shore, the sound of the pebbles as they are dragged along the beach by the receding waves. These pebbles are once again pushed up the sloping beach as the tide returns. Thus there is constant sound and motion that begins and ceases and begins again. The trembling rhythm seem to symbolize some kind of unending sorrow.

Lines 14-20 carry forward this notion of eternity by harking back to the time of Sophocles. This 'granting roar' was probably also heard by Sophocles long ago on the shores of the Aegean sea and it was this that perhaps induced in his mind the sense of the miseries in human life which are reflected in his great tragedies.

What can one do in such a situation? The poet appeals to Lucy once more. He believes that if they love each other truly, they will be able to discover some value in life. Loss of religious faith had made it impossible to believe that the universe was to some extent adjusted to human needs. He says that the world they can see before them is beautiful like a dream. But in spite of its varied beauty it cannot offer either joy.

The image of the sea is present throughout the poem. But in the last 3 lines we are taken to a 'darkling plain'. The sea is calm at the outset. Slowly a 'granting roar' is discernible, an ebb and flow that turns the poet's thoughts to meditate on the loss of faith with which humanity now beset. This loss of religious faith is depicted by the image of receding tide with its melancholy, long, withdrawing roar'. What is the result of this loss of faith? Without religious faith to invest life with some meaning and sense of value, the world is like and anarchic battlefield in the dark where people ignorant of their friends and foes are engaged in a hideous clash.

Q11. Write down a critical comment on poem "The Death of Sohrab"

Ans. In spite of the epic grandeur of the poem, based on Persian mythology, the language of 'Sohrab and Rutum' is surprisingly clear and unambiguous. The passage we have just read is the final part of the long poem. We know that Rustum had been separated from his wife long ago and had head that he had fathered a girl, Rustum fought for the Persian army and his exploits of valour were known far and wide. Sohrab on the other hand, knew of his illustrious father while fighting with the Tartar army. When the two armies faced each other on the banks of the Oxus, it was the bravest soldier from each side that was asked to confront his counterpart. Sohrab represented the Tartars while Rustum fought for the Persians. Both heroes fought bravely and neither side had the advantage until Sohrab's blow brought the mighty Rutum down.

Furious, Rustum shouted his own name before charging at this unknown but brave youth. On hearing the name Sohrab, who knew Rustum was his father was completely disarmed and Rustum's spear penetrated his side, wounding him mortally.

Sohrab smiled at him and removed the spear from the wound in his side, somewhat relieving the pain. But blood flowered freely from the wound and gradually life ebbed with this flow. The stream of red blood flowed down his white body which looked dull and soiled like the bruised petals of white violets. These flowers were plucked by the children from the bank where they grew. As the children had been called away indoors by their nurses out of the heat of the sun they left the flowers to wilt outside. Sohrab's head languished and his limbs became lifeless. Pale and motionless he lay with his eyes closed, breathing heavily. Heavy gasps of breath shaking his body seemed to activate him as he opened his eyes and looked weakly at his father's face. By now he had lost all his strength and his spirit left his body rather unwillingly. It seemed as if the spirit regretted leaving such a magnificent body full of youth and beauty.

The Sohrab lay dead on the sand coloured with his blood. Rustum covered his face with his cloak and sat by the side of his died son. Just as the black concrete pillars that Jemshid had erected to support his house in Pesepolis which now lies in ruins amidst broken stairs with the pillars strewn down the mountain side, in the same way the mighty Rustum lay like the ruined pillars by his son's side. A cold fog rose from the river. As the assembled armies broke up, a hum of sound could be heard as the men went towards their camps, lit the fires which were visible in the fog and took their meals. The Persians were located in the south on the open sands and the Tartars by the sands of the Oxus, Rustum was now alone with his son and his colossal loss.

The final stanza is a **coda.** A coda is an independent and often elaborate passage introduced after the end of the main part of the movement. As we know the tragic tale of Sohrab and Rustum has ended with Sohrab's untimely and tragic death in the pervious stanza itself. In the final part, we are told only of the Oxus flowing on its variegated course to merge with the sea. Here calm and majestic nature is contrasted with the tragic destiny of human beings.

Q12. Write your views (critical analyse) of poem "The Darkling Thrush"

Ans. Hardy is alone – it is evening and everything around him looks bleak and dreary. It is also the last day of the year and the century. Instead of looking forward optimistically to a 'Happy New Year' and the start of the twentieth century, Hardy seem to regret the passage of time.

Hardly tells us that one evening when the grey frost had thickened the air, he leaned against a gate leading to a small wood. The evening light was fading and it being winter, the whole landscape looked gloomy and desolate. The disorderly stalks of vines could be seen silhouetted against the sky like the broken strings of a lyre. And all the people, who lived in the neighborhood, barring hardly, had gone to the comfort of their warm homes. The landscape looked so bleak and desolate that in the dark It looked like the corpse of the bygone century laid at rest. The cloudy sky seemed to be the burial place of the century and the wind seemed to sing its funeral dirge. With death there is birth and renewal but now the germ of birth seemed hard and dry and no sign of life was visible. Everything on earth seemed to share the utmost melancholy and listlessness that Hardy felt. Nature seems to be in sympathy with the poet's mood.

In this bleak landscape, suddenly an energetic and joyous voice burst forth from the dull leafless branches, singing an evening song. It was the song of a small, thin, old thrush with feathers ruffled by the cold wind. It seemed that the thrush had decided to express itself thus in the growing darkness.

The poet is sad at the passage of time and the futility of human existence. This gloom is heightened by the bleak winter weather and the dark evening. In spite of such gloomy surroundings, and aged thrush bursts out in full- throated joyous song that brings a feeling of hope to the poet's heart. The thin aged bird braves the winter blasts and still continues to sing. The final message that comes through clearly establishes the fact that a blithe spirit can surmount life's difficulties, however bleak and unyielding they might at first seem. This joyous spirit is infectious and can also infuse joy among those who feel dejected and depressed. The frail bird, small and makes it noble.

This is very short poem yet it is packed with images that invest it with layers of meaning. Hardly is known for his particular genius for condensation. In the first stanza itself, he has captured a whole landscape, the time of year, the time of day, as well as his own mood as people return to their houses. He works by suggestion rather than by detailed description.

Q13. What do you conclude from the poem "God Forgotten"

[June 2007, Q4]

Ans. Hardy's titles are usually loaded with meaning. The poet here refers to planet earth which has broken all ties with God so that He can no longer hear their cries for help. God is still in touch with all the other planets but it is earth which chose to break away and must now face the consequences of being forgotten by God. This theme has been dramatized by Hardy by presenting a dialogue between God and himself.

This poem is a fantasy and by suspending your disbelief for a moment try to imagine the narrator standing face to face with God.

What is God's first response to his representation? It is one of surprise for He seems to have forgotten the existence of earth altogether. It is only on being reminded again that He faintly recalls that 'tiny sphere I built long ago'. He had created this planet as one among millions but once He discovered that His aims had failed. He lost interest in it.

God says that the other heavenly bodies were in constant touch with him and it was rather strange that earth should expect any attention after its utter decadence. In comparison all other planets were pure and faultless. In spite of all this, God is moved with sympathy at the plight of human beings. He then tells the poet that if he had done nothing to rectify the ills of humankind, it was only because He did not know of them. God directs His heavenly Messengers to set out immediately and put an end to human problems. When the narrator returns home after his interview with God, he expects to find His Messengers solving terrestrial problems. Clearly this did not happen and he chides himself for his childish expectations. Knowing fully well that it is native to expect such miracles, narrator would still like to hope in moments of crisis that such divine help will be forthcoming.

In short, Hardy is mounting a direct attack on the idea of Providence. According to Christian belief, those who do good deeds are rewarded with heaven. In Hardy's scheme of things there are no such easy assurances. On the contrary, he seems to believe.

Q14. Write critical comment on "Nightingales"

Ans. The first person speaker need not necessarily be the poet himself but may be a fictional persona; as we have seen. Here however, the poet addresses the nightingales as if they were persons. The poet feels that the mountain from where the nightingales hail must be extremely beautiful. Their valley homes must be fertile and it is from the bright streams and their musical flow that the nightingale probably learnt their song. The poet wonders where those enchanted forests were that the nightingales inhabited. He then wishes that he might be able to wander in those woods, among the flowers that bloom the whole year in that divine atmosphere.

The nightingales then respond, saying that the mountains where they hail from the barren and the streams dry. Their song is not the song of the joy but is the song of unfulfilled longing and desire, a pang of the heart. The nightingales say that they cannot express their longings and unfulfilled hopes even though they are famed for their art. The nightingales believe that no cadence or sign express the depth of their sorrow.

This lyric is structured in the form of a dialogue. The poet addresses the nightingales in the opening verse. He has come to the conclusion that as the nightingales sing so beautifully, they must live in some beautiful divine abode. However, the response from the nightingales is surprising – they do not live in enchanted forests but in bleak and barren mountains. Their song is not a song of joy but a cry of pain and unfulfilled hopes.

The stanzas are of 6 lines each. As we have seen the poem is visually beautiful not just in content but also in form.

Bridges also uses personification extensively. The nightingales are personified when the poet addresses them as 'ye'. His images are ethereal and evocative.

The poet can hear the beautiful song of the nightingales but he cannot hear the note of pain and longing concealed therein. The song evokes images of ethereal valleys of flowers that bloom forever to poet's mind. But the reality is quite different. It is from an abode of barren mountains and dried streams that the nightingales come singing secretly in the dead of night of their unfulfilled hopes and desires.

Q15. How do Tennyson's describe the scene help the narration in the Shalott?

Ans. Tennyson, like many other Romantic and Victorian poets, often based his poems on medieval stories. Here the poet refers to the story of the legendary King Arthur. Developed in the Middle Ages, the story tells of the noble and generous kind and his knights of the Round Table, all of whom are famous for their chivalry. But gradually the perfect scenario is somewhat disturbed by court intrigues and the illicit affair of Arthur's wife Guinevere with his trusted knight Sir Lancelot. King Arthur was mortally wounded in a battle and carried away by fairy queens from where, according to legend, he will return when his country needs him. In this poem, reference is made to Camelot, the Court of King Arthur and to Sir Lancelot who was the most famous knight in Arthurian legends.

It is at this point that Part I ends, as you can see. The dreaded curse befalls the lady, here mirror 'cracks from side to side' and the magic web flies out of the window. The lady goes down to the riverside, writes her name "The

Lady of Shalott" on a boat, lies down in it, setting it adrift. By the time the boat passes by the palace of King Arthur, the lady is dead. Sir Lancelot and his merrymaking fellow knights merely watch the mysterious lady with interest and awe. This extremely moving poem must be read in full.

This poem then tells us the story of the Lady of Shalott. It is a narrative poem. But as you will see, this poem also has beautiful descriptions that make the scene come alive as in a brilliant painting. In his word pictures, Tennyson is like Keats. The Lady of Shalott was first published in 1832. It was revised and included in the two volumes of *Poems* of 1842.

The poet describes a river that runs towards Camelot and the towers of which are visible in the distance. The river is flanked on either side by fields through which runs a road. As people go up and down this road, they can see an island in the river full of flowers and a grey castle where the Lady of Shalott lives. No one has ever seen her. Her existence is only confirmed by her song that can sometimes be heard by reapers late at night. The busy road and the boats plying in the river suggest a normal life which is in direct contrast to the complete seclusion of the island.

Sweetness is a virtue that searches with patience for the good in every person and situation

Brahma Kumaris

Chapter – 5

The Modern Poets

Q1. Critically appreciate the poem "The Lake Isle of Innisfree" by W.B.Yeats?

Ans. Yeats outgrows this fondness for decoration and moves to compose spare line drawings, composing a poetry that can be called more masculine, more intellectual.

Yeats's poetry has an air of deliberation that makes him appear to be claiming for his work a certain sort of protection. He impresses one as the man in the poet's mask. He always seems to demand to be listened to on his own terms. And that is why perhaps most of his poems strike up a prophetic note, warning humanity itself to pay attention and heed.

In The Lake Isle of Innisfree the poet dreams of escape to the idyllic island and the simple life. Yeats later in described this poem as his first lyric with anything in its rhythm of his own music. In fact, Yeats often expressed the desire for a solitary life, and the island was even associated with Irish folk-legend. The poem begins with a deliberate Biblical echo, and the first three words "I will arise" take us to the Prodigal Son mentioned in the Gospel according to Saint Luke. It is important to note here that prodigal son, referred to in one of the parables of Jesus, is a wasteful and improvident person who ultimately decides to renounce his lustful life, arise and go home. This Biblical echo here is symbolic indeed. The poet puts across his desire to renounce his busy life of hectic activities, arise and go home to his Lake Isle and build a tiny room there with interwoven twigs and branches forming the structure. He would life to plant nine rows of bean (nine being a mystical number), build up a bee-hive and live alone in the clear open space in the forested area with the bees pleasantly murmuring right through. It should be noted here that the phrase "nine bean rows" gives a lifting music and the superb evocation of sound in "the bee-loud glade" suggests a neat contrast with the voices of human beings.

The second stanza develops still further on this picture of the solitary life. The poet admits that he will find peace in this island, because according to him, peace comes by moving away from the busy life and light of everyday to a place life this where the cricket makes its own noise by rubbing its wings together and the evening is crowded with the wings of the linnet. The noises of nature are actually conductive to peace and instead of the jarring light of the morning we find here the weak light of the midnight and the purple glow of the noon.

The third stanza begins again with the same words that opened the first stanza. This artistic repetition of "I will arise and go now" re-enforces the main theme of the poem and adds to the urgency of it all. The poet now seems to have become very intense in his desire to leave it all and go home, for now he seems to be obsessed with this idea and, night and day, he even hears the water of the lake lapping by the shore. Even when he stands on the roadway or on the grey pavements of the street, he hears this sound in the very depth of his heart. The poem ends with a deeply penetrating simplicity. This poem is remarkable indeed because of its unique simplicity, a simplicity that is echoed in the descriptions of nature. The three stanzas have alternate lines rhyming, but with a fine variation of the length of the lines, a rhythmic control and an intimacy of vision that make it a compelling, endearing poem. It has been rightly described as quaint and airy, simple, artful, and eloquent to the heart.

Q2. Give the summary of the poem "The Folly of being comforted" by Yeast?

Ans. 'The Folly of being comforted' is a love poem of a kind very different from those presented by Yeast. Yeats is more pointed, epigrammatic and colloquial. It will be mist relevant to remember here that in 1888. Yeats was introduced to Maud Gonne and fell violently in love with her. But to his surprise. Maud Gonne married John MacBride, a red haired, high spirited Celt who had led the Irish Brigade with the Boers. Maud Gonne's marriage hit Yeasts very hard. He stood aghast, angry as well as miserable for, according to him, John MacBribe scarcely seemed suited to share the life of an unconventional and delicately nurtured woman life Maud Gonne.

The poetry which comes here is conversational in tone. The first stanza presents one part of the conversation in detail. The poet refers directly to a comforting statement made by an ever kind friend of his. He is told that his well-beloved's hair has already started turning grey and that little shadows have started emerging near her eyes. The poet is also told that gradually, as time passes, she will learn to be wise, and all that he needs is to be patient.

In the second stanza comes the poet's reaction to these comforting words. His heart seems to writhe in pain and hiss that he has not a bit of comfort. Tome will only restore the beauty of the beloved because her essential nobility of character will shine more beautifully. The poet even repents that she was not like this whem the entire summer was in her purview.

The third stanza, made up of only two lines, gives an epigrammatic thrust with the poet observing that only if his well-beloved had turned her head and actually seen him his heart would have known the utter foolishness of being comforted.

Thus this poem can be called a cynical little composition certainly autobiographical in tone and connected with Maud Gonne's marriage to Major John MacBride. The theme deals with the loss of the poet, and the language is a simple expression of that the last line of the first stanza and the first line of the second stanza could be taken as forming one line) are evocative of depression. The voice of Yeats here is musical, but touched with melancholy, the tones rising and falling in a continuous flow of sound. When emphasis is needed, he introduces a hard metallic note (like "Heart cries No" with which the second stanza begins). The poem indeed reminds one of a clash of sword-blades. Teats here seems indeed to be discoursing with himself rather than to be persuading others. It is interesting to note that while Yeats' verse generally appears to be often elaborate and full of complex symbolism, this poem has an utter simplicity of style. Yeats her makes everything very hard and clear.

Q3. Analysis the poem "The Second Coming" by Yeast?

[June 2007, Q5]

Ans. 'The Second Coming' speaks of the coming of a new spirit, and the image presented is of a brazen-winged beast which Yeats considered to be always at hand but just outside his field of vision. The Christian doctrine of Christ's second appearance on earth forms the basis for the poem, and the title is obviously derived from Christianity. It is important to remember here that this poem was written in January 1919, and therefore shortly after the First World War and the Russion Revolution, during the Black and Tan War in Ireland, and just before the rise of Fascism (Mussolini came to power in 1922). Thus the poem is generally concerned with the disintegration of modern society with the spread of anarchy and the consequent violence and bloodshed.

The poem opens with an analogy. The falcons spiraling flight is a gyre at the centre of which is a whirling centrifugal force which is about to cause total disintegration, to precipitate a catastrophe. While some critics see the falconer as man who can no longer impose a discipline or his power over nature, which is therefore falling apart, other critics see the falcon as man losing contact with Christ or more generally with ideals which enabled him to control his life – religion, philosophy, poetry – and with all traditional ties.

In the first stanza (made up of eight lines). Yeats talks of an abandonment of the ceremoniousness which he believed essential to a life of true dignity. For the soul to be 'innocent', it must be protected from the vulgarity of the market-place by ritual, or ceremony, and by custom hallowed by tradition. There is opposition between natural and supernatural, love and hate, war and peace subjective and objective.

It is important to observe here that according to Theosophical belief, every cycle of history has its special deity, so that a new god comes regularly to replace the old. A time of upheaval, therefore, such as has been depicted, would seem to denote the end of the one such cycle and to imply the coming of some new deity. The first stanza, therefore, presents certain determinism. The end of an age which always receives the revelation of the character of the next age is represented by the coming of one gyre to its place of greatest expansion and of the other to that of the greatest contraction. Something disastrous has happened in modern civilization. Through the falcon is not a pet but is meant for killing, and thus symbolizes death. The second line of the first stanza suggests that in the modern times this control has been lost and murderous instincts cannot be kept in control. There is complete chaos, and no restraint.

The second stanza presents hope (emphasized by the repetition of "surely"). The point of saturation has nee reached. It is time for divine intervention. Another Saviour is needed. There will come a rescuer.

It will be important for us to understand at this point what is meant by *Spirits Mundi* W.B. Yeats is supposed to have believed that the souls of the dead could communicate with writers and artists, and in so doing they were drawing on a general storehouse of images, a kind of corporate imagination which is *Spirits Mundi*. With this the poet's vision ends, but he proclaims that now he knows. What he knows seems to be that the beast; having spent the two thousand years of the Christian era in 'stony sleep' has been roused by a nightmare. The image of the 'rocking cradle' is an imagery of birth, urging the monster to be born, and the fact that it moves lazily towards Bethlehem, points at the horrifying contrast between the birth of Chirst and that of the 'shape'. The poet's uncertainty, despite the seeming assurance "now I know", appears to be expressed by the fact that the poem ends not with an assertion but a question what is the nature of the slouching brute about to be born?

The poet is needed in a mood of be wilderment. The idea which the sphinx stood for are being reborn. The animal in man is again being awakended. The suggestion is that if Christ refuses to come, probably the second deity/ monster will be born. The vision of the creature about to be born may be prophetic. The prophecy is, in fact, a curious blending of Christian association with the bestial, as the beast moves towards Bethlehem – perhaps as a terrible corrective to the world in which the poet finds himself.

Q4. Analysis the poem "Journey of the Magi" by Eliot".

[Dec 2006, Q6]

Ans. The Magi were the three wise men who received news of the birth of the baby Jesus and went to see him with gifts. The poet narrates their journey in an anti-romantic vein. Here we discover Eliot's optimism.

Eliot thought that there was very little religious verse that reached the highest level of poetry.

'Journey of the Magi' has many layers of meanings. It is at one level just the narration of the experience of one of the wise men on his journey to Bethlehem. It is also an account of the introspection that the wise man goes through after he gas completed the journey. The poem it appears that the wise man is doing it after about 2000 years of his actual journey making him a contemporary of ours.

On another level, it is the experience of enlightenment of every man. The moment of revelation, or on a lower level, of initiation (at the level of rituals), is a moment both of birth and death – birth into a new order and the death of the old' birth of a new outlook and the death of the old way of life.

The first stanza of the poem symbolically, tells you about the various inconveniences that the wise men faced on their way to Bethlehem. The first five lines of the poem make a single sentence and they are in direct speech. The poem is this given an urgency and directness that is lost in indirect speech and narration. The wise men also, however, looked back from their shoulders towards their summer palaces and 'the silken girls bringing sherbet'.

The second stanza throws a ray of hope. After the night's troublesome journey they descend into a 'temperate' valley with 'smell of vegetation'. There is the water-mill "beating" darkness. Early in the dawn the water in the river looks dark. The fan of the water-mill that is rotated by the running stream is thus seen as beating darkness, Beating here also means defeating. Then there are three trees symbolizing the crufixation of Jesus Christ. Jesus also atoned for the original sin of Adam, who disobeyed God, beguiled by Satan. In a way Eliot yokes together images grand and mundane, suggestive of the same experience of the presence of God in subtle ways. There is a suggestion. Christ was betrayed by one of his disciples – Judas – for pieces of silver. Here in the poem there is a tavern scene where three persons are at the gaming table. The three wise men reach 'the place' in the evening.

The account of the journey is over by the end of the second stanza. The third is meditation on the journey that was performed years ago. The text deliberately leaves gaps and holes through an elliptical use of language. Who would be glad of another death" Certainly the wise men – contextually speaking. However, the personal pronoun is 'T' not 'we'. Christ died to save mankind. Would he die another death to save us? The suggestion cannot be ruled out.

There is a completely different level at which were would also like to understand the poem. It was written in the year 1927 the year in which Eliot also became a British subject and joined the Anglican Church. Both, we cam imagine, must have been great acts of affirmation. Eliot declared himself a 'classical in literature, royalist in politics and Anglo-Catholic in religion. These are acts of affirmation for a septic such as Eliot was and the poem is a record of Eliot's growing optimism in his own capacity as a poet and hope of a better world to be.

Q5. Sum up the poem "Marina" by Eliot". [Dec 2006, Q6]

Ans. T.S. Eliot is not only a poet but also a critic. He moulded the taste of his age both through his poetry and criticism. Poetry, Eliot said, 'is not the expression of personality, but a escape from personality' – and 'the more perfect the artist, the more completely separate in him will be the man who suffers and the mind which creates'. ('Tradition and the Individual Talent'. 1917. Thus Eliot disapproved of criticism that sought to link works of art with their artist' lives. However, at times when we do so, we appreciate Eliot's poetry better. 'Marina' is another poem of the phase of optimism in Eliot's life. Eliot expresses it through the central symbol of Marina, daughter of Pericles in Shakespeare's play. Marina was born at sea and was thought to have been murdered by those in whose charge she had been left. She was miraculously restored to her father when she became a woman. Marina thus is a symbol of life where death had been accepted. She is a symbol of joy in place of the sorrow to which the poet had reconciled himself. Contrary to this spirit is the epigraph from Seneca's *Hercules Furens.* Hercules in a fir of madness, unknowingly, kills his children and after he returns to sanity wishes to seem then alive and discovers his loss. Why is the epigraph, in spirit, contrary to the poem? Perhaps because Eliot believed in the dual nature of truth. Truth, in itself was neither good nor bad. You observed this in the last stanza if 'Journey of the Magi."

'Marina is a poem of arrival, unlike the 'Journey'. Notice the feeling of satisfaction and hope that come out of the first and last stanzas. Pericles's ship is reaching some island. In the opening stanza it was 'grey rocks'. In the last stanza it is 'granite islands'. Notice the rise in the spirit of certainty. We hear the Wood thrush's song through the fog in the first stanza. In the last stanza they 'call' Pericles. There is the warmth of an invitation. The poem evokes images that suggest fulfillment of a wish of a long cherished desire. The images in the poem picture for us the mind of Pericles. They also present the image of a poet who has begun to seen the 'granite island' in place of the 'Waste Land' he had seen before.

Q6. Critically appreciate the poem "On This Island" by Auden and Spender?

Ans. Poem is one of place an scene and it suffers from none of the strain of some of Auden's other poems. In fact, this poem is the first piece in a collection of his poems with the title *Look Stranger!* (entitled in the U.S.A. *on this Island*) containing Auden's more serious poetic output of the thirties. Auden also probably wrote part of the commentary for a production by Strand Films on behalf of the British Travel Association, entitled Beside the Seaside, in which poetry had been applied as a general emotional commentary. It was apparently for this film that he wrote the poem entitled 'Look Stranger, on this Island now' though it was not used in the soundtrack.

The first stanza presents a neat little exposition in which the poet introduces us to the scene itself. Somewhat like Wordsworth in his sonnet entitled *Composed Upon Westminster Bridge*. Auden here invites us to look at a natural scene at a particular point of time and be conscious of the glory and splendour of that particular sight. Auden asks the stranger to look at the beautiful scene of that island as revealed by the rays of light primarily for the pleasure of the onlooker. The stranger is advised to stand firmly and silently there so that the swinging sound of the sea may leisurely pass into his ears like a meandering river.

In the second stanza, the poet presents a slight shift in his perspective, and asks the stranger to pause at the ending of the small field and notice the chalk walls of the cliff falling towards the sea. The stranger is asked to notice the narrow horizontal shelves of these walls braving courageously the blow of the waves, and observe the rounded pebbles on the seashore crawling toward the sea-waves which break into white forum. The stranger can also see a gull entering and resting on the steep side of the cliff.

The third stanza presents a still different perspective in which we obtain a more open-ended, over-all view. The poet presents an almost cinematographic description of the ships in the distant horizon moving out in various directions on different missions. This full view, the poet hopes, may enter the very consciousness of the on looker and move in to the individual memory very much like the clouds that float over the clearly reflecting mirror of the harbour and wander all through the summer through the water of the sea.

The poem is remarkable for the beauty of its imagery. You must have noticed that the phrases "channels of the ear" "sucking surf", present powerfully descriptive images that add to the impact being created by the poet. The "sound" is allowed to wander "like a river", and a comparison has been made between the two movements. The first line of the third stanza presents a simile "like floating seeds the ships." And the comparison made is indeed unique. The last but one line of the third stanza presents a Metaphor "harbor mirror" where the harbour has been identified as a mirror. Figure of speech which the poet has used here to add effectiveness to his poetic style is known as onomatopoeia. You must have also noticed that the poet has not used any fixed rhyme scheme. The free verse used by him gives to the poem a certain ease and fluency. The poem, therefore, presents a remarkable technical facility, and one can easily find many brilliant and powerful lines, Auden's easy mastery of free verse contributes to a new lyrical quality. The poem reminds one of Byron's Rollon. Thou Deep and Dark Blue Ocean' which you read in Unit 9 in Block III. For both Auden and Byron present tender and true poems, showing rhetorical powers at their best.

Q7. Justify the title unknown citizen. [June 2007, Q5]

Ans. In this poem, written after he became an American citizen, W.H. Auden emerges primarily as a satirist. The title seems to have been deliberately chosen to echo the name on the grave of the Unknown Soldier buried ceremonially after the First World War. Here the poet pungently describes an average citizen who has been analyzed by the computer and statistics but whose individually seems to be still unknown.

The poem has an interesting superscription, full of ironic suggestions. JS/07/M/378 is the number which denotes the citizen in the records of the Bureau of Statistics. And although a marble monument has been erected by the state in his honour, the human being has been ironically summed up in a mere number, not in a name which would have certainly sounded more personal. Moreover, the marble monument itself has something cold about it.

The first four lines of the poem introduce us to this unknown citizen who has been found by the Bureau of Statistics to be someone against whom no official complaint has been registered. There is an artistic indirectness in such a presentation which aptly reflects the poet's satiric vigour. The reports on the behaviour of this unknown citizen confirm that he was saintly in his conduct. Ironically enough, "saint" has been described as an "old fashioned word", being used "in the modern sense."

The poet talks about the official work of this unknown citizen. Even here there is a subtle indirectness in the presentation and the words seem to meander. One comes to know that this citizen worked in Fudge Motors and retired serving the greater community of people. He never got a firing from his job and yet he also paid his Union dies and never refused to join a strike. He was popular with his friends and liked a drink (indicating that he was of a sociable nature.

Another facet of the individual's personality. The Press seems to be agreed that he purchased a newspaper everyday, and that he reacted normally to the advertisements flashed in the newspapers. (There seems to be a tongue-in-the-check humour here, and a subtle commentary has been made on the very life of the average modern man.) This unknown citizen was fully insured and his health card showed that he had visited the hospital once and was cured.

This satiric commentary on the plight of the modern man seems to have been done with greater concentration. The research done by Producers indicate that this unknown citizen took a great advantage of the installment plan and possessed everything needed by a modern human being – a phonograph, a radio, a car, a Frigidaire (This is a lightly mocking comment on the materialistic society of toady in which utmost importance is given to such material goods.) The researchers into Public Opinion are satisfied that this citizen held proper opinions according to the need of the hour. When there was peace, this citizen cried for peace, and when there was war, she went in for war. (This hints at the basic opportunism in the very inner personality of this citizen.

In the last the poem concludes by talking about the personal self of this individual. This unknown citizen had, in fact, married and had five children. But his five children are described by the Eugenist as just "the right number" for "a parent of his generations." And the teachers of these children report that this citizen never interfered with their education. The poet admits that it is absurd to ask such questions, for, if anything had been wrong, they should have heard.

Q8. Discuss the poem "I think Continually of those Who Were Truly Great" by Stephen Spender.

Ans. In this poem, Stephen Spender pays a glowing tribute to those great people who were dynamically conscious of their glorious traditions. Spender here exalts the geniuses who apprehended the true and the beautiful. And the entire poem becomes a rich fusion of the doctrine with a suggestive complex of emotions and images. The poet presents a magnificent illustration of the victory which the genius of man pursues, and which he wins by virtue of the force of creative enterprise. The setting of this cosmic drama, its actors, its incidents, the pains and the joys of a world restored to its primal purity by a supreme act of liberation, all bear the touch of a sovereign grandeur, of a pathos vast in its scope, of a bright of graceful magic.

In the first stanza, the poet presents himself as continually thinking about those valiant who, from the womb, remembered the history of the soul through the corridors of light where hours were suns, eternal and rejoicing. (This picture reminds us of the celestial light found in Wordsworth's Ode on the Limitations of Immortality from Recollections of Early. Spender remembers this who made their lips the lyre and the trumped of a prophecy and who carefully saved from the branches of Spring the desires which appeared to be organically falling across their bodies like the flowed.

The second stanza takes us to the heart of the matter. The poet here admits that what is actually important is to be perpetually aware of the continuity of the stream of consciousness flowing from eternity. It is vitally important never to permit the daily movements of everyday routine to suffocate and kill with its pollution the blessing of the human spirit. This idea again takes us back to Wordsworth's 'ode on the Intimations of Immortality' by voicing a similar adoration for the ancient world of purity and innocence.

The third stanza presents a world that seems to be full of Romantic imagination. The reference to Nature can be found here in plenty. The poet takes us to a plane of reality that can be compared with the one Keats reaches to in his 'Ode to a Nightingale' in which he cannot see what flowers are at his feet. Spender her carries us on his wings of Imagination to a world near the snow, near the sun, in the highest fields where the names of these valiant geniuses are honoured by the waving grass and the ribbons of white cloud. These great people who fought to preserve life and possessed inspiration seem to have signed their names on the bright atmosphere as it were. They have indeed left footprints, not only on the sands of time but also in the very air we breathe.

The poem is remarkable for its numerous poetic images. The "corridors of light" where the hours are suns, "endless and singing" the lips "touched with fire", the "ageless springs" – are powerfully evocative, The reference to Nature made in "Spring branches", "blossoms", "rocks", "morning simple light", "grave evening", "snow", "sun", "white cloud", "whispers of wind", "listening sky", "vivid air", remind us of the Romantic poetry of Wordsworth, Shelley and Keats. The Simile in the last line of the first stanza ("desires falling..... like blossoms") adds to the picturesque quality of the poem. Indeed, Spender lends this poem a sweet and liquid harmony, sonorous and sexual, pure in its vehement intensity. The flowing ease with which the words merge into one another, at the same time as the ideas they call forth join up together, goes to prove that for Spender, the psychological melody and the cadence of syllables, the one as spontaneous as the other, naturally formed but one music.

Q9. Give central idea of the poem 'The express by Stephen Spender?

Ans. The Express has been regarded as a typical poem by Stephen Spender glorifying the Express Train. The train here becomes a symbol of the modern industrial civilization. The glorious march of the train to its destination is vividly captured by the poet, who considers this machine as an object of great beauty. It is interesting to note that the movement of the lines of the poem mimes the majestic journey of the train. The Express, according to the poet, excels all beautiful objects of nature in beauty and elegance. In this respect, the world of machine seems to have been to Spender what Nature was to Wordsworth.

The first three lines of the poem set the train in motion. After the first forceful blowing of the engine's whistle, the movement of the pistons announces the departure of the train, which moves away from the station smoothly and majestically as a queen. There is so much beauty in this machine and feminine qualities are attributed to it. Moreover, the train is personified.

First stage of the train's movement. A cross-section view is also given of the surrounding area through this description. The train passes the houses that humbly crowd outside (and these humbly crowding houses give a picture of the average humanity desperately trying to make both ends meet). It moves past the gas work and then by the cemetery in which the gravestones have printed the heavy page of death. The train next leaves the town and goes into the open countrywide where she picks up seed and becomes mysterious. She now controls herself perfectly like a stately ship moving on the ocean.

The poet focuses his attention on the various sounds emitted by the train. At first, the Express sings quite low. Then the sound becomes more loud, and ultimately it seems to break into a loud madness. Her whistle screams at curves and tunnels. Her brakes and bolts produce their own music too.

The joyous rhythm of the train is also desired. The Express speeds through the metal track and shows up starting features of the landscape. In the next seven lines, night sets in. The train seems to have moved beyond Edinburgh or

Rome, even beyond the very end of the world. And in the night one can notice only a very clear line or phosphorus, the fiery smoke sent out by the train on the edge of the high sky. The train appears now to move like a comet through flame, carried away in the dream as it were. Neither any song of the bird, nor any large branch laden with honey buds can ever match this train wrap in her own music.

The passenger and the train are shut together in darkness where no one can interfere and all identity seems to be lost. The poet talks about the physical selves of the passengers when he says that in this state of communion, the bodies seem to be dashed together by the storm of desire in the flesh, and generations appear to be leaping into creation through the veins. The forceful joy makes the heart a powerful sun bringing ripeness to all.

The poet moves from the train to the unique associations that she gives rise to, when he admits that while lying with the Express in this eternity, the passenger will start to dream of all women. The whole train of romantic associations will be let loose and the passenger will come to realize that the Express, in fact, represents all the women that have ever bee.

This it is evident that this poem has admirably captured the various movements, sounds, moods and association set loose by the Express Train. The poem is remarkable for its suggestive expressions and realistic description. The expressions life "black statement of pistons" (line 2) "heavy page of death, printed by gravestones" (line 6-7), "rectitude of their breasts in the night" (line 41) and "fingers tangled in their yellow hair" (line 42) are indeed so very thought-provoking. The Similes "gliding like a queen" (line 3) "parallels clean like the steel of guns", (line 20) "like a comet through flame" (line 25) "her heart, as a moon" (line 38), "the scent.... Like the calm earth in summer" (line 43) add to the richness of the poem. It is not only the train which has been personified. Even the houses crowd outside humbly (line 5) as if they too were living beings. The poem indeed is a powerful evocative tribute paid by a man to the machine.

W.B. Yeats

(1) In a short paragraph of so words explain what thoughts and feeling are expressed in this poem.

In this poem, the poet dreams of escape to the idyllic island of Inn is free and the simple life there. According to the poet, peace comes by dropping away from the busy life to the solitary life of such an island where the sounds of Nature are conductive to peace.

(2) Is Innisfree a real island?

Yes, Innisfree a Real Island

(3) If Inn is free a real island, where is at situated

The lake isle of Inn is free is situated a Long Gill Cannily Sligo.

(4) Comment critically on the echo generated by the first three worth, "I will arise" 30 words.

The echo generated the first three words "I will arise" is Biblical; taking us to the Prodigal san meantime's in the gospel according to Saint Luke. Here prodigal son, referred to the parables of Jesus.

(5) The rhyme scheme of the poems

The rhyme scheme of the poem is abab, cdcd, efef.

(6) Express in not more than 50 words remain theme of the poem.

The poem is a love poem. It deals with the personal loss of the poem. Maud Ganne, with whom Yeats had fallen violently in love, has married John Mac Bride. This poem shows the aghast angry and miserable poem. The poet tells that how foolish is to be comforted.

(7) What is the tune of the poem?

The time of the poem is cynical.

(8) From the list balas, tick the 5 epithets that best describe the style of the poem?

The 5 epithets that first describe the poet are

(a) Colloquial (b) pointed (c) epigrammatic (d) conversional (e) musical

(9) The name the verse pattern that has been used?

Rhyming coupled has been used in the poem.

(10) What do the sonorous lines of the poem evoke?

The sonorous lines of the poem evoke depression

(11) Express in 75 words main gist of the poem.

In the poem "The Second Coming" is about the coming of the new spirit. The poem speaks of desintrigation of modern society with the spread of anarchy and the consequent violent and blood shed. Modern man is shown uncontrolled and uncontrolling. The fine of divine intervention has come, and other saviors needed. But the rough beast that more towards Bethlehem to be born is a terrible thing like sphinx with the head of a man and the body of a lion.

(12) Explain in 25 words what Yeats means by the 'gyri' in the first

stanza.

Gyre means a movement in spirit circle or spirals. In the poem Yeats want to express trig 'Gyre', that history is a process conceived of a turning on a great wheel a three dimensional figure, as sphere, which he refers to as gyres.

(13) What does Yeats suggest through falcon?

Yeats suggests the cruelty and terror in modern times.

(14) Clarify in 20 words, what Yeats mean by Spirits Mundi in 2nd stanza.

Yeats believed the souls of the dead could communicate with writers and artists. I doing so they draw a general storehouse of images, a kind of corporate imagination which is 'Spirits Mundi'.

(15) How does the poem end?

The poem ends in the moods of bewilderment

(16) Sum up in 50 words the main girl of the poem.

The poem Yeats presents a beautiful description of the grace and enduring splendor of the swans in the lake of cook. The poem expresses his unhappiness generated in him due to the passing of time. The poet has grown old white the swans are still grateful and graceful.

(17) What sort of life did Yeats find at Cobe.

At Cobe, Yeats found a life of order and labour where all outward things appeared to be signature of an inward world.

(18) Identify 3 main characteristics of the verse pattern used.

(i) Six line verse

(ii) Alternative lines rhyming

(iii) Each verse climaxed by a couplet

(19) Explain the following terms

Companionable streams – The warmth Yeats envied love by lover – every of the swans who have mated while the poet could not be united with his beloved.

(20) Which Yeats do you find in this poem?

We find austere Yeats in this poem

T.S. Eliot

(1) Who was T.S. Eliot's grandfather? What did he do?

Revi Williams green leaf Eliot was T.S. Eliot's grandfather. He was founder of Washington University and 1872 became its Chancellor. His mother wrote a biography of her father-in-law.

(2) Name 3 persons who influenced Eliot's anti-romantic attitude.

3 persons who influenced Eliot's anti-romantic attitude are Irving Bibfit, F.H. Bradley and T.E.Hulme.

(3) What do you know about Eliot;s interest in Sanskrit and Indian philosophy.

From 1911 to 1914 T.S. Eliot studied Indian Philosophy and read Sanskrit form Charles Lenman. He also wanted to embrace Buddhism fat did not do so because the Buddhist way of life was difficult to be practiced in a western milieu. Hence to he becomes Anglo Chattosic Forsaking his parents' faith-Protestantism.

(4) You will notice that the last five lines of the extract from 'Precludes' have not been scanned.

The showers beat
On broken, blinds and Chimney pots
A lonely cab-horse, steams and stamps
And then the lighting of the lamps

(5) Briefly recall 3 reasons for Eliot using free verse.

Free verse is capable of carrying the reader/listener along forcefully when he would doze; However it would check his enthusiasm as it rises to passion. Passion blurs our vision and makes is incapable of reasonable action. The irregularity of the metrical effect would enforce the modern reader to think about life aria him

(6) With the help of two sets images from the first and second stanzas has Eliot it an anti-romantic poet.

Compare the images of 'silken girls bringing shortest' with 'wanting their liquor and area' is the first stanza. In the second you may compose the images of the 'water will beating the darkness 'with the 'three trees in the low sky. For a detailed discussion read the analysis.

(7) Who is the narrator of this poem and does it any way compare with 'My last Duchess' you reading Block in.

The narrator of the poem is one of the wise men who went to see Jesus soon after his birth at Beth Lehman. However the narrator can be anyone who undertakes to discover something or work sincerely in the light of his faith like 'My Last Duchess', Journey of the Magi is alsoi dramatic monologue.

Auden and Spender

(1) Express the theme of the own words.

The poem invites the stranger to look at the picture of the sea from Daver Cliff in the West Country of England and by be conscious of the glory of that particular sight. It is an artistically plotted objective description of a natural scene dome with a gradually widening perspective.

(2) Comment critically on the superscription to JS.

The simile is in "Like floating seeds the ships' in the first line of the third stanza. It aptly presents the numerous ship" in the first lime of the third stanza aptly presents the numerous ships scattered on the distant horizon, which seem to be floating like seeds and also appearing to be tiny, like the seed themselves.

(3) Quote two examples of the poet's skillful use of alliteration and explain their significance in the poem.

Two examples of use of alliteration are:

(i) 'swaying sound of the "sea"

(ii) "shingle scrambles – sucking of surf

(4) Identify the figures of speech in the following expressions.

(i) knock of the tide – Onomatopoeia

(ii) harbour mirror - Metaphor

(5) Name the verse pattern that has been used in this poem

Free verse

(6) In the short Para of 75 words, explain what thought and feeling are expressed in this poem.

In this poem Auden describes a common citizen in analyzed by the statistic, but his individuality seems to be still unknown. With a humor the poet satirically comments on the ironic fact that this human being has been summed up in a mere number not in a name which would have certainly sounded mere personal. The poem is in fact a sardonic elegy on the modem human being.

(7) Comment critically on the superscription to JS/07/14/328.

The superscription to JS/07/14/328 is the number which denotes the citizen in the records of the Bureau of Statistics, and it sardonically comments on the fact that the human being has been reduced to a mere number, and not even a name is there to humor and remember him.

(8) What is the rhyme scheme of the first 4 lines.

abab

(9) What aspect of the unknown citizens; personality is highlighted by the words, "when there was peace, he was for peace when there was, he went".

He was opportunistic.

(10) What does the poet mean which he says "Had anything been wrong, we should certainly have heard."

Poet has commented sardonically. Nowadays much stress on the information given by the computers and press has been placed. We totally depend on keen even to find out about the well being of the individuals. It ironically register the fact that only apparently average citizen was alright.

(11) Express in not more than 75 words on the theme of the poem.

The poem is a tribute to those valiant people who were dynamically conscious of their part. It is vitally essential for us to be aware of the continually of our glorious trading. The great people who are conscious of this ever following stream of consciousness actually and have fought to preserve life have been hammered by the various subject of nature.

(12) Explain the meaning of the lines.

It is of vital importance to never permit the daily movement of everyday routine to suffocate and pollute the blossoming of the human spirit.

(13) Make a list of five objects of nature referred to in 3rd stanza.

The snow, the sun, the highest fields, waving gross, and white cloud are the five objects of nature.

(14) Quit a simile from the poem and comment on its apt.

The simile is in desires falling ——— like blossoms (last line of the first stanza). It makes the poem more picturesque.

(15) What does the poet mean which he says 'and left the two similes are:

(i) Gliding likes a queen – there train is persons feed as a glorious queen. It moves from the station majestically as a queen.

(ii) Like a comet through flame – here train appear to move like a comet through flame, carried away in a dream as it were.

(16) What is the "two streamline brightness of phosphorous"?

The phrase "low streamline brightness of phosphorus" refers to the fiery smoke sent out by the train that can be visualization the edge of the high sky as a clear line.

(17) The vivid air signed with their honour?

The poet means to say that the signatures of these valiant can be notices in the air itself.

(18) Explain in 75 words main gist of the poem.

The poem glorifies the Express Train the train here becomes a symbol of modern industrial civilization. The train is described moving as majestically as a queen and the various stages of its journey are described. The train excels all beautiful objects of nature in beauty and elegance.

(19) What is the black statement of the pistons.

The black statement of the pistons refers to the movement of the pistons of the railway engine, which announces the departure of the train.

(20) Explain what the poet meant by "'she moves entranced wept in her............ever equal.

Is the above lines, the poet observes that the music of the moving train is so melodious that this there any song of the first nor any large branch idea with honey buds can even match this serious effect.

Chapter – 6

The American Poets

Q1. Write a short note on the poetic devices used in "Brahma".

Ans. Brahma is a poem by Ralplm Waldo and he used various poetic devices. The poetic devices used by Ralplm are :

(i) Brahma is a lyric of four stanzas and that each stanza has four lines hence it contains four quatrains.

(ii) Pairs of opposites like shadow and sunlight for and near are used to indicate that Brahma transcends these states of qualities.

(iii) Alliteration is also used along with consonance.

(iv) The rhyme pattern is followed is ab ab cd c def ef gh gh.

(v) Inversion is also a part of this poetry.

(vi) The sloke of Bhagvad Gita inspired Emerson to write "Brahma".

The exigencies of consonance demanded the poet to use or instead of and but the use of or makes the word they in the line organ material.

Q2. Interpret the poem "Brahma" in terms of Indian thoughts?

Ans. Rampln Waldo Emerson was deeply interested in Indian philosophical concepts such as Brahman, Atman, Karma, illusions, Representation Men, are permeated with the aroma of Indian thought.

About the inpact of Indian thought an Emerson. Mahatma Gandhi – an admirer of Emerson wrote as follows "The essays to mind contain the teaching of Indian wisdom in a western guru.

Brahma is one of the popular poems of Emerson. A discerning reader of this poem can easily see the influence of Indian thought in the author. According to ancient Indian thought, there is one Supreme Power that governs universe. This supreme power is the origin of all beings and final destination of all souls. Through a ceaseless cycle of births and death through nobility of finally merges with Brahman or over-soul.

Brahma or over soul has no beginning no middle, and no end. It has ever been there. It can neither be created hot destroyed. Slayer, slaying and slain are not real, they are only appearances. For the soul cannot be killed. So if one can think he is the killer or of another thinks he has been killed both are ignorant of the ways of Brahma. The soul lives on only the body dies.

These lines are taken from Bhagvad Gita and it shows Indian impact on the poetry of Emerson.

Q3. Write the outline of the poem "Hamatreya".

Ans. Bulkeley, Hunt, Wilard, Hosmer, Meriam, Flint were some of the earliest settlers in Massachusetts. They produced hay, corn, roots, hemp, flax, apples, wool and wood in their land. Each of them who owned the land walked amidst his farm saying: "This land is mine and my progeny's. I feel as if these springs of pure water and the flags (a kind of plant) know me as intimately as does my dog. We sympathize with each other; and my action has a flavor of the soil."

But where are all these owners now, asks the poet. They are all dead and buried in their own grounds. Now new settlers – who are as foolish as their forerunners – plough the same lands with the same sense of possession.

Earth laughs – in the form of blooming flowers – at the boastful cultivators, who are proud of possessing the earth – which cannot be their forever. They steer the plough in the fields but cannot keep away from the grave.

While ploughing the fields they connect a ridge with a valley, a book with a pond and aspire to bring under their possession the lands which they do not possess now. They say to themselves. "This piece of land will suit me for a pasture; and I can use that piece of land as park. We must have clay, lime. Gravel, and granite. We also need misty lowlands for growing peat. This piece of land is good; it lies to the south. It will give us satisfaction, if on our return from across the seas. We find our lands in the condition of which in left them." Alas! The foolish owners of the land do not know that Death will turn them into some mounds on the earth.

Now earth speaks: "Stars shine forever; and the shores of the seas are also old. But where are the old men now. Of course, the lawyers' deeds pass from one generation of inheritors to another generation. Inheritor change, but the land remains there, covered with woods, valleys mounds, and rivers. But the inheritors, lawyers, and laws have all gone floating like foam on the stream of water. These men called me (i.e. the earth) theirs and believed that they possessed me. But they – who wanted to stay on forever have all gone. How can I be theirs if they cannot possess me. In fact, it is I who possesses them; for, after death they become a part of me. After listening to Earth-Song, the poet's avarice disappeared.

Q4. Write a note on the poetic used in "Hamatreya"?

Ans. Poetic devices in Hamatreya are :

(i) Hamatreya' can be considered a good example of free verse. It has irregular line lengths; it lacks regular stress patterns and rhyme.

(ii) There are three speakers in the poem

(a) The landowners

(b) The Earth

(c) The poet

(iii) The flat and un poetic language of the landowners reflects their mundane and materialistic approach towards life. Hence even in the use of proper names in line (I0 and in the list of items grown on the soil (in line 3), Emerson, deliberately, didn't infuse a pattern.

(iv) In contrast to the landowners 'flat language, the language of the earth is poetic. You can find various poetic devices in the language used by the earth.

For example, 'alliteration' is present in the following lines:

"......boastful boys (18)

"Stars abide

Shine down in the old sea

Old are the shores'

"I who have seem much (31-33)

Such have I never seen" (35-36)

"Field like the flood's foam

The lawyer and the laws" (49-50)

Moreover, 'Rhyme' can be seen in the following lines :

"Mine and Yours

Mine, not Yours

Earth endures" (28-30)

And 'Rhetoric' can be found in the following lines:

"But where are old men?" (34)

"But the in heritors?" (48)

"But I hold them?" (59)

(v) The language of the poet as one who understands the transient nature of human life after listening to the song of earth – is also poetic. For example :

'Pathetic fallacy' which means attribution of human capacities and feelings to natural objects – is present in the following :

"How graceful climb those shadows on my hill" (7)

"I fancy these pure waters and the flags
know me, as my dog" (8-9)

"Earth laughs" (13)

"Earth-Song"

Q5. Interpret "Hamatreya in lines of Indian thought.

Ans. 'Hamatreya' was published in 1847. 'Hamatreya' is a variation of the term 'Hail Maitreya', which means 'Hail, Mother Earth!' The poem deals with the theme of the transient life of mand and the permanence of Earth. Reminger Vaid gives a different interpretation. Referring to an entry in Emerson's Journal in 1845, the critic says: "Emerson had copied into his 1845 Journal a long passage from **the Vishnu Purana.**

'This earth is mine – it is may son's belongs to my dynasty' – have all passed way …… Earth laughs as if smiling with autumnal flowers to behold her kings unable to effect the subjugation of themselves'….. The passage includes a Song of the Earth, recited to a disciple names Maitreya of which the name 'Hamatreya' is a variation. The passage concludes: 'These were the verses, Maitreya, which Earth recited and by listening to which ambition fades away like snow before the wind'. This makes Hamatreya the name of a disciple and the lines, "Hear what the Earth say's which precede the Song of the Earth are addressed by the Guru (in vishnu Purana) to his disciple."

'Hamatreya' tells us about the mortality of man. No man can live or return his possessions forever. The early settlers of Massachusetts walked proudly declaring that some particular plot of land belonged to them. They are dead and buried and are possessed by the land of which they considered themselves to be the proud owners.

These early settler were followed by others. The newcomers told the line of their forerunners in increasing their possessions. They too – like their forerunners – did not see Death lurking at the corner. The earth laughs at them and says that they could not possess her forever, but she possessed them as they became a part of her.

This exquisite lyric contracts the short, transient life of men with the permanence of Earth of Nature. Like the earlier poem, 'Brahma', this lyric also brings out the Indian influence on Emerson. The language used in this poem is simple and musical.

Q6. Write a note on Passage to India? [June 2007, Q6]

Ans. Through the poem Passage to India Whiteman came to the conclusion that the historic sequence of events had a spiritual meaning. He wanted to harmonize past with the past with the present and he was keen won proving that the past was a part of the present. As a mystic poet, he thought that he must give a new faith to inspire they future generation.

But, to get into the past, the history of mankind, one should know the contribution of Asia in general and of India in particular so, the poet wanted his fellowman to understand myths and fables of old Asia's Africa's fables. He asked the captains the voyagers the explores, the engineers and the archived to appreciate the beauty of temples fairer than lilies and admire the lefty and dazzling towers, financed red as rises, burnished with gold.

According to Whiteman, the poet's role would begin in this context. The poet would sing the divine songs about the deeds of voyagers and scientist. Finally the poet would fuse nature and Man together and the spiritual Union would be achieved. The poet would tell his soul about the "Passage to more than India. Passage to India is indeed, a passage to more then India. The poem tells about the poet's faith in the one ness of all, his pride in the achievements of mankind in the filed of science and technology, his conception of the role of poet and finally the Union of human soul with the universal soul.

The poem symbolizes first, the physical exploration carried out by the navigator and explorers through Railroad and Seas. Secondly it symbolizes mankind's exploration. Thirdly it symbolizes the intellectual exploration to white the past, the present and future. Fourthly the poem also symbolizes man's spiritual exploration which will lead to a human soul with the universal soul.

Q7. Write a brief note on the poetic devices used in Passage to India."

Ans. Poetic Devices used in 'Passage to India' by poet are:

(i) Whiteman, perhaps, was the first poet to exploit to the full the possibilities of free verse. There is a rare compatibility between his form and his themes: the long, unrestrained line in its free flow captures in its very form the spirit of democracy and freedom.

(ii) Whiteman's unit of rhythm is the phrase instead of the food and his unit of thought is the line instead of the sentence.

(iii) One of the salient features of Whiteman's poetry is 'the catalogue'.

(iv) 'Repetition' is another feature of the poetry of the Sage of Mauhattan

(v) 'Consonance' is the repetition of a sequence of consonants, but with a change in the intervening stressed vowels. For example: deep diving.

(vi) Another literary device used by Whiteman is 'assonance' which is the repetition of identical or similar vowel sounds – especially in stressed syllables – in a sequence of nearby words.

(vii) Whiteman's style can be called functional. It was admirably adapted to describe the immigrant and emigrant. American on the move, the still unshaped landscape of a new condiment, the energy and the romance of pioneering and the dreams of a nation sure of an illimitable future.

(viii) The brilliance of Whiteman's lines sometimes arises from his use of concrete vivid imagery, at other times from a pilling up of simple details, and at other times from a use of telling metaphor.

"The old, most populous, wealthiest of earth's lands
The streams of the Indus and the Ganges and their
Many affluents,
(..)
The tale of Alexander on his warlike marches suddenly
Dying

....

"The flowing literatures, tremendous epics, religion, castes, Old occult Brahma interminably for back, the tender and junior Buddha."

All these poetic devices make the poetry effective and more interesting.

Q8. Write a brief note on the art line of "O Captain! My Caption?

Ans. O Captain! My Captain is a poem given by Whiteman. The poet's grief is expressed through the is of symbol and metaphor. The United States is compared to ship whose war fought under Lincoln's leadership is called a dangerous Voyage. As the Captain is brave and skillful, he brings the ship home after the completion of the voyage. The people are naturally happy and they want to humor their Captain. But they cannot do so for their Captain is assassinated at the very moment of victory. The people eagerly wait on the shore of their Captain but unfortunately he is dead finally the poet is left alone on the deck of ship where his captain lies felled and dead.

"O Captain! My Captain!" is one of the well known poems of Whiteman. It is an elegy on the death of Abraham Lincoln, who was the President of the USA from 1860 to 1865. Being kind and gentle, he could not bear the sight of the wretched and subhuman existence of the negro-slaves of the Southern States of his country and thereby, he wanted to abolish slavery. The Southern States at this juncture decided to break away from the Northern States. Abraham Lincoln as the President of the country did not approve of the decision of the Southern States and decided to fight a civil war in the interest of his country. He fought the war bravely and skillfully and saved his country from disintegration. But hardly a year later Lincoln was assassinated by an actor, John Wilkers Booth, in a theatre. Consequently, the entire nation plunged into mourning. Walt Whiteman, who was an ardent admirer of Lincoln, felt that the death of his leader was a personal loss. This accounts for the poignancy of the poet's grief in the elegy. Moreover in the death of Lincoln Whiteman found the symbol for the suffering and death of a number of soldiers he had himself witnessed. For this reason, his expression of grief has a universal appeal.

Q9. Write a brief note on the poetic device used in O Captain! My Captain?

Ans. (i) 'O Captain! My Captain!' is not a formless poem. In fact, it is Whitman's best poem in rhyme and near regular metre. It is a poem in three stanzas of eight lines each, each stanza having a regular rhyme pattern.

(ii) We have already said 'O Captain! My Captain!' is an elegy. An elegy is a formal and sustained poem of lament for the death of a particular person. The present poem, is a lament for the death of Abraham Lincoln.

(iii) 'Metaphor' is used by Whitman in this poem. The USA is the ship and its captain, is the president, Abraham Lincoln. The war waged against the Southern States was the voyage undertaken by the captain.

(iv) Whiteman's style is functional.

(v) Literary device used by Whiteman is "assonance" which is repetition of identical or similar vowel sounds.

(vi) Alliteration is another device used by Whiteman.

(vii) One of the most important feature of Whiteman's poetry is the Catalogue.

Q10. Give the Outline of the poem "A PSALM of Life" by H.W.Long fellow?

Ans. The poem contains the response of a youngman to a Psalmist. In the first stanza, the Youngman asks the Psalmist not to tell him that life is an empty dream or life is unreal. In the following stanza, the youngman emphatically states that life is real and that the grave is not its goal. He further says that the body comes from and returns to dust, but not the soul.

In Stanza 3, he states that neither enjoyment nor sorrow is the goal of life. Action is the main aim of life. In Stanza 4, he feels sorry that we waste our time in thinking about graves and funerals without bothering about the greatness of art. Continuing in the same vein, the youngman says (in the fifth stanza) on should not be like the dumb cattle driven by others; but one should be like a hero in the struggle and strife of life. Again, in the sixth stanza, the emphasis is on action in the present, without caring for the past or the future. Further, he suggests that God's grace will be bestowed on men of action. In the seventh and eight stanzas, the youngman says that the lives of great men inspire us to become great and leave our footprints on the sands of time and footprints will be followed by the less fortunate brothers. In the concluding stanza, the emphasis is again on action and the capacity to wait.

Q11. Write a critical appreciation of 'A Psalm of Life'?

Ans. 'A Psalm of Life' is a simple, lucid, and meaningful poem. It is a satire on the writers of holy hymns and religious preachers whose sermons are suffused with pessimism, fatalism and defeatism. The speaker, in the present poem, is a Youngman. Being young, his emphasis is on optimism and action. He is frank and forthright in making categorical statements.

He exhorts people to be heroes in the struggle of life and to become great by emulating greatmen. Finally, he implores people to 'learn to labor and to wait.' In the present poem, the emphasis is on action, but not on the fruits of action.

Further, Longfellow did affirm in 'A Psalm of Life', the masculine creed of action, without bothering about 'enjoyment' or 'sorrow', as a means of creating values. This affirmation is a manifestation of the philosophy of pragmatism. Though the message conveyed by the poem is meaningful and useful, it is didactic.

Q12. Write a brief note on the poetic devices used in poem?

Ans. The devices used in poem are below :

(i) The poem contains seven stanzas. Each stanza follows the rhyme scheme ab, ab. To all the stanzas are rhythmic.

(ii) Alliteration is used in a number of places.

E.g. Soul – slumbers

grave – goal

spoken – soul

dum – driven

(iii) The words have been chosen well. The choice of words contributes to the simplicity and lucidity of the poem.

(iv) The metre employed in poem is trochaic. That is the feet employed throughout consists of long syllable followed by short syllable.

(v) The literary device "alliteration" is employed in present poem in number of places.

(vi) It is an example of free verse.

(vii) The language of the poet as one who understands. The transient nature of human life after listening to the song is also poetic.

Q13. Write a brief note on outline of the poem Raven?

[June 2008, Q9]

Ans. A raven having crammed the word 'nevermore' and having escaped from the custody of its owner, is driven at midnight in December through the violence of a storm and seeks admission into a room through a window. The window is that of the chamber of a scholar, occupied half in poring over a volume and half in dreaming of his beloved who is no more. The window being thrown open at the tapping of the bird's wings, the bird itself sits on the most convenient seat. The scholar, who is amused by the incident and the oddity of the visitor's behaviour, demands of its, in jest and without looking for a reply, its name. the raven answers with its customary word 'Nevermore'.

The 'Nevermore' finds an immediate echo in the melancholy heart of the scholar, who, giving utterance aloud to certain thoughts suggested by the occasion, is again started by the bird's repetition of 'Nevermore'. The scholar now guesses the state of the case, but is impelled by the human thirst for self-torture, and in part by superstition, to propound such queries to the bird as will bring him, the lover, the most of the luxury of sorrow, through the anticipated answer 'Nevermore'. From that moment the lover (in the scholar) no longer sees even the fantastic in the bird's behaviour, but speaks of him as a 'grim', ungainly, ghostly, gaunt, and ominous bird of yore.

Q14. Critically appreciate Poe's poem 'The Raven'?

Ans. There is a pet raven named grip in Dicken's **Burnaby Rudge,** while reviewing the novel. Poe felt that Dickens might have made more of the bird: "Its croakings night have been prophetically heard in the course of the drama. Its character might have performed, in regard to that of the idiot, much the same part as, in music, the accompaniment in respect to the air." Here was the germ of the poem. Poe may have been influenced by the verse of Thomas Holley Chivers, and was almost certainly indebted to "Lady Geraldine's Courtship" by Elizabeth Barrett Browning, to whom he dedicated **The Raven and Other Poems.**

'The Raven' in 'The Philosophy of Composition', Poe wrote : "It is my design to render it manifest that no one point in its composition is referable either to accident or intuition – that the work proceeded, step by step, to its completion with the precision and rigid consequences of a mathematical problem."

According to Poe, if a literary work is too long to be read at one sitting, the immensely important effect derivable from unity of impression must be dispensed with. For the above reason, Poe thought the proper length for his poem should be one hundred lines. It is, in fact, a hundred and eight lines.

Beauty is the sole legitimate province of the poem. According to Poe, the pleasure which is at once the most intense, the most elevating, and the most pure is found in the contemplation of the beautiful. As melancholy is the most legitimate of all the poetical tones, Poe has chosen it as the tone for the poem.

The refrain in the present poem 'Nevermore' is chosen to suite the tone of the poem i.e. melancholy. And the topic of the poem is the death of a beautiful woman, namely, Lenore, who was the beloved o the scholar. Finally, the locale for the poem is the scholar's chamber – a chamber rendered sacred to him by memories of his beloved who had frequented it. The room is represented as richly furnished.

The **denoument** (or resolution of the conflict) takes place when the raven's reply 'Nevermore' to the lover's final demand if he shall meet his mistress in another world.

Q15. Write a brief note on the poetic devices used in the poem "The Raven"?

Ans. Poe's poem entitled "The Raven" is a beautiful poem with the well chosen meaningful refrain. It is model for budding creative writers. The poetic devices in the poem are :

(i) The metre employed in the poem is trochaic. That is, the feet employed throughout trochees) consist of a long syllable followed by a short syllable.

(ii) In the refrain of the poem, i.e. 'Nevermore' the most sonorous vowel 'o' and the most producible consonant 'r' are used.

(iii) The literary device 'alliteration' is employed in the present poem in a number of places.

(iv) It is considered a good example of free verse.

(v) The alliteration is also present along with Rhyme.

(vi) The language of poet as one who understands the transient nanutere of human life after listening to the song of earth – is also poetic.

Q16. Give the poetic device used in "Because I could not stop for Death"?

Ans.

(i) The poem contains six stanzas which do not follow a definite rhyme scheme. But the rhythm changes with movement the pattern of action in the poem.

(ii) The balanced parallelism of the first stanza is lightly quickened by the alliterating 'labour' and 'leisure'

(iii) The poetess visualises Death as a person. Don't you think that here the figure of speech, 'personification' is used?.

(iv) In the fourth line of the poem, we find the familiar device of using a major abstraction (i.e. Immortality) in an indefinable manner. In the last stanza, we notice the presence of familiarity with the experience of eternity.

(v) Every image present in the poem is precise. The images are not only beautiful but fused with the central idea the third stanza especially shows Emily Dickinson's power of use.

(vi) You will find 'Consonance' in the following words :

Grazing Grain

Gossamer – Gown

Tippet – Tulle

Horses – Heads

Q17. Give outline of the poem "Because I could not stop for Death"?

Ans. The present poem, in which Death is one of the characters, contains six stanzas. In Stanza I, the poetess visualises Death as a person whom she knows and trusts. As she cannot stop for her, he is considerate enough to stop for her. The carriage holds only her, Death, and Immortality. In Stanza 2, it is stated that they drive in leisurely manner and he, too, is not in a hurry. As a response to his politeness, she is willing to put aside her work.

In Stanza 3, the poetess notes the daily routine of the life she is leaving behind. Children playing games during school racess catch her eyes and later the gazing grain. The poetess now says that they have passed the setting Sun. But in Stanza 4, she corrects, herself by saying that the Sun has passed them. Being aware of the dampness and cold around, she becomes suddenly conscious of her dress.

In Stanza 5, the house of the poetess is identified. It is the slightly rounded surface 'of the ground' with a scarcely visible roof and a cornice 'in the ground'. We realize here that Death, as a person, has gradually receded into the background. In Stanza 6, the poetess about the cessation of all activity. She, finally, says the last objects before her eyes are the heads of the horses of the carriage heading towards eternity.

Q18. Critically comment on the poem "Because I could not stop for Death". [June 2006, Q7]

Ans. 'Because I could not stop for Death' is a beautiful poem on the subject of the daily realization of the imminence of death. It is a poem about the final departure – the departure from life; it is an intensely conscious leave-taking. Funeral ceremony is the theme of a number of poems written by Emily Dickinson. The present poem is the best in that category. The poem contains layers of meaning.

Death, which is conventionally associated with rudeness, suddenness, and impartiality is projected here as a kindly and leisurely gentleman. Moreover, Death, like a compassionate suitor takes the poetess out of the woes of this world into the bliss of the next. Although, the poetess is aware that this is the last ride and his carriage can only be a hearse, its terror is subdued by the 'civility' of the driver. The metaphor of a gentleman taking a lady for a carriage ride is dropped after two stanzas.

The poetess intensely conscious leave-taking is rendered with economy and pose in the third stanza. As a result, an objectively presented scene emerges instead of the sentimental grief of parting. The sequence of items in the third and the fourth stanzas denotes the usual route of a funeral procession – past the school playground, then the village, and on to the remote burying ground.

In the last stanza, the movement of the poem slows down almost to the stop. 'We paused' contrast with the sights 'we passed' in the earlier stages of the journey. The identification of her new 'house with a tomb' is achieved by the use of only two details : a 'roof' that is 'scarcely visible' and a 'cornica' – the moulding around the coffin's lid – that is 'in the ground'.

By delineating vividly the commencement of a journey by carriage to eternity, with Death as the coachman, the poem gives concrete expression to the hope for immortality. The idea of achieving immortality by a ride in the carriage of death is confronted by the concrete fact of physical disintegration as the poetess pauses before 'a swelling in the ground'. But the tomb is not the final destination of the poetess. The final destination is clearly stated at the end as 'Eternity'.

One critic has described the driver as 'amorous but genteel' and another has noted 'the subtly interfused erotic motive'. Further, the carriage drive was a standard mode of courtship more than a century ago.

The aforesaid description is certainly not that of conventional burial clothes. Instead it suits a bridal dress. In the days of the poetess, the term 'Gossamer' was not applied to fine-spun cloth but to a thin, filmy substance formed by a spider – like insect. By using the term 'tippet' (which is the flowing scarf-like part of the disctive hood of holy orders) for a bridal veil, the poetess is suggesting a heavenly marriage.

Thus 'Because I could not stop for Death' is one of the finest poem of Emily Dickinson in which the poetess suggests that Death should not be accepted calmly and politely as befits a gentle woman receiving the attention of gentleman.

Q19. Write a critical appreciation of the poem "I heard a Fly Buzz"?

[Dec 2006, Q7]

Ans. In 'I heard a fly Buzz – when I died', a fly comes at the wrong time – like many things in life - as an irritant which distracts the attention of the people from the magnificent approach of death. But the fly signals the presence of death. The fly comes between light and the dying person, blocking the physical sight, but, at the same time, allows the dying person see the radiance of immortality.

Further, in the third stanza, the poetess talks about distributing her keepsakes' – the tokens of her life. The only heavenly music or a semblance of it was the 'blue uncertain stumbling buzz'. In this stanza, mystery is evoked by a single word 'blue'. The presence of a buzzing fly, the distribution of 'keepsakes' and the attempts of a soul to prolong life suggest that the whole poem satirises the traditional view of death as a peaceful release from life's presence and a glorious entrance into immortality.

'Because I could not stop for Death' and 'I heard a Fly Buzz' are the pre-visions of the poetess own death. In neither of these two poems does death present himself as absolute in brutal majesty nor in the role of God's dreadful minister. The transaction is easy and homely for the author and a lot of knowledge in these matters having attended upon death beds and being aware that the terror of the event was mainly for the observers.

Q20. Give outline of the poem 'I heard a Fly Buzz"

Ans. In the first stanza he poetess tells about the buzz of a fly which interrupts – rather ludicrously – the approach of death. She describes then the atmosphere of the sick room: the stillness in the room is like the deceptively calm centre of a storm which is deceptively calm. The second stanza describes the dry-eyed onlookers as they come closer in the room in order to witness the last dying moments. In line 7 the final death-struggle is described as an 'onset' when the king comes in with the treasures of paradise. The third and the fourth stanzas contains the climax. The final acts of a dying person are described with detachment. The pun in 'signed' and 'assignable' illustrates death's supreme power and the worthlessness of the documents, empty phrases and a corrupting body which one left behind. When the soul waits for death, the buzz of a fly interrupts the grand moment.

Q21. Give poetic view of the poem "I Heard a Fly Buzz – when I Died"?

Ans.

(i) The poem entitled 'I heard a Fly Buzz – when I Died' contains four stanzas. None of the stanzas follows a rhyme pattern.

(ii) In the first stanza, the word 'stillness' is repeated twice indicating the stillness of the imminent death.

(iii) In the third stanza, the literary device 'alliteration' is used

E.g. Blue – Buzz – Between

Q22. Write a critical appreciation of "The Road Not Taken"?

[Dec 2006, Q7]

Ans. The Road Not Taken is one of the most popular lyrics of Robert Frost. It was published in 1916 in the volume of poems entitled **Mountain Interval.** Frost's imagination set as work by the difficulty of choosing one of the two roads which diverge at a particular point. The problem of making a choice is an important theme in Frost's poetry and it is also the theme of the present poem.

'The Road Not Taken' is a great lyric which records a personal experience of the poet. But, from the personal and the individual, the poet rises to the universal and the general. The poet's experience becomes symbolic of human experience in all times and countries. The difficulty of making a choice is a universal experience.

Moreover, it was the choice of poet Robert Frost made which determined his destiny and made him a poet different from others. It is thus that even minor decisions have far reaching consequences. A step once taken or way once chose can never be retraced.

Further, the emphasis, in the present poem, on the importance of making a choice comes close to the thinking of Indian philosophers. "Progress happens at sub-human level; progress is willed at the human," said Professor Sarvapalli Radhakrishnan.

Similarly, if you look back at 'Stopping By Woods' you would appreciate the way the poet thinks about the promises to keep and the miles to go before he sleeps. His manner was dispassionate; there was no attachment to the fruits of actions. Does no Frost's approach similar to the Indian concept of 'Nishkam Karma' (action without attachment)? You must ruminate over this point.

Q23. Write a brief note on the poetic device used in "The Road Not Taken"?

Ans.

(i) In 'The Road Not Taken' there are four stanzas and each stanza contains five lines. Each line consists of eight syllables; though variations are definitely introduced to impart the casualness and the informality of the spoken language.

(ii) The language used in the lyric is simple, lucid, epigrammatic and terse.

(iii) It is a personal lyric. So it does not contain the dashes, parentheses and the pauses, which characterise the dramatic lyric.

(iv) The rhyme scheme is a-b-a-a-b.

(v) It is a good example of free verse.

(vi) Alliteration is present.

(vii) The language used is indicative of the personality of speaker.

(viii) The language of poet as one who understands the transient nature of human life after listening to the song of earth is also poetic.

(ix) Writers style can be called functional.

Chapter – 7

The Indian Poets

Q1. Comment on Indian Poetry in English? **[June 2007, Q7]**

Ans. The term Indian Writing in English has acquired a wide currency during the past few decades. Indian literature in English is no longer regarded as a sub-standard variety of English. It has now gained a certain standard and individuality of its own. The beginning in Indo Anglian poetry were made under adverse circumstances – "adverse" in the sense that the country was still groaning under the burden of a foreign government. The British had subjugated India. During this time 3 significant factors emerged and acted as a solvent of the doubts and perplexities of the situation. They were 1) the new intellectualism and renascent nationalism among the Indians, as symbolized by Raja Ram Mohan Roy; 2) the perseverance of the Christian missionaries; 3) the persuasiveness and metallic clarity of Macaulay's prose style. These factors went a long way in defining the course of Education in India.

English came to be regarded as the official language and many Indians accepted it as the medium of expression. Those who were gifted began to use it creatively in their prose and poetry.

Indian poetry in English may be said to have emerged under unfavourable conditions but as conditions changed, this brand of poetry became more and more homely, indigenous and patriotic.

In examining the phenomenon of Indian poetry in English, one comes up, first of all against the paradox that it did not seriously begin to exist till after the withdrawal of the British from India. An important characteristic of Indian verse in English in the mid-twentieth century has been its emergence from the mainstream of English literature and its appearance as part of Indian literature. It has been said that it is Indian in sensibility and context, and English in language. It is rooted in and stems from the India environment, and reflects its moves, often ironically.

An Indian writing in English, there are at least two problems and sooner or later, he has to come to terms with them. The first is the quality of experience he would like to express in English. The Indian who uses the English language feels, to some extent alienated. His development as a poem is irregular. And it is partly because of this that there is, today, no perspective at all in which to evaluate this phenomenon.

The second is the difference in the idioms he uses. There has always been a time-lag between the adoption of the living, creative idiom of the English speaking peoples and the Indians writing in English in India. And this time-lag is not likely to diminish, although it has today considerably narrowed down. It is true that the historical situation is responsible for it. Besides, there is no special Indian English idiom either. Either in India rarely approaches the liveliness and idiosyncrasy of usage one finds in African or West Indian writing, perhaps because of the long traditions of literatures in the Indian language. It is not surprising, therefore, that writers in English are conscious of their Indianness because, at the bottom of it all, one suspects a crisis of identity.

Q2. Critically appreciate the images in "Palanquin Bearers" in Sarojini Naidu

Ans. 'Palanquin Bearers' gains richness through the images which lie inherent in the native consciousness. It explodes with lovely romantic images. The quick succession of images shows the Shelleyan impact. No fewer than seven similes emphasize her beauty, she "sways like a flower", "skims like a bird", "floats like a laugh", "hangs like a star", "springs like a beam" and "falls like a tear"; the bearers of her palanquin bear her along like a "pearl on a string"

There are vivid and concerete images executed with gnomic terseness like skimming on the foam of a stream, a beam springing on the brow of the tide and a tear falling from the eyes of a bride.

There are also some vague images in the manner of the Pre-Raphaelites, like a laugh from the lips of a dream, swinging like a flower in the wind of a song and hanging like a star in the dew of a song.

The image "She falls.....bride" is highly imaginative and suggestive. It embodies the age-old story of an Indian bride's sadness, whatever be the cause – separation from the parents etc.

The whole setting of this poem is romantic. The movement of the poem suggests the rhythmic march of the palanquin -bearers through the streets. The bearers sing gaily of the beauty of the lady. A soft music leaps up in the air as the palanquin-bearers bear the blooming beauty along. The tone here is in complete rapport with the heart beats of the beauty inside. The palanquin, the bearers, the inmate inside the song and the springy movement all fuse into one another.

The poem consists of 2 stanzas each of six rhymed lines. The first and the fifth lines in each stanza serve as a refrain. The rhythm is of comparatively swift movement corresponding with the swaying movement of the palanquin, and the rise and fall.

The tune and movement go together in this song, where we have what is rhetorically called, the kinesthetic image, or the image of felt motion 'swaying', 'skimming', 'floating'. It may sound nostalgic but it is very true to the Indian experience. The image indicates a lightness of touch, a buoyancy, and create a dram like atmosphere.

Even though the setting of the poem 'Palanquin Bearers' is specifically Indian, it acquires its appeal from a certain exoticism of setting or certain ideals or emotions which inspire them. The emotions suffusing 'Palanquin Bearers' is not confined to India alone. The sadness of a departing bride and the joy of those escorting here to her new home and unraveling, like diving agents, the stages of the inexorable march of human life, is expressed through a rocking rhythm and cosmic imagery.

The poem seems to be an allegory on the movement of time gleefully carrying man towards an unknown but inevitable destiny, which can either be "like a laugh from the tips of a dream" or "like a tear from the eyes of a bride". Possibly both.

Q3. Analysis the poem "The Bird of Time" by Sarojani Naidu?

Ans. The poem "The Bird of Time" rings with melody throughout and suggests the totality of life wherein pleasure and pain hold an even scale. The poem consists of two stanzas of nine lines each.

In the first stanza, the Bird of Time has been addressed and asked about the subject matter of her songs. The reply is that the songs are about the varied emotions of human life i.e. joys, sorrows, troubles, , fights, hopes, faith, peace and death.

In the second stanza, she has been asked to disclose the location where she learned the "changing measures" of her song. And the reply that comes is: that almost any situation has been able to evoke and inspire the Bird of Time to sing. It may have been the forest or the waves at the sea-side. It could have been the laughter and happiness of a new bride. It may have been the dawn of hope or the dawn of despair; or the emotions of pity, hate or pride. Therefore any situation or emotion has been capable of inspiring the songs of The Bird of Time.

The poetry of Sarojini Naidu embodies her bold defiance of fate. Eternal joy can be experienced only by those who have strength and courage to defeat the deceptive designs of fate. In this poem, when the poetess asks the bird about the sources of its profound joy its delightful music, it points to the precious possession emanating from the triumph over fate :

The desire to escape from the hard realities of life does not touch the valiant souls that aspire to defy and defeat fate. They learn to pass through easily the moments of failure and frustration and to extract peace and joy form them. Sarojini herself lived a life of this type. She continually suffered from ill health and gloom and often longed for peace and poise, but soon her indomitable spirit would come out of such a state of despondency triumphantly and she would rush to the joyful realm of dreams and hope. The variety of emotions that goad the bird in the poem to burst in spontaneous music makes it a typical Indian bird.

Sarojini Naidu is a gifted artist who shows in all her poetry a great flair for ornamental and highly sophisticated style which abound in lovely similies, metaphors, images and symbols.

Q4. Sum up the poem "Bangle-Sellers" by Sarojini Naidu?

Ans. This poem throws light on Sarojini Naidu's conception of Indian womanhood. According to her, the lives of women should be radiant, the lustrous tokens of which are the delicate bright rainbow-tinted bangles. The first duty of a woman is to be happy, since her happiness radiates happiness to those who come into contact with her. To be a happy daughter and wife is the goal to which Indian women ought to aspire. Marriage to an Indian woman means much more than to a man since the woman is in most cases economically dependent. It is therefore a turning point in her life. Sarojini symbolized the heart's desire of a bride with the rich red colour of her bangles.

The would be bride responds to the laughter of the intimate companions of her girlhood as they tease her about her coming marriage. She sheds tears as she leaves her father's house for her husband's. Hence Sarojini Naidu speaks of the bridal laughter and the bridal tears which like the bangles she wears are, Tinkling, luminous, tender and clear.

'Bangle Sellers' confines itself to the different states in a woman's life, relating each stage to the bangles appropriate to it. Thus the "rainbow-tinted circles of light" carried by the bangle sellers to the temple fare are 'Lustous tokens of radiant lives/for happy daughters and happy wives'.

The focus here is only on the radiance and not on the desolation at all. Sarojini Naidu mingles description with reflection in 'Bangle Sellers'. It is beautifully executed and shows her descriptive skills with sustained thought.

Q5. Give various specialities of the Nissim Ezekiel poem "Night of the Scorpion". [June 2007, Q7]

Ans. A poem of human interest, 'Night of the Scorpion' has a delicate family situation as its setting. The poet's mother stung by a scorpion is given multiple treatment, bringing in its sweep the world of magic and superstition, science and rationality and material affection.

Though Ezekiel is a poet of the city, in this poem he gives a living truthful rural picture. The scene of a mother stung by a scorpion on a rainy night in the village brings in its wake the two worlds of superstition and scientific temperament into focus. The neighbours swarming like flies and trying to mitigate her pain by various methods reveal the essence of community life. The father embodies the sceptic, rational approach. A feeling effect is achieved in the last lines when the mother heaves a sigh of relief on her children being spared. The experience is distinctly Indian and the imagery vivid and sensitive. The neighbours concern for a speedy recovery is expressed through lines that are incantatory in effect.

'Night of Scorpion' evokes superstitious practices we haven't still outgrown. It enacts an impressive ritual in which the mother's reaction, towards the end, to her own suffering ironically cancels out earlier response, both primitive and sophisticated. The interrelationship between the domestic tragedy and the surrounding community is unobtrusively established. The poem also demonstrates the effective use of parallelism.

The various specialities of the Nissim Ezekiel poem "Night of the Scorpion" are :

(1) Irony : Two kinds of Irony are seen to operate in the poetry of Nissim Ezekiel : one closely allied to satire, where the poet stands at a distance from the object looked at; the other, closely allied to compassion where the poet examines the experience as if from within. Examples of first kind are more numerous among his early writings; they are less common in the later period. In the middle poems, the two kinds of irony appears to co-exist.

The early poems are greatly influenced by British poets, Eliot, Auden and Empson. The taut line, the tell-tale imagery, the finished stanza.

'Night of Scorpion', in which Ezekiel evokes the rural milieu, illustrates the operation of a kind of irony. Here we have a situation in which the speaker moves among other characters. For all the humour at the expense of the peasants, there is also an involvement in the situation on the part of the speaker. He is moved. It provides a fitting finale to the narrative.

Example : My mother only said

Thank God the scorpion picked on me
and spared my children

The shift from the speaker to the mother is significant. The return to the mother is a celebration of the liberation from foreign influence.

(2) Indian Colour : In his poem Nissim Ezekiel has done a tremendous job in depicting the Indian milieu. In many of his poems we come across a visilant criticism of the Indian 'Night of the Scorpion' involves one entire community in case of scorpion biting. The mother is senseless. A big preparation goes on. Each one in his manner prepares to cure "the Evil one". The methods of superstitious practices are the main aim of the poet. But the poet never forgest to describe the plight of the victim. "My mother twisted".

Thus we see a kind of faithful description of the immediate situation by Ezekiel. He has an eye for details and paints them without distortion. With his simple diction Nissim Ezekiel gives stress on his ironical statements. It is difficult to miss the Indian smell and the concealed statements in his poetry.

(3) Style and Technique : The engrossing narration and description of the poem are made effective also through the free verse. This poem is much more relaxed and open worked than Ezekiel's formal poetry, with a new quality of natural colloquialism in diction and tone:

Example : I remember the night my mother
was stung by a scorpion. Ten hours
of steady rain had driven him
to crawl beneath a sack of rice.

In the poem the abandonment of capitals at the start of each line, the dramatic casualness of the recalled crisis, the long paragraph set off abruptly from the three-line climax, all of which give 'Night of the Scorpion', a new feel, a new appearance, a sense of unhurried lucid progression through time. And yet the poet is only partially able to escape old habits. On closer inspection we hear behind the arras of free verse regular iambic lines insisting upon their own pattern. The casual flow of the newly-loosened sound is several times violated and made awkward as the metrical pulse appears and tires to assert itself:

Example : They clicked their tongues
With every movement that the scorpion made
his poison moved in mother's blood, they said

Or

I watched the holy man perform his rites
to tame the poison with an incantation.

Now Ezekiel achieves the maturity to allow the regular iambic metre to remain only in the form of an undercurrent. "Night of the Scorpion" is an interesting poem, containing a fascinating tension between crisis and mocking social observation, but the discrepancies of the poem confuse the tone, which swings between the natural and colloquial reporting of experience and a more removed literary formality. The poem finds a happy conclusion in the last lines where the typical Indian mother expresses satisfaction in the fact that her children were spared.

Q6. Give a comment on Nissim Ezekiel's poem "Enterprise"?

Ans. The poem 'Enterprise' is one of the serious poems of Ezekiel and is moulded out of the fallouts of frustration in a barbaric city.

'Enterprise' is an allegory of the pilgrimage theme with a suggestion of futility. The journey from the city to the hinterland is a metaphor for contrived change from frustration to fulfillment.

The group ignores the thunder which is nothing but the inner voice of man. It should have guided the group. Man deprived of the inner voice or insensitive to the call of his own soul invariably rushes into impediments.

At the end of the journey there is complete disillusionment. Was the journey worth undertaking? Instead of bringing any sense of fulfilment, the 'trip had only darkened every face'. The futility of the whole enterprise, the struggles on the way, the deprivations the group undergoes and the failure to compromise the intention of the journey with its end are succinctly brought out in the final clinching line of the poem. While many poets are satisfied with just a glimpse of the truth, Ezekiel probes the feelings of the personal loss and deprivation till ultimately he reaches the core of truth. This is one of his man characteristics. Scores of his poems are obviously written for personal and therapeutic purposes.

In this poem, 'Enterprise', a situation is viewed with an ironic angle with a hope that it would offer some consolation, a still point or some momentary stay against the feelings of loss and deprivation. The enterprise which was started as a pilgrimage ultimately filled a sense of loss in the group members. 'Some were broken, some merely bent' Ezekiel says. The concluding stanza throws light on the whole event.

This is the tragedy of modern humanity where every enterprise ends in futility. Life is like pathless wood and there is no purpose in taking up any enterprise. The Vedic man according to Nissim Ezekiel's philosophy moved from darkness to light. Hence this enterprise was meaningful. But the modern man is simply misfit for noble missions. Like Eliot's Prufrock or Auden's 'hero' he wastes a valuable life afflicted by fear in trivial acts.

The pilgrims in the 'Enterprise' ignore the call of conscience and consequently some are broken, some bent. The poet who is making the emotive use of language and through that emotive use of language he reaches the conclusion. 'Enterprise' begins in delight and ends in wisdom. The delight is in talking up the enterprise, in taking up the action. Without action no human being can live. Wisdom constitutes in the darkened faces and in their discovery that there was nothing unique about them. The poem can be meaningfully related to Lord Krishna's conception of Karma Yoga which expects us to remain active and to submit ourselves to law and duty.

Q7. Analyse the poem "My Grandmother's House" by Kamla Das?

Ans. Kamala Das's reminiscences of childhood are associated with Nalapat House, her family home in Malabar, and her grandmother whom she loved dearly. These recollections are always linked with feelings of nostalgia and wistfulness.

In this poem the house is presented with concern and pathos and the poetess expresses her poignant feelings of yearning for this house. She wishes to go back to it. The words 'windows' and 'air' are qualified by the two prefixes "blind", and "frozen" respectively. There is a rich ambiguity in the phrasing which makes very real the suffering of the poetess. Her heart is itself like a dark window where the fresh air does not blow. Images working on several layers of response, or enrich the poem's texture. One of the favourite images is that of the window where she sits and enjoys the cool refreshing breeze of the past. This recurs to the extent of becoming an obsessive image.

The image emphasizes, the languishing desire of the poetess for a sentient peep into her past and resurrect her dreams and desires. With the dereliction of the old house, the windows have become blind. Only the heart of the reunion with the house will melt the ice and the window will again be restored to old life. The crumbling of the old house and the death of the old woman leave their impact on the poetess also. With them crumbles her own life of innocence and the cherished values.

Q8. Critically appreciate the poem "The Blood" by Kamla Das?

Ans. Blood shows an admirable restraint in tone and tautness of language. The remorse that Kamala Das feels at having failed to abide by the values associated with the old house and the grandmother is more clearly expressed in the poem "Blood" which runs at two levels literal and allegorical. At the literal level it describes the remote ancestry and the old blood of her family of which her great grandmother was the living example. The poetess promised to her to rejuvenate the house when she grew up and was very rich.

The poem is touchingly autobiographical, and her nostalgia for the old house and for the great grandmother who lived in it and gave it an everlasting character is convincingly evoked. That Kamala Das does not idealise the house and the people who are associated with it, is not only evident in the matter-of-factness of he reminiscential mood; but in the fact that the sense of the history of the house is evoked in terms of the poet's own childhood memory of it and in the way this memory acquires a renewed but ironic significance under the pressure of the poet's immediate poetic concern.

The poet does not attempt to reach out into the history of the house of three hundred years beyond what she herself knows of it. At present it is a decrepit house with the walls 'cracked and torn and moistened by the rains', and with the fallen tiles, the whining and groaning windows and the rats scampering past the door. The grandmother, 'really simple' and 'fed on God for years', and proud of her 'oldest blood' is portrayed with humour and detachment. The forces or disruption and decay are at work and the poet's memory of the grandmother who was hurt to see the house die is poignant.

More than the pathos of the memory of her grandmother, it is the poet's preoccupation with death and decay, so innocuously impaled in the image of the crumbling house which she loves so much that emerges as the dominant theme. The lines, short and chiseled, have a solemnity of tone and a gravity of mood which comes not from melancholia but from a sense of feeling life on the tips of her senses, as it were. Even when Kamala Das speaks of defeat and emptiness and the inevitable darkness which is imminent, the assured clear outline, the somber control of nerve, and the poise of movement which is at once graceful and firm show tha the poet is in command of herself in a moment of personal reckoning.

In 'Blood' the great grandmother is vividly portrayed through a rich cluster of details, such as her riding an elephant and visit to a Shiva temple when she was young.

The series of images portray the grandmother and, by implication serve as a memory of the days gone by. They also reveal the poet's wistful longing to have been born in those days and to have lived with full breath in the open air. The most remarkable phenomenon about the images of Kamala Das is that they emerge from the cultural sources of the typical Indian background and they also define her identity. They have the sharp indigenous smell and their treatment is expressly individual in the specific context of emotions and feelings.

Q9. Write the special features used in by Ramanujan in his poetry?

Ans. The special features of his poetry are :

(i) Imagery : The imagery for which Ramanujan is well known becomes conspicuous only in the last lines. Not only on the crotch...evokes the images of a terribly unforgettable past, of the nasty associations of childhood. It was on the 'crotch of a tree' that the children had met to feed their sensation in innocent days. The passion raging hard within the woman is beautifully translated into words in the subsequent lines. The last lines of the poem are strongly suggestive and evocative. The term sneezing is full of implications. On the one hand, it indicates the consummation of passion on the tree; on the other hand, it hints at tone of the popular love-pranks in the street. Ramanujan's verse displays the quality of indirection and suggestiveness which goes with an unusual aesthetic appeal. The lines above are rich in erotic suggestiveness.

(ii) Versification: Ramanujan is deliberate writer who takes his tools into account before letting them appear on his page for the reader. He chooses monosyllabic words for the sake of effect and concentration. He employs rhyme and rhythm to enhance the charm of his art. There is no superfluous word or phrase in his poems. Terseness is the hallmark of his verse. Subtlety is his touchstone with and irony makes his poetry lively and delightful.

The poem is delightfully readable for its lucidity of language and for its employment of literary devices shorn of embellishments. The lines and stanzas vary in length and thereby keep monotony and roughness at bay. A stanza may be of ten lines or of one only. Clearly, this sort of variation has been a favourite device with 'new' poets, and Ramanujan falls in their line. He opts for free verse in place of regular rhymes, and for stress rhythm in place of traditional syllabic rhythm. This poem is no exception to his general practice. Very deftly, he shifts the scene in this poem from a 'village' to 'cities' where one has an immense scope of sin and corruption. The swift change of years is also skillfully arranged in it. The girl has now matured in age. As a full-blooded woman, she is out to seek illicit love in cities. Adulthood has come for her not without its repercussions. Seen in this light, the poem becomes kaleidoscopic, and the total effect created by it is almost astonishing.

Q10. Analysis the poem "River" by Ramanujan and also give its style?

Ans. This poem is on the river Vaikai which flows through Madurai, a city that has for about two thousand years been the seat of Tamil culture. As an evocation of the river the poem succeeds admirably. At the same time, the river becomes "a point of departure for ironically contrasting the relative attitudes of the old and new Tamil poets, both of whom are exposed for their callousness to suffering, when it is so obvious, as a result of the floods".

The poets of yore sang only of the floods (1.15), not of the ruins and ravages caused by them. The old poet paid a casual visit to the river when it was in its fully fury, and when the people talked of its speedy rising, submerging the 'cobbled steps' and the 'bathing places', and when the stories were whispered around about the sweeping off the 'three village houses' and the drowning of 'one pregnant woman' and 'a couple of cows/named Gopi and Brinda'. His visit was no more than a pleasure-trip or a curiosity trip undertaken in a sportive mood, for he remained totally indifferent towards the losses and sorrows of the people.

The same sort of the attitude has also been adopted by the new poets. These poets never versified the agonies and miseries of the people – of the drowning of the pregnant woman, with perhaps twins in her belly who died before their birth, of the carrying away of three village houses and a couple of cows. Of course, they waxed rapturous and poetic over the ruins and floods, but they had no time to think of the destroyed innocent creatures.

This poem is a welcome attempt at showing the poet's concern about the sufferers and the bereaved. Skillfully it shows his sympathy for them. It is, thus, a realistic portrayal of the people's unmerited suffering at the hands of cruel and uncontrollable. Doomsters, who often heap 'travails and teens' on humanity. The poet's love for all creatures – not only for human beings, but also for animals.

Style of the poem is :

The poem 'A River' has a sweet and simple language. There is nothing to be read between the lines. The variation in the length of lines and stanzas is to be seen here too, as usual. The poet's compassion is conveyed directly, without the help of imagery or symbolism. The tone is obviously ironical, particularly into the portrayal of the indifferent attitude of the old and new poets towards the destructive role of the river. They are equally to blame for being 'poetic' at the cost of human lives and property. The false assumptions of the poets who live in ivory towers are exposed herein. The poem hits hard at them and their vanities. Their false notions are partly due to their ignorance of the rural life and its acute problems, since they are born and bred in cities. The three village houses, the pregnant woman, the coins, and the river itself are part and parcel of the rural life. And then the old city of Madurai owes greatly to the river for its being the 'seat of Tamil culture'. If we keep the cultural efflorescence of many big Indian cities in mind, we shall discover that it was mainly due to the positive contributions of the rivers and the seas, which served as the real source of conveyance and transportation in those good old days.

The big cities of India like Delhi, Agra, Kanpur, Allahabad, Varanasi, Patna, Calcutta, Bombay, Madras, Madurai, and many others are all situated on the banks of the rivers and the sea. The attitude of the poets become all the more laughable and despicable when we consider these cities as the direct result of the positive role of the rivers and the seas.

Speaker in the poem expresses an attitude through his particular use of the language, by his choice of words, imagery and syntax.

The reality of the floods doesn't seem to affect anyone; its havoc goes unnoticed even by the 'new' poets who, one would have thought, could be expected to be socially conscious but are not. Their claims to be new or modern are exposed. The poem is thus an oblique comment on the sterility of much of contemporary Tamil poetry – an opinion which isn't overtly stated. It is the speaker's attitude in the poem that helps us to make this inference.

Q11. Give interpretation of the poem "A Missing Person" by Jayant Mahapatra?

Ans. This short poem is an autobiographical piece in which Mahapatra is deeply involved. It, in fact, etches the contours of the lingering loneliness of Mahapatra's own mother which he observed in his early years and whose memory tormented him for long until years later when he "decided to put the whole thing on paper in an exercise of exorcism"

My father was away most of the time, touring the primary schools of the subdivision on his study BSA bicycle; and in the house my mother, physically ill, would be moving about in the listless darkness; my younger brother at her heels. We didn't have electricity in the house (it was a luxury for us), and the veranda with its adjoining little courtyard seemed to float in a ghostly atmosphere, filling me with a sense of insecurity… And the picture of my mother, holding on to the oil lamp in the shadows, the sooty flame swaying in the breeze, seemed to establish itself firmly in my mind… An inexplicable loneliness linked itself with the sad eyed oil lamp of my mother.

The poem is a recollection of the creative moment of Mahapata. It is out of this silence of the lonely body that one is able to speak, out of the condition of being absent from oneself and unable to find comfort in any self-reflection.

To write, means never to be whole. Only that which is not whole, after all, would look to reflections for completion. And the reflections, including those of art are illusions. Our personal identify will always be that of "A missing person". He expresses this convincingly in "A Missing Person".

The Indian woman has not yet found herself. Celebrated and reversed as she is in ancient Sanskrit lore, she is at a loss to place herself in the modern world. In the darkened room with the lighted lamp in her hand she cannot see her own reflection in the mirror because she is always "at the edge of sleep" a **tamasic** slumber that obliterates all awareness of the self. The oil lamp she holds in her hand is the knowledge that knows her lonely physical self in relation to the universal. The mirror is a common image used in Sanskrit to represent oneself hence the appropriateness of its use in the present context.

Ignorant of her true identity a woman becomes a missing person in the society. She is unable to fill the gap for lack of knowledge of her own potentialities. She thus deprives humanity of something priceless. The meaning is well conveyed with a sustained symbol and the language honed of all unnecessaries. The phrase "drunken yellow flames" works at 2 levels, both as the inner source of knowledge and as **agni** that destroys the physical "lovely body". The logic on the other hand is not as effectively constructed as the deliberate aim seems to be to obfuscate logic with illogicality. The method by itself could, if used with conviction, reveal a greater awareness, a wider perception, a holistic view but in this poem it succeeds only in descending to the level of the ludicrous. The dual personae of this poem is intended to contrast the man has attained wordly success, with the one who has been exploited.

Q12. Define the Indo-Anglian poetry with help of suitable poets?

Ans. Indo-Anglian Poetry has by all means, a bright future. Like the poetry being written in any other Indian languages, this brand of poetry has become part and parcel of modern Indian literature. It has a distinctive taste and expresses effectively the varicoloured Indian life. It embodies nationalistic sentiments and aspirations, and that is one of the strong reasons for its popularity today. Several critical studies, special numbers and anthologies that have appeared on this branch of Indian literature in recent years speak of its popularity and significance.

In the present context one can only recall the remarks of Rabindranath Tagore regarding Bengal's response through literature to the call of the West: "It has a future for it is quickened with life and it carries within itself a hope that one day it will become a great channel for communication of ideas between adventurous West, and the East of the immemorial tranquility.

Indo-Anglian poetry has now come to stay on its own strength, and the prophecy of the Nobel Laureate of India has been eventually realised.

At the outset we had set for ourselves as one of our aims the task of enabling you to enjoy and appreciate poetry by six of the famous Indian poets writing in English. The poem by Rabindranath Tagore ('I ask for a moment's indulgence to sit by thy side' and 'This is my prayer to thee my Lord') The text and the finer appreciation was pointed out to you. Similarly, we took up Sarojini Naidu ("The Bird of Time", 'Bangle Sellers' and Palanquin bearers'), Nissim Ezekiel ('Night of the Scorpion' and 'Enterprise'), Kamala Das ('My Grandmother's House' and 'Blood') A.K.Ramanujan ('A River' and 'Look for a Cousin on a Swing') and finally Jayant Mahapatra ('Indian Summer' and 'A Missing Person')

In taking up all the poems we have seen to it that apart from the explaining literal meaning, the other finer points of the poem have also been taken up.

Comprehension Exercises

Q1. What are the basic themes of both the poems of Rabindra Nath Tagore?

Ans. The poem "I ask for a moment's indulges to sit by thy side" is based on relationship between God and the poet. It emphasizes the intimate relationship of love existing between the Poet and the God. To sit face to face with the Lord of Love with and to sing The Mystic Muse of Life shows the necessity of atmosphere of serene silence for the poet. He is waiting for the sweet music of bees in flowering grove. The dramatic atmosphere is pained in the mystic words of muse.

The poem "This is my prayer to Thee My Lord" is expression of the will of shedding of the life of attention led by a single individual. It is prayer to The Lord to remove darkness of ignorance from the heart of the poet. The poet wishes to get strength not only to bear up to his joys and troubles but also to be able to selfless serve the Lord with a human heart. He also to be gifted with the fortitude to serve and love the poor and unfortunate. He never wanted to be a coward in the face of the rude and mighty. He asks God to raise up his mind from the insignificant. He wants to be merged with the will of God with love and devotion.

Q2. What are the various images that can be seen in the poem "The Palanquin Bearers"?

Ans. 'Palanquin Bearers' has images which lie in the native consciousness. It is loaded with lovely romantic images. Here we have both concrete and abstract images. There are vivid and concrete images mingles like skimming on the foam of stream, a beam springing on the brow of file etc. There are some vague images as a laugh from the lips of dream, swinging like a flower of the wind of a song and hanging like a star in the dew of song. The image 'She falls…bride' is highly imaginative and suggestive. It depicts the age-old story of an Indian bride's sadness, due to separation from the parents. The images indicate the lightness of touch buoyancy and create a dream like atmosphere.

Q3. How does the poem 'The Bangle Seller' throw light on Sarojini Naidu's conception of Indian women?

Ans. In the poem the poetess says that the lives of women should be radiant. The lustrous tokens of which are the delicate bright rainbow –tinted bangles. The first duty of a woman is to be happy her happiness radiants happiness to those who are related to her. An Indian woman ought to be happy daughter and wife. An Indian woman has to adjust more than a man in a marriage as she is economically depended. She symbolises the desire of a bride with rich red colour of her bangles. She speaks of the bridal laughter and tears which like the bangles she wears.

Q4. What are the some of the contrasts present in poem 'Night of the Scorpion'

Ans. The contrast is somewhat central to the poem. The contrast is based on clash of values. The deep, traditional widespread superstition of illiterate rural folk and the half baked urban educated, rational element represented by the father of person and muted tongue-in cheek, sareastic attitude of pesona. The contrast is between the superstitious village peasant. The town bred, rational, sceptic father who tries everything. The extended meaning of the poem makes it a parable of the conflict between the Gods and the demons and makes it a tale of sufferings and explanation.

Q5. Compare and contrast 'Enterprise' with Eliot's The Journey of the Magi?

Ans. 'Enterprise' is an allegory of the pilgrimage theme with a suggestion of futility. The journey from the city to the hinterland is a metaphor for contrived change from frustration to fulfilment. The group ignores the thunder which is nothing but the inner voice of man. Man deprived of the inner voice invariably rushes into impediments. At the end of the journey there is complete disillusionment. Was the journey worth undertaking. The pilgrims here are like The Magi in Eliot's poem.

Q6. In the poem "Looking on a Swing" what are the images you can find?

Ans. The imagery becomes conspicuous only in the last lines. The images of a terribly unforgettable part, of the hasty associations of childhood evokes on the crotch. On the crotch of the tree the children used to feed their sensation in innocent days. The last lines of the poem are strongly suggestive and evocative. The last lines of the poem are strongly suggestive and evocative. The term sneezing indicated passion on the tree and it hints one of the popular love pranks in the street. Ramanujan verse displays the quality of indirection and suggestiveness which goes with an unusual aesthetic appeal. The lines are rich in erotic suggestiveness.

Q7. What does Jayant Mahapatra put across in his poem "A Missing Person"?

Ans. The given poem is auto biographical. The poem is a recollection of the creative moment for Mahapatra. It is out of this silence of the lonely body that one is able to speak. He feels unable to find comfort in any self-reflection which is not whole, would look to reflection for completion. The reflection, including those of art are illusions. Our personal identity will always be "that of a missing person" a woman's inability to find herself. The true meaning and purpose of her existence trouble Jayant Mahapatra. He expresses this convincingly in his poem.

Q8. What can you say about the style employed in A.K.Ramanujan?

Ans. Ramanujan is a deliberate writer. Her chooses mono syllabic words for the sake of the effect and concentration. He employs rhyme and rhythm to enhance the charm of his art. There is no superfluous word or phrase in is poems. His touch tones wit and irony make his poetry lively and delightful. The reader feels delight in reading his poems due to lucidity of languages and its literary devices. The lines and stanza vary in length and thereby keep monotony and roughness at bag.

QUESTION PAPERS
EEG-06

EEG-6 : UNDERSTANDING POETRY
June, 2006

Note : Question No. 1 and Question No. 2 are **compulsory**. Answer any **three** questions from the rest. Answer **five** questions in all.

Q1. Write short notes on any *four* of the following :

(i) Sonnet

Ans. The Sonnet is a verse form of fourteen lines, usually of iambic pentameter with an elaborate rhyme scheme. There are two distinct kinds 1) The English or the Shakespearean Sonnet and 2) The Italian or Petrarchan Sonnet. The new type of style is developed by English Sonnet variation which is called Spenserian sonnet.

(a) The English or Shakespearean Sonnet : The Sonnet is organised either into twelve lines and a couplet to make it 12 + 2 = 14 or three quatrains (3 × 4) and a couplet (12 + 2 = 14) with a correspondingly organised rhyme scheme such as a-b-ab-c-d-efgg. Usually the quatrain, expresses the thoughts of the poem and it is summed up in the concluding couplet.

(b) The Italian or the Petrarachan Sonnet : The Italian Sonnet is in iambic pentameter and it is divided into two parts :

(i) The octave (8 lines) and

(ii) Setet (6 lines)

The octave has the rhyming pattern abba-abba while the sestet has cde-cde. The octave expresses in figurative language what is restated in direct language in the sestet.

(c) The Spenserian Sonnet : It is a variation of the English sonnet with the different rhyme scheme abab-bcbc-cd-dee. Writing a poem in fourteen lines demands a high degree of discipline on the part of poet. With a codified rhyme scheme, the poet has to use specialised vocabulary and at the same time choose the appropriate word to express his emotional intensity. Hence the Sonnet as a verse from is characterised by the tightness of rhyme in iambic pentameter and includes in its themes love time, friendship honour, duty, art, nature.

(ii) Image

Ans. The fundamental idea about images in literature is that they evoke visual response in the reader. That is why descriptive poetry uses images for effective picturisation of men and women scenes and seasons. This basic meaning of the "image" is thus provided by the context. The image is what they name but there are other meanings of this term. An image is more than visual perception. It is sense perception reproduced in the mind. It is a reflection of sense impressions conveying a mood or emotion. A rose for example not only provides us with sense images in term of its colour, texture, but it also conveys the sense of loveliness, tenderness, softness and also sweetness. A poet thus use the image of a rose to express his attitude towards his mistress or his beloved and addresses her as "my rose". The image goes beyond verbal analysis and connects in with assumptions, which give poetry a deeper meaning.

Example : A violet by mossy stone
Half hidden from the eyes
Fair as star, when only one
Is shining in the sky

Wordsworth compares Lucky first to a violet flower and then a single star. The violet flower brings to our mind a dainty flower, beautiful and fragile. After directing our attention to a half hidden violet. Wordworth evokes the image of a shining star when the sky is bare. There lines show the effectiveness of image in the poem.

(iii) Symbol

Ans. Symbol derives the sustenance through the suppression of direct Metaphor. The symbol evokes unseen worlds. It reveals a hidden order that lurks behind our perceptive everyday reality. A poem which speaks of the fading of rose has for its theme the transience of beauty, of all things bright and beautiful. There the poet uses the rose as symbol. Symbolism thus attempts to penetrate into World of ideas beyond reality and this it achieves through suggestiveness, evoking an object little by little.

Example : The White moon is setting behind wave
And time is setting with me.

These lines are symbolical, evoking an emotion of melancholy through the symbolic association of these words moon, wave, whiteness, settling time along with the last melancholy cry O!

(iv) Lyric

Ans. The Lyric is a short poem that expresses emotion and is meant to be sung but lyrics written after 15th century though not meant to be sung, nevertheless tend to retain their mellifluous quality and rhythm. The lyric lends itself to the expression of intense personal joy or pain or offers a contemplative mood. The lyric expresses the poets emotional response to an event or scene or to the recollection of an emotion. Thus the lyric is essentially an emotional or reflective soliloquy.

Many of the long poem in modern period have also used the devices of lyricism to express the "peak moments" of the poet but by chaining these fragmentary sequences together, the lyric in 20th century has allowed for more complex attitudes than those of the earlier period.

It express the instant emotion felt at that very moment and which follow out in the form of poetry.

As a lyric is composition spontaneously written at the white heat of passion, it is not limited to expressions of joy or elation.

(v) Ode

Ans. The Ode is most elevated and complex variety of lyric, written to celebrate a public occasion or some high and serious theme. The ode originating from Greece and Rome influenced the English poets of 17th century. The ode is of two kinds:

(a) Pindaric – These odes were composed to be chanted to music for dance and this resulted in its developing an elaborate stanzaic structure.

(b) Horatian - It was often personal and reflective and had a greater degree of Solemnity.

From 17th to 19th century, the ode was considered a poetic ideal both for its high seriousness and technical design. The greatest English poets who wrote odes were Gray Wordsworth, Shelley and Keats.

Q2. Explain any *four* of the following passages with reference to their contexts :

(i) But thy eternal summer shall not fade.
Nor lose possession of that fair thou ow'st;
Nor shall Death brag thou wander'st in his shade,
When in eternal lines to time thou grow'st.

Reference : These lines have been taken from the Shakespearean Sonnet "Shall I Compare Thee to the Summer Day". This Sonnet is addressed to a friend. The speaker is in the twin roles of friend and poet. It is full of scale immortalisation of art and through art. In this sonnet, the poet sets up the power of time and then introduces the power of his verse as a defence against time.

Context : These line suggests a comparison of youth's beauty with that of summer and then appears to reject it by claiming permanence for the youth and against the inevitable transience of summer's glory. The focus is on the apparent comparison and contrast between order of youth and the order of nature but it shifts through the liens to affirm the eternity of Time and Art. The subtle transition is effected by the phrase "eternal lines to time" Thus the apparent contrast between the summers of youth and nature in this quatrain yields to an underlying similarity. Both nature and youth alike tend to lose their beauty and brightness only to regain them when they are framed within the confines of Eternal Time and Art.

(ii) **Weep no more, woeful shepherds, weep no more,**
For Lycidas, your sorrow, is not dead.
Sunk though he be beneath the watery floor
So sinks the day-star in the ocean bed.

Reference: These lines have been taken from John Milton's Lycidas. Lycidas begins on a note of despair consequent upon the premature death of Edward King, kind but as the poem progresses. The poem Lycidas effectively blinds the Christian, Classical and Humanist element.

Context: These lines shows the accident that ended brings life. By giving king the name of Lycidas a classical, name, the poem framed within pastoral convention. Milton returns one more them of the Lycidas death and re-invocates the Muse to aid him to sing his elogy. Alpheus a legendry river of Arcady who pursued the nymph. Arethusa with great passion, till the nymph was turned into fountain by Diana. Hence, the invocation to Alpheus for poetic inspiration and Muse of the Theocritus and other Greek bucolic poets in general. This poem shows the vision of hope and expectations.

(iii) **Thou art slave to Fate, chance, kings and desperate men,**
And dost with poyson, warre and sicknesse dwelle.
And poppie, or charmes can made us sleep as well,
And better than thy stroke; why swellest thou then?

Reference: These lines have been taken from "The Holy Sonnet" by Donne. The tone in the Donne's poem is one of the scorn and raillery at the beginning and mock compassion towards the close. According, to him Death's claims to power and tyranny and then shifts the tone in the couplet to affirm immortality for man vis-à-vis mortality for Death. The incongruity of Death dying makes the couplet strikingly witty. Those whom death intends to overthrow do not die but it is death which shall ultimately die.

Context : According to the poet due toe fact a slave can be ring death is also powerful thing. Death is a thing which makes a man witty. It also let the man to sleep put man's courage is much powerful and man can kill the death by his courage.

(iv) **Here rests his head upon the lap of Earth**
A Youth, to Fortune and to Fame unknown;
Fair Science frown'd not on his humble birth,
And Melancholy mark'd him for her own.

Reference: These lines have been taken from the poem "A Country Churchyard" by Thomas Gray. Through this poem the poet gives description of the churchyard the poet does not give a pictorial representation of the place, by opt image. He evokes a sense of weariness, darkness, gloom, and parting and thereby sets the scene of poem.

Context: Through these lines poet describes that here lies a youngman, who had known neither fortune nor fame. He was of humble birth but fair science did not frown upon his humble birth. He was apart from the rest of the villagers as he possessed both intelligence and melancholic sensitivity. It is this made him respond to their suffering with generosity and compassion. The lack of earthly riches was amply compensated by heaven's bounty that gave him a generous heart and genial soul. No one need know further his merits and faults for he has earned his repose in he bosom of the lord.

(v) After twenty hours
it lost its sting.
My mother only said
Thank God the scorpion picked on me.
And spared my children.

Reference: These lines have been taken from the Night of the Scorpion by Nissim Ezekiel. The poem of interest, Night of the Scorpion has a delicate family situation as its settling. The poet's mother is stung by a Scorpion is given multiply treatment bringing in its sweep the world of magic and superstition, science, rationality and material affection.

Context: These lines are said by poet's mother who is now out of danger after twenty hours. She became conscious and thanked god that Scorpion picked her and spared her children. This shows the love and affection of a mother towards her children who even thanked got after so many problems and long pain.

Note : Attempt any three of the following.

Q3. Attempt a critical appreciation of Milton's sonnet "On his Blindness".

Refer to Chapter-1, Q.No.-10

Or

Attempt an analysis of Shakespeare's sonnet "Shall I Compare Thee To A Summer's Day?"

Refer to Chapter-1, Q.No.-5

Q4. Attempt a critical reading of William Wordsworth's poem "Tintern Abbey".

Refer to Chapter-3, Q.No.-1

Or

Write a critical appreciation of Shelley's "Ode To The West Wind."

Refer to Chapter-3, Q.No.-12

Q5. Discuss Tennyson as a lyric poet giving illustrations from the prescribed poems.

Ans. The poetry of Tennyson is continuation of the Romantic traditions on one level while on another it is also an expression of the spirit of its age. In general term one night well say that while Romantic poetry emerged as a product of poet's individual mind and experiences. Romantic poem comes direct from the heart and lyrics come easily to give speciality to the poem.

Now : Refer to Chapter-4, Q.No.-2

Or

Trace the development of thought in "Meeting At Night".

Ans. The poem opens without a preamble. We are transported straight to the narrator's boat being rowed in the grey sea. In the distance, the long line of the shore looks dark in the night. The golden half-moon seems suspended low in the sky. The reflection of the moonlight on the waves gives them the appearance of the tousled golden curls of someone who has suddenly woken up from sleep. The narrator's boat reaches a small bay. The prow of the speeding boat comes to a stop in the soft, wet sand.

The narrator then continues his eager journey on foot, walking along for about a mile on the warm beach that smells of salt water and fish (In literature, you will find in general that warmth and summer and pleasant smells are associated with happy and fulfilled love whereas winter and cold are associated with parting and sorrow). The lover then crosses three fields till he comes to a farm. He taps at a particular window. He can hear the sound of a matchstick striking a box after which a blue flame of lighted match becomes visible. He then hears his beloved's voice which is softer than their heart beats. The voice is full of joy and fear – joy at his arrival but fear? It is probably the fear of being discovered. The journey concludes happily as the two lovers join in a passionate embrace.

The first feature of the poem to strike you is its brevity and intensity. The lady is not described, the meeting is barely mentioned. It is only through selective details of the journey that the excitement of the meeting is built up. The eagerness with which the lover anticipates the meeting with his beloved is conveyed in the quick pace and rhythm of the poem. The rhyme scheme of the two short stanzas is ab cc ba; de ff ed. The lines are in pentameter through you will notice that the metre is quite irregular and therefore it is difficult to determine its exact category.

The musical quality of Browning's poem is ensured, however, by his extensive use of alliteration: Look at 'long black land', 'yellow half-moon large and low' startled little waves that leap'. The persistent 'l' sound conveys a liquid lilting effect that captures the peace and quiet of the moonlit night.

The reflection of the moonlight on the waves is conveyed in the effective image of a head of curly golden hair of someone who has woken up with a start. The poem is almost like a painting with its vivid portrayal of a 'grey' sea, 'black' land and 'yellow' moon. The subdued colours of the first two lines give way to a more vivid image as a pace of the lover's journey is conveyed. Not only does Browning make us see but he also makes us smell the 'sea-scented beach'. He makes us hear the 'sharp scratch' of the lighted match and finally makes us feel the 'two hearts beating'. In short, the poem is richly sensuous – an effect that is suited to its romantic theme.

Q6. Write a critical appreciation of Hardy's poem "The Darkling Thrush".

Ans. Though the poem Darkling Thrush by Hardy states the mind is often projected on the outside world. In 'The Darkling Thrush' the gloomy landscape seems gloomed. Hardy is in a pessimistic mood. The thrush is the only cheerful creature around him but even the birds song fails to inspire chear him.

Hardy is alone – it is evening and everything around him looks bleak and dreary. It is also the last day of the year and the century. Instead of looking forward optimistically to a 'Happy New Year' and the start of the twentieth century. Hardy seems to regret the passage of time.

Hardy tells us that one evening when the grey frost had thickened the air, he leaned against a gate leading to a small wood. The evening light was fading and it being winter, the whole landscape looked gloomy and desolate. The disorderly stalks of vines could be seen silhouetted against the sky like the broken strings of a lyre. And all the people, who lived in the neighbourhood, barring Hardy, had one to the comfort of their warm homes. The landscape looked so bleak and desolate that in the dark it looked like the corpse of the bygone century laid at rest. The cloudy sky seemed to be the burial place of the century and the wind seemed to sing its funeral dirge. With death there is birth and renewal but now the germ of birth seemed hard and dry and no sign of life was visible. Everything on earth seemed to share the utmost melancholy and listlessness that Hardy felt. Nature seems to be in sympathy with the poet's mood.

In this bleak landscape, suddenly an energetic and joyous voice burst forth from the dull leafless branches, singing and evening song. It was the song of a small, thin, old thrush with feathers ruffled by the cold wind. It seemed that the thrush had decided to express itself thus in the growing darkness.

The poet is sad at the passage of time and the futility of human existence. This gloom is heightened by the bleak winter weather and the dark evening. In spite of such gloomy surroundings, an aged thrush bursts out in full-throated joyous song that brings a feeling of hope to the poet's heart. The thin aged bird braves the winter blasts and still continues to sing. The final message that comes through clearly establishes the fact that a blithe spirit can surmount life's difficulties, however bleak and unyielding they might at first seem. This joyous spirit is infectious and can also infuse joy among those who feel dejected and depressed. The frail bird, small and insignificant against the vastness of nature is still striving – and it is this persistence that makes it noble.

This is a very short poem yet it is packed with images that invest it with layers of meaning. Hardy is known for his particular genius for condensation. In the first stanza itself, he has captured a whole landscape, the time of year, the time of day, as well as his own mood as people return to their houses. He works by suggestion rather than by detailed description.

Or

Write a note on the imagery in the poems of T.S. Eliot.

Ans. (a) Who was T.S. Eliot's grandfather? What did he do?

Revi Williams green leaf Eliot was T.S. Eliot's grandfather. He was founder of Washington University and 1872 became its Chancellor. His mother wrote a biography of her father-in-law.

(b) Name 3 persons who influenced Eliot's anti-romantic attitude.

3 persons who influenced Eliot's anti-romantic attitude are Irving Bibfit, F.H. Bradley and T.E.Hulme.

(c) What do you know about Eliot;s interest in Sanskrit and Indian philosophy.

From 1911 to 1914 T.S. Eliot studied Indian Philosophy and read Sanskrit form Charles Lenman. He also wanted to embrace Buddhism fat did not do so because the Buddhist way of life was difficult to be practiced in a western milieu. Hence to he becomes Anglo Chattosic Forsaking his parents' faith-Protestantism.

(d) You will notice that the last five lines of the extract from 'Precludes' have not been scanned.

The showers beat
On broken, blinds and Chimney pots
A lonely cab-horse, steams and stamps
And then the lighting of the lamps

(e) Briefly recall 3 reasons for Eliot using free verse.

Free verse is capable of carrying the reader/listener along forcefully when he would doze; However it would check his enthusiasm as it rises to passion. Passion blurs our vision and makes is incapable of reasonable action. The irregularity of the metrical effect would enforce the modern reader to think about life aria him

(f) With the help of two sets images from the first and second stanzas has Eliot it an anti-romantic poet.

Compare the images of 'silken girls bringing shortest' with 'wanting their liquor and area' is the first stanza. In the second you may compose the images of the 'water will beating the darkness 'with the 'three trees in the low sky. For a detailed discussion read the analysis.

(g) Who is the narrator of this poem and does it any way compare with 'My last Duchess' you reading Block in.

The narrator of the poem is one of the wise men who went to see Jesus soon after his birth at Beth Lehman. However the narrator can be anyone who undertakes to discover something or work sincerely in the light of his faith like 'My Last Duchess', Journey of the Magi is alsoi dramatic monologue.

Q7. Write a critical appreciation of the poem 'Because I Could Not Stop For Death' by Emily Dickinson.

Refer to Chapter-6, Q.No.-18

EEG-6 : UNDERSTANDING POETRY
December, 2006

Note : Question No. 1 and Question No. 2 are **compulsory**. Answer any **three** questions from the rest. Answer **five** questions in all.

Q1. Write short notes on any *four* of the following:

(i) Myth

Ans. Myths are stories about gods or heroes of superhuman dimension, intended to support religious beliefs. They are valued for their universality and timelessness. Sometimes the myths relate to natural and animal motifs which explain fertility rites and the cycle of seasons with their alternations of growth, fruitfulness, decay and death. The myth thus derive sustenance from symbolism, whereby their meanings are dependent on the context in which they are used. Myth in modern literature is looked upon as a system of signs which helps the poet to express complex thoughts that do not easily lend themselves to expression in direct language. One of the most influential poems of the 20th century. **The Wasteland** by T.S.Eliot, uses the primitive myth about fertility rites to show he spiritual barrenness of the modern world. Literature derives from myth, for myth expresses a satisfying and lasting account of the experience of man. The mythological stories and legends that have come down to us over the ages help to establish and conceptualise difficult ideas through identifying the correspondence between the past and the present experience.

(ii) Metaphor

Ans. The use of a phrase which describes one thing by stating another thing with which it can be compared. When the comparison is made between two unlike things without the connectives 'like' and 'as', it is called metaphor. The meaning is suggested by the image. **Metaphor is an implied comparison.** It is a figure of speech in which we use a name or descriptive term or phrase for an object or action to which it is not literally applicable. Whereas in a simile there is a direct comparison, a metaphor suggests the comparison between two things not usually thought of as similar.

E.g. "The fog comes
on little cat feet"

Cat feet move silently and softly. The reader can understand how the poet feels and sees the fog setting slowly and gently. Take the phrase: "the Winter of our discontent" – Here, to convey the abstract quality of discontentedness, the poet has employed the figurative term 'Winter', which not only illustrates the quality, but also adds to the idea of bitterness, barrenness and waiting. So in a metaphor, the literal and the figurative meanings re-inforce each other. (Remember that the above metaphorical phrase can be made into simile if it is stated thus : "Our discontent is like winter")

(iii) Ballad

Ans. The Ballad: A ballad is a simple, straightforward poem set to tune. There are two distinct kinds of ballads – the traditional ballad and the literary ballad. The traditional ballad is popular in England and in Scotland in the 15th century was a specific form of narrative poem which has become a part of the world of folk-song. By the end of the 17th century, the emphasis shifted from narration to music as the prime constituent of the ballad. The traditional ballads deal with episodes from well-known stories rendered impersonally. The literary ballad which came into vogue at the end of the 18th century and continued to be popular in the 19th century was not set to music.

The main characteristics of a ballad are :

(a) The ballad is full of refrains. This is known as the **incremental repetition** (a device which repeats what has been said before, sometimes lines, sometimes words) Stock epithets are also often repeated.

(b) The ballad is remarkable for its straightforward narration and it concentrates on striking details. It is compressed and tends towards the dramatic with a good deal of action and dialogue in the course of narration.

(c) The ballad is a poem in short stanzas usually of four lines, having eight and six syllables alternately. You will read an extract from Coleridge's ballad *THE RIME OF THE ANCIENT MARINER*..

(iv) Dramatic Monologue

Ans. The Dramatic Monologue: Dramatic Monologue is a poem in which a single speaker – not the poet – speaks at a critical moment or situation in which he finds himself and he is seen addressing one or more persons who do not speak but whose presence we strongly feel. This form makes the reader follow the story from the point of view of the speaker who is involved in the action and it also throws light on his character. Dramatic poems are short and compressed and the reader is called upon to draw a good deal of inference about the character and situation.

(v) Elegy

Ans. The Elegy: As the lyric is a composition spontaneously written at the white heat of passion, it is not limited to expressions of joy or elation. Intense sorrow or pain or mournful contemplation can also give rise to poems of lyrical kind which are known as elegies. The Elegy is classical in its origin and is a composition in verse. But in its treatment of the subject matter, it is tied to a limited range of plaintive musing. In this form heightened emotional tension is restrained by the use of pastoral convention and the employment of pastoral characters like the **shepherds, nymphs,** and **satyrs** gives the poem an impersonal touch.

(vi) Ode

Refer to June 2006, Q.No.-1(v)

Q2. Explain any *four* of the following passages with reference to their contexts:

(i) **Shall I compare thee to a summer's day?**
Thou art more lovely and more temperate:
Rough winds do shake the darling buds of May,
And summer's lease hath all too short a date:

Refer to June 2006, Q.No.-2(i)

(ii) **Return, Alpheus, the dread voice is past,**
That shrunk thy streams; return, Sicilian Muse.
And call the vales, and bid them hither cast
Their bells and flowerets of a thousand hues.

Refer to June 2006, Q.No.-2(ii)

(iii) **Fade for away, dissolve, and quite forget**
What thou among the leaves hast never known,
The weariness, the fever, and the fret
Here, where men sit and hear each other groan;

Reference: These lines have been taken from John Keat's Ode to a Nightingale. In this poem keat's skill in word painting and verbal coinage are given. This poem is Keats craftsmanship is remarkably in evidence in this poem.

Context: In this stanza, there is reiterate the poet's desire to fade far away and forget the fretful fever and stir of the world. Wine is sought as an opiate to support him in his desire for oblivion so as to forget all the painful experiences of life which include 9 poignant reference to the brother Tom's death and where but to thing full of sorrow. The poem imagines the bird to be happy because it does not belong to the world of human. To be human is to experience the "weariness, fret and fever of existence."

The poet also aware that he is human and therefore even if he were to fly away into the nightingale world, he cannot forever stay there is happiness. His depression is thus implicit in his desire for escape. Keats is seen struggling against the inevitable impermanence of human beauty, youth and happiness. He is striving for some enduring principle of permanence which he associates with the song of nightingale.

(iv) Ah, love, let us be true
To one another! For the world, which seems
To lie before us like a land of dreams,
So various, so beautiful, so new,
Hath really neither joy, nor love, nor light,
Nor certitude, nor peace, nor help for pain;

Reference: These lines have been taken from the Dover beach poem by Mathew Arnold. This poem evokes the romantic feelings it each poet. The mood is one of the melancholy and nostalgia for the loss of faith. Once again Arnold outlines the human condition and feels that love can somewhat lessen the pain of isolation and sufferings.

Context: In these lines the poet appeals to Lucy once more. He believes that if they love each other truly, they will be able to discover some values of life from the sea image. The poet moves to starting new image of field with battle ringing in dark where it is not clear who is a friend and who is a enemy. The ebbing and flowing of the waves and the consequent grating road is evoked. The image of sea is present throughout the poem.

(v) When finally we reached the place,
We hardly knew why we were there,
The trip had darkened every face,
Our deeds were neither great nor rare.
Home is where we have to gather grace.

Reference: These lines have been taken from the Enterprise by Mission Ekekiel. The poem "Enterprise" is one of the serious poems of Ezekiel moulded out of the fallouts of frustration in Barbaric city. The poem can be meaningfully related to Lord Krishna's conception Karma Yoga which expects us to remain active and to submit ourselves to law and duty.

Context: After a long journey and a thunder, the pilgrims complete their journey. This line shows the futility of the whole enterprise the struggle on the way, the deprivation the groups undergoes and the failure to compromise the intention of the journey with the ends are succinctly brought out in final clinching life of poem. The pilgrims in the Enterprise ignore the call of conscience and consequently same are broken, some bent. The poet who is making emotive use of language and through emotive use of language.

Q3. Write a note on metaphysical poetry with suitable illustrations from the poems you have read.

Refer to Chapter-2, Q.No.-1

Or

Bring out the personal elements in "Lycidas".

Refer to Chapter-1, Q.No.-8

Q4. How, according to Wordsworth, are man and nature related? Illustrated from the poems prescribed in your course.

First : Refer to Chapter-3, Q.No.-1

& Refer to Chapter-3, Q.No.-4

Through these poem this is shown that man and nature are related. Both depends on each other. If one is died then other will also.

Or

Write an essay on Shelley as a romantic poet with special reference to the prescribed poems.

Refer to Chapter-3, Q.No.-13

Q5. Discuss Tennyson as a lyric poet giving illustrations from the poems prescribed for you.

Refer to June 2006, Q.No.-4

Or

Write an essay on Browning's philosophy of life with reference to the poems you have studied.

Ans. Browing has been often considered a "difficult poet. There may be several reasons for his difficulty.

(a) Sometimes, Browing has a tendency to say too much in too few words.

(b) At other times there are sudden jumps from one thought to another. So it is difficult to keep pace with these quick transitions.

(c) Browing was also a very learned man. He opposed that his readers could easily understand the vast range of allusions that he introduced in his poems.

But till then Browing's poetry is a rewarding experience. A poem can have different interpretations and therefore no single interpretation can qualify. Poems are to be enjoyed we will recall a lyric poem that has a song like quality. The subject matter is usually personal and poem express deeply felt emotions and states of mind. His poem's are similar to dramatic analog. In his poem philosophy of life is seen and it is easy to understand and also easy to adopt.

Q6. Write a short note on Eliot's modernity while quoting from "Journey of the Magi" and "Marina".

First : Refer to Chapter-5, Q.No.-4

& Refer to Chapter-5, Q.No.-5

Both these poem shows the modernity of the writers thought. He created the taste of special kind of literature. Eliot's poetry conceals its meaning that it is the core of his experience.

Q7. Write a critical appreciation of "The Road Not Taken" by Robert Frost.

Refer to Chapter-6, Q.No.-22

Or

Write a critical note on the poem "I Heard a Fly Buzz When I Died" by Emily Dickinson.

Refer to Chapter-6, Q.No.-19

EEG-6 : UNDERSTANDING POETRY
June, 2007

Note : Question No. 1 and Question No. 2 are **compulsory**. Answer any **three** questions from the rest. Answer **five** questions in all.

Q1. (a) Write short notes on any *two* of the following :

(i) Simile

Ans. It is a comparison made between items from different classes with the help of connectives such as 'like' or 'as' or 'than' or by the use of verb such as **'appear'** or **'seems'.** You can understand from these connectives that the items compared are of distinctive classes. If the objects compared are from the same class, there is no simile present – E.g. "Bombay is like London."

Read the following line to recognise the presence of simile:

"The holy time is quite as a Nun"

Similes are easy to recognise and understand. The comparison is of two otherwise unlike things such as **"The holy time"** and **"The Nun".** Yet the meaning is apparent and the comparison strengthens the meaning.

(ii) Symbol

Refer to June 2006, Q.No.-1(iii)

(iii) The Lyric

Refer to June 2006, Q.No.-1(iv)

(iv) Apostrophe

Ans. It is type of figurative speech. It is an address to a person or thing who is not listening for example Wordsworth, a 19th century poet addresses a 17th century poet Milton.

Through this poetry style we feels that this belongs to us. In poetry it's function as decorative element and richly suggestive or complex attitude an feeling.

(b) Scan *one* of the passages given below and supply brief comments on the prosodic features of the passage scanned:

(i) **I am monarch of all I survey,**
My right there is none to dispute;
From the centre all round to the sea
I am lord of the bird and the brute.

(1) These lines trace the imagery of a person.

(2) Connotations of beauty and fragrance is also found in the lines.
(3) Metaphore is also found.
(4) The verbs at the end lend force and strength to the action described.
(5) It turns, the contrast between sea and bird.

(ii) May thou month of rosy beauty,
Month, when pleasure is a duty,
Month of bees and month of flowers,
Month of blossom laden bowers.

(1) beauty and duty
flowers and bowers
End rhyme is used
(2) Metaphore is also seen in this lines.
(3) Inversion is also a attraction.
(4) These lines also compelled into write elegy.
(5) Synecdoche and apostrophe are also a part of the poem.

Q2. Explain any *four* of the following passages with reference to their contexts:

(i) Since brass, nor stone, nor earth, nor boundless sea,
But sad mortality o'ersways their power,
How with this rage shall beauty hold a plea,
Whose action is no stronger than a flower?

Reference: These lines have been taken from the poem "Since brass, nor stone, nor Earth, nor boundless sea" by Shakespeare. Beauty is so frail that it can neither escape mortality nor arrest the ravages of time. There is no strong force that can prevent the destruction of beauty that takes place with the inexorable march of time.

Context: According to the poet, the glitter of brass, the hardness of stone, the vastness of earth and the expansiveness of sea are in themselves a marvel of beauty, forces and power of the twin but order of nature in all its awesome majesty is subject to mortality like any other created things on earth. Sad mortality is terrible destruction of a fatal kind.

Beauty is compared to delicate flower when measured against the rage of time and mortality, beauty in physical terms no stronger than a flower.

(ii) Thine ages askes ease, and since thy duties bee
To warme the world, that's done in warning us.
Shine here to us, and thou art every where;
This bed thy centre is, these walls, thy spheare.

Reference: These lines are taken from the poem "The Sunne Rising" by John Donne. The poet and his beloved are still in bed as the sun rises in the morning. The poetry is playfull chides the sun not to disturn him and his mistress and to attend to other matters. The poet mocks at the sun for imaging itself to be all powerful for can shut out its beansky closing eyes. This poem is specially based on mutual love.

Context: The poet says that the majestic sun has been relegated to the role of an ancient tired workman compelled to do his daily duties of waking and warming the world. The lover suggests that the sun can minimize it movement by remaining static in his room and shining on him and his mistress – who constitute the whole world. The poet has established the lovers superiority and he is not longer irascible as at the beginning. On the contrary, he welcomes not to tell him that life is an empty dream or life is unreal that the grave is not its goal. He further says that the body comes from the returns of dust but not the soul. Through these lines the Youngman says that the lives the great men inspire us to became great and leaves our footprints on the sands of time and these footprints will be followed by the less fortunate brothers. In the concluding stanza, the emphasis is again an action and capacity to wait the intrusion of the sun by extending his permission to shine on them and thereby save its labour.

(iii) We look before and after,
And pine for what is not:
Our sincerest laughter
With some pain is fraught;
Our sweetest songs are those that fell
of saddest thought.

Reference: These lines are taken from the poem Skylark by Shelley. In this poem, the poet contrasts the perfect happiness of the bird with the sad state of man whose "sweetest songs are those that tell of saddes thought"

Context: According to the poem he wants to learn from the Skylark, be it a bird or a spirit, the source of its ethereal joyousness. He has never heard that love or wine has influenced a poet to such joyousness. As against that the man is torn by regrets for the past and fears for the future; even the sincerest of our delight has a touch of sadness in it and our most touching songs are those that sing the tragedies.

(iv) We returned to our places, these Kingdoms,
But no longer at ease here, in the old dispensation,
With an alien people clutching their gods.
I should be glad of another death.

Reference: These lines are taken from the poem "Journey to Magi" by T.S.Eliot. This poem is about the tree wise man who received news of the birth of the baby Jesus and went to see him with gifts. The poem narrates their journey in an anti romantic vein.

Context: The account of the journey is over by the end of second stanza. In this stanza there is a meditation on the journey that was performed years ago. There is a suggestion, Christ was betrayed by one of his disciples - Judas for piece of silver. Here in the poem there is a tavern scene where three person are at the gaming table. Piece of silver exchanged by them remind us of Christ's betrayal. The three wise men reach the place in the evening.

(v) Lives of great men all remind us
We can make our lives sublime,
And, departing, leave behind us
Footprints on the sands of time;

Reference: These lines are taken from the PSALM of Life by H.W.Longfellow. The poem contains the response of the Youngman Psalmist.

Context: This poem starts with the Youngman who ask the Psalmist

(vi) Softly, O softly we bear her along,
She hangs like a star in the dew of our song;
She springs like a beam on the brow of the tide,
She falls like a tear from the eyes of a bride.

Reference: These lines have been taken from the poem "palanquin Bearers" by Sarojini Naidu. This is first poem in the first section of "The Golden Threshold" which has three sections fold, songs, music and peace. Images is the speciality of this poem.

Context: These lines the embodies the age old story of an Indian bride's sadness, whatever be the cause-separation from the parents. There are the poetess try to show the image of a bride. The birds are sad due to departing bride and joy of those escorting her new home and unraveling like divine agents, the stages of the inexorable march of human life.

The poem seems to be an allegory on the movement of time gleefully carrying man towards an unknown but inevitable destiny which can either to "like a laugh from the tips of dream" or like a tear from the eyes of bride.

Q3. Discuss any three Biblical references used by Milton in his sonnet "On His Blindness".

Refer to Chapter-1, Q.No.-11

Or

Examine "The Rape of the Lock" (Canto III) as a mock-heroic poem.

Refer to Chapter-2, Q.No.-5

Q4. Discuss the theme of the poem "Ulysses".

Refer to Chapter-4, Q.No.-3 (Long Answer)

Or

Hardy's philosophy that Providence is indifferent to human suffering is amply illustrated in his poem "God-Forgotten". Discuss.

Ans. Hardy's philosophy the providence is indifferent to human suffering in amply illustrate in the poem "God forgotten"

Now : Refer to Chapter-4, Q.No.-13

Q5. Write a critical appreciation of Yeats' poem "The Second Coming".

Refer to Chapter-5, Q.No.-3

Or

Discuss W.H. Auden's poem "The Unknown Citizen" as an elegy on the modern human being.

Refer to Chapter-5, Q.No.-7

Q6. Write a critical appreciation of Robert Frost's poem "Stopping By Woods On a Snowy Evening".

Ans. The poem is not just a record of something that once happened to the poet. It expresses the conflict between the demands practical life with its obligation to other and poignant desire to escape into a land of reverie.

The poet's consciousness seems to be on the verge of freeing itself from ordinary life belt the poet remember that his journey has a purpose and he has promises to keep and miles to geo before he can yield to the dream like release which the woods offer.

There is overt symbolism in the poem yet the reader finds his vision deserted in expression common to all. The wide scope of meaning becomes obvious in the last four lines. There state the inflict in a simple realistic way further the depth richness and significance of the lyric is brought out only on a symbolist reading sleep and darkness, suggest death and the word suggests enchantment each other. The words which the poet enjoys looking upon are opposed to promise sleep becomes a deserved reward in contrast to the unearned pleasure of looking at the woods.

Or

Trace the influence of India in Whitman's poem "Passage to India".

Refer to Chapter-6, Q.No.-6

Q7. Nissim Ezekiel's poem "Night of the Scorpion" depicts an authentic rural picture. Comment.

Refer to Chapter-7, Q.No.-5

Or

Indian poetry is Indian in content and sensibility and English in language. Comment with suitable examples.

Refer to Chapter-7, Q.No.-1

and Refer to Chapter-7, Q.No.-12

EEG-6 : UNDERSTANDING POETRY
June, 2008

Note : Section A is *compulsory*. Answer any three questions in Section B

SECTION A

Q1. Explain any *four* of the following with reference to context supplying brief critical comments where necessary.

(a) When wasteful war shall statues overturn,
And broils root out the work of masonry,
Nor mars his sword nor war's quick fire shall burn
The living record of your memory

Reference: These lines are taken from "Mot Marble, Mor the Glided Monuments by Shakespeare. This is a sonnet. The subject is power of art. This sonnet exists is a living record of his friends memory. It is in itself a strong monument which recognize not only its power but also recognises the existence of the friend and lover throughout the history of mankind.

Context: According to the writer, the day of judgement marks the end of the world. So long as lasts, his verse will last and so long as the verse lasts, his friend will last. But he emphasis the shifts at this point in the couple when the poet asserts the immorality of his friend not just through the lines of poetry but in his own symbol of love. Love has the power to resist the passage of time and poet's proper mode of love is poetry.

(b) Was it a vision, or a walking dream?
Fled is that music: - do I wake or sleep?

Reference: These lines have been taken from the poem "Ode to a Nightingale by John Keats. This poem is a rich tribute to the song of a Nightingale. It speaks of the poet's identification with the bird. The voice at the end is skeptical and questions where the poet had genuinely experienced heightened feelings of ecstasy or was it but a subjective half dream. The dramatic tension in the poem is built around the poet's initial identification on with the bird and later separateness from it.

Context: In these lines Keats opens up the world of the legend, of fairy tales, a world that is in the sub-conscious and present in all of us. The poet describe the fairy land as "Forlorn". These fairy lands are Forlorn because they are not of men. They have become inaccessible for no man can ever return of them.

Comment: The conflicting tendencies towards mortality expressed the attraction and fear also. Thus the poem maintains the dramatic debate between two voices of the poet.

(c) An aged thrush, frail, gaunt, and small
In blast-beruffled plume,
Has chosen thus to fling his soul
Upon the growing gloom.

Reference: These lines have been taken from the poem "The Darkling Thrush" by Thomas Hardy. It is unique distinction of being a major poet. There is a different type of integration carried. The poet's state of mind is often projected on to the outside world. "The Darkling Thrush", the gloomy landscape seems gloomier. Hardy is in pessimistic mood. The thrush is only cheerful landscape seems gloomier and it is cheerful creature around him but even birds song fails to inspire in him.

Context: The landscape looked so bleak and desolate that in the dark it looked like corpse of the bygone century laid at rest. The cloudy sky seemed to be the burial place of the century and the wind seemed to sing its funeral digre. With death there is a birth and renewal but now the germs of birth seemed hard and dry and no sign of life is visible. Everything on earth seems to share the utmost melancholy and listlessness that Hardy felt. Nature seems to be in sympathy with poet's mood.

(d) .... and experience
The ceremony of innocence is drowned;
The best lack all conviction, while the worst
Are full of passionate intensity

Reference: These lines have been taken from the "Second Coming" by William Yeast. This poem indicates the coming of a lay to her own house after a long time on someone death. There is a relief on her face due to her returning. She is quiet happy with her returning. There is a opposite between natural and supernatural, love and hate, war and peace, subjective and objective.

Context: These lines presents a certain determinism. The end of an age which always receives the revelation of the characters of the next age is represented by the coming of one gyre to its place of greatest expansion and the other to that of the greatest contraction. Something disastrous has happened in modern civilization. Through the falcon, Yeasts suggests the elemore of cruely and terror and found in the modern time. This suggests that in the modern times this control has been last and murderous instincts cannot kept in control. There is complete chaos and nor restraint. This age is such that the best cannot do anything even the nobles are futile. It is indeed a sheerly destructive age. This shows the loneliness of a human but till she is happy as she is in her own house.

(e) Exult, O shores, and ring, O bells!
But I, with mournful tread,
Walk the deck my Captain lies,
Fallen cold and dead.

Reference: These lines have been taken from the O Captain! My Captain by Whiteman. Through this poem poet's grief is expressed through the symbol of metaphar. The united states is compared to the ship and whose captain is Abraham Lincon. The captain is brave and skilful, he brings the ship home after the successful completion of voyage. Finally the poet is left alone on the deck of the ship where the captain lies fallen.

Context: Answer 7 – Chapter – 6

Q2. Scan *one* of the following passage and comment on its prosodic feature.

(a) My days among the Dead are passed;
Around me I behold,
Where'er these casual eyes are cast,
The mighty minds of old:

(1) The poet has employed the technique of inversion.
(2) Metaphysical poetry and imagery is shown by the lines.
(3) There is a tone of playful irony
(4) There is also a use of Hypebale

(b) Touch her not scornfully;
Think of her mournfully,
Gently and humanly;
Not of the stains of her –
All that remains of her
Now is pure womanly.

(1) These lines are consist of two consecutive lines of iambic peta meter verse whose end words rhyme.
(2) Close couplet is used.
(3) There is reorganization of metre for satire.
(4) The poet gives a tremendous range and variety of tone.

Q3. Write brief notes, illustrating your points with the help of examples, on any *two* of the following:

Symbolism: A Symbolism derives its sustenance through suppression of direct metaphor. The symbol evokes unseen words. It reveals a hidden order that lurks behind our perceptive everyday reality. A poem which speaks of the fading of rose has for its theme the transience of beauty, of all things bright and beautiful. There the poet uses the rose as a symbol. Symbolism thus attempts to penetrate into a world of ideas reality and thus attempts to penetrate into world of ideas beyond reality and this it achieves through suggestiveness evoking an object little by little.

E.g. The white moon is stling behind the white wave
And time is setting with me O!

These lines are symbolical evoking an emotion of melanchy through symbolic association of these words – moon – wave – whiteness and setting time along with last melan chaly cry O" !

Spenserian : It is a type of Sonnet. It is variation of the English sonnet with the different rhyme scheme abab – bcbc – cdcdee. Writing a poem in fourteen lines demand high degree of discipline on the part of poet. With a codified rhyme scheme, the poet has to use a specialized vocabulary and at the same time choose the appropriate word to express his emotional intensity. The sonnet as a verse from is characterised by the tightness of rhyme in iambic pentameter and includes in its themes love, time, friendship, honour, duty, art and nature.

Stanza: A Stanza is a group of lines in the repetitive pattern, forming division of poem. The distinguishing characteristics of an English stanza are

(a) Number of lines

(b) The number of feet in each line

(c) The metre

(d) The rhyme scene

There are variations and we have stanza of two lines called a couples or a three line stanza known a triplet and four line the quatrain. Similarly, the line can be iambic pentameter, trochaic to tetrameter. The stanza can be rhymed or unrhymed.

E.g. So long as men can breathe or eyes can see
So long live this, and this gives life to thee

(couplet)

He must not float upon his watery bier unwept, and welter to the parching wind. Without the need of some melodies fear

(triplet)

End rhyme : Rhyme is the repetition of identical sounds at the end of lines. Though rhythm is basic poetry, rhyme is not and End rhyme is the one kind of rhyme in which rhyming words are at the end of line.

E.g. Shall I compare thee to a summer's day?

Thou art more lovely and more temperate
Rough winds do shake the darling buds of May
And summer's lease bath all too short date
day – May
Temperate – Date
These are the end rhyming words as they are in the end of the lines

SECTION-B

Answer any *three* questions. Each question carries 20 marks.

Q4. Examine "Lycidas" as a postoral elegy?

Refer to Chapter-1, Q.No.-12

Q5. Comment on Alexander Pope's use of (a) the heroic couplet (b) the mock heroic in T*he Rape of the Lock*

Refer to Chapter-2, Q.No.-5

Q6. Discuss 'Tintern Abbey' as a autobiographical poem.

Refer to Chapter-3, Q.No.-3

Q7. How do Tennyson's description of scenes help the narration in 'The Lady of Shalott'?

Refer to Chapter-4, Q.No.-15

Q8. Assess W.H.Auden as a modernist poet.

Ans. Wystan Hugh Auden (1907-73) has been considered to be the most representative of the English poets who wrote with pronounced Marxisdt affinites during the 1930s. Auden became a member of the Communist Party in 1932 but only to break away from it in 1939 when the Nazi-Soviet Pact was signed. As a poet, Auden is concerned primarily about the social and psychological maladies that have contaminated the modern world. He resorts to plain, matter-of-fact language, and a bitterly ironic style. His drift away from Marxism gradually brought him nearer to religion and some of his poems show a marked proneness to Christian motifs and parallels. His poetical works include Poems (1930). *The Orator* (1932), *Look Stranger* (1936), *Another Time* (1940), *New Year Letter* (1941). *For the Time Being*: A Christmas Oratorio

(1944), *The Age of Anxiety*: A Baroque Eclogue (1947), *The Shield of Achilles* (1955), *Homage to Clio* (1960), *About the House* (1966) and *Epistle to a Godson* and other Poems (1972).

In 1945, Auden became an American citizen and his "The Unknown Citizen" was written soon after. Auden seems to have been profoundly fascinated by W.B.Yeats in spite of the latter's romantic, mythical vision of life and poetry and regarded him as one of the greatest poets of the century. In fact, Auden's poem 'In Memory of W.B.Yeats' is an elegy on the death of the poet. Poetry for Auden was no more an instrument to effect desirable changes in the society but a happening that modified the psychic reality of a few readers. According to Auden, a poem once composed and released by the poet was no more under his control but lived its own life, continually formed and re-formed in the minds of the people. Auden's development as a poet, however, has not been of the radical nature of W.B.Yeats or T.S.Eliot, to both to whom, he owes much.

Q9. Critically appreciate Poe's poem 'The Raven'

Refer to Chapter-6, Q.No.-13

Q10. Compare the poetic art of Sarojini Naidu that of Kamala Das

Ans. Sarojini Naidu too was more than a poet. She was one of the most illustrious Indians who contributed to the cultural, political and a social advancement of the nations in numerous way. Even before plugging into the freedom movement, she had impressed the west by her remarkable poetic genuine. Some poets said her Queen of India in her poems. Her earlier compositions were entirely "Western in feeling imagery and totally without individuality".

Sarojini Naidu wrote poetry where images and metaphors can readily out of her imagination. Her poetry is intensely emotional and passionate. The influence of British Romantic poets can be perceived on her poetry but what makes it interesting and relevant to tradition is the sustenance from the twin indigenous source. Her poetry continues to delight the readers by sheet simplicity and sweetness.

Naidu's poetry presents Kaleidoscope of Indian scenes, sights, sounds and experiences transmuted into a fantastic vision of colour of rhythm. While Kamla Das poetry is effected by English poetry, her poetry is autobiography. Her poetry lives up to his expectations. In a sense it is psychic striptease that her poetry enacts. Much of poetry is basically an expression of sweating self.

With the change of outlook and setting forth of women's liberation, many of the modern women poets have taken resource to frank expression of which some striking examples are to be found in her poetry. Her frankness gives strength to her poetry. Taking her cue from the modernist movement in poetry, she believes in the sincere treatment of material. In trying to establish intimate tone she gives unabashed expression to her personal theme.

Kamla Das's to retreat into the past is a major preoccupation with her. In essence, it is symbolic retreat into the realms of innocence simplicity and purity.

EEG-6: UNDERSTADING POETRY
December, 2008

Note: Section A is ***compulsory***. Answer any three questions in Section B.

SECTION A

1. Explain any four of the following passages with reference to the context, supplying brief critical comments where necessary:

(a) She'is all States, and all Princes, I,
Nothing else is.
Princes doe but play us; compar'd to this,
All honour's mimique; All wealth alchemie.

(b) These are thy toys, and, as the snowy flake,
They melt into the yeast of waves, which mar
Alike the Armada's pride, or spoils of
Trafalgar.

(c) I was ever a fighter, so - one fight more,
The best and the last!
I would hate that death bandaged my eyes, and
forbore,
And bade me creep past.

(d) We returned to our places, these Kingdoms,
But no longer at ease here, in the old
Dispensation,
With an alien people clutching their gods,
I should be glad of another death.

(e) Two roads converged in a wood and I –
I took the one less travelled by,
And that has made all the difference

(f) And cradled fair sons on the faithful breast.
Who serves her household in fruitful pride.
And worships the gods at her husband's side.

Q2. Scan one of the following passages and comment on its prosodic features:

(a) Perishing gloomily,
Spurr'd by contumely,
Cold inhumanity,
Burning insanity,
Into her rest.

(b) Now fades the glimmering landscape on the sight,
And all the air a solemn stillness holds,
Save where the beetle wheels his droning flight,
And drowsy tinklings lull the distant folds:

Q3. Write brief notes, illustrating your points with the help of suitable examples, on any two of the following:
Metaphor, Elegy, Oxymoron, the Petrarchan sonnet, Enjambment

SECTION B

Answer any three questions
Q4. Comment on Gray's use of poetic devices in "Elegy Written in a Country Churchyard".

Q5. Discuss Coleridge's use of the supernatural in The Rime of the Ancient Mariner.

Q6. Assess Matthew Arnold as a poet with reference to his poems in your course.

Q7. Attempt a critical appreciation of the "Journey of the Magi".

Q8. In what way does Indian philosophy influence "Hamatreya"?

Q9. Compare and contrast the use of imagery by Jayant Mahapatra and A.K. Ramanujan in their poems.

EEC-6: UNDERSTANDING POETRY
June, 2009

Note: Section A is ***compulsory***. Answer any 3 question in Section B.

SECTION A

Q1. Explain any four of the following passages with brief critical comments:

(a) Turning and turning in the widening gyre.
The falcon cannot hear the falconer;
Things fall apart: the centre cannot hold;
Mere anarchy is loosed upon the world.

(b) Since brass, nor stone, nor earth, nor
boundless sea,
But sad mortality O'ersways their power,
How with this rage shall beauty hold a plea,
Whose action is no stronger than a flower?

(c) Let not ambition mock their useful toil
Their homely joys, and destiny obscure;
Nor Grandeur hear with a disdainful smile
The short and simple annals of the Poor.

(d) Made weak by time and fate,
but strong in will
To strive, to seek, to find and
not to yield.

(e) Lives of great men all remind us
We can make our lives sublime,
And, departing, leave behind us
Footprints on the sands of time.

(f) Softly, O softly we bear her along,
She hangs like a star in the dew of our song;
She springs like a beam on the brow of the tide,
She falls like a tear from the eyes of a bride.

Q2. Scan any one of the following with special reference to prosody:

(a) How fleet is the glance of the mind
Compared with the speed of its flight!
The tempest itself lags behind
And the swift winged arrows of light.

(b) Touch her not scornfully
Think of her mournfully.

Gently and humanly;
Not of the remains of her
All that remains of her
Now is pure womanly

Q3. Write brief notes with examples of your own on any two of the following:
(a) Sonnet
(b) The Ballad
(c) Personification
(d) Metaphor
(e) Onomatopoeia

SECTION B

Answer any three questions:

Q4. Discuss the use of symbolism and allegory T.S. Eliot's 'journey of the Magi'.

Q5. Critically appreciate the poem
'Stopping by Woods on a Snowy Evening'
by Robert Frost.

Q3. Comment on the sense of harmony and music in Tennyson's poem 'Lines from the Lotos-Eaters'.

Q4. Discuss Kamala Das's 'My Grandmother's House' as an autobiographical poem.

Q5. Comment on 'Shelleyan thought' with special reference to the peom 'Ode to the West Wind'.

Q6. 'Alexander Pope is a maker of great moral satires'. Comment.

Q7. Discuss Milton's 'On His Blindness' as an example of a sonnet in the Petrarchan tradition.

EEG-6: UNDERSTANDING POETRY
December, 2009

Note: Section A is *compulsory*. Answer any 3 questions from Section B.

SECTION A

Q1. (a) So long as men can breathe or eyes
can see,
So long lives this, and this gives life to thee.
(b) But no longer atease here, in the
old dispensation
With an alien people clutching
their gods.
I should be glad of another death.
(c) She's all states, and all Princes, I,
Nothing else is.
(d) Nor certitude, nor peace, nor help
for pain;
And we are here as on a darkling
Plain
Swept with confused alarms of
struggle and flight,
where ignorant armies clash by night.
(e) Life is real! Life is earnest!
And the grave is not its goal;
"Dust thou art, to dust returnest",
Was not spoken of the soul.
(f) After twenty hours
it lost its sting.
My mother only said
Thank God the scorpion picked on me
and spared my child

Q2. Scan *one* of the following passages and comment on its prosodic aspect:
(a) Know then thyself, presume not
God to scan,
The proper study of mankind is man.

(b) Not a drum was heard, not a funeral note,
As his corpse to the ramparts we hurried;
Not a soldier discharged his farewell shot,
O'er the grave where our hero we buried.

Q3. Write brief notes on *any three* of the following:
(a) Elegy
(b) Alliteration
(c) Apostrophe
(d) Heroic couplet
(e) Ode
(f) Simile

SECTION B

Answer *any three* questions.

Q4. Discuss Pope's 'Rape of the Lock' as a mock heroic poem.

Q5. Discuss Robert Browning's 'My Last Duchess' as a dramatic monologue.

Q6. Bring out Robert Frost's robust optimism with special reference to his poem' Stopping, by woods on a Snowy Evening'.

Q7. 'The wild Swans at Coole' is a commentary on W.B. Yeats's personal unhappiness.' Comment.

Q8. What is Sarojini Naidu's approach towards Indian women in the poem 'The Bangle Sellers'? Explain.

Q9. Critically examine Shelley's 'West Wind' as an agent of preservation and destruction.

Q10. Discuss the theme of immortality in Shakespearean Sonnets.

EEG-6: UNDERSTANDING POETRY
June, 2010

Note: Answer questions 1 and 2 and 3 more from the remaining ones.

Q1. Explain *any four* of the following passages with reference to the context, supplying brief critical comments where necessary:

(a) Not Marble, nor the gilded monuments of princes shall outlive this powerful rhyme; But you shall shine more bright in these contents. Than unswept stone besmear'd with sluttish time.

(b) One short sleepe past, wee wake eternally. And death shall be no more, Death thou shall die.

(c) In such an ecstasy!
Still wouldst thou sing, and I
have ears in vain.

(d) I cannot rest from travel: I will drink Life to the lees.

(e) A cold coming we had of it just the worst time of the year. For a journey, and such a long journey.

(f) Now she looks for the swing in cities with fifteen suburbs and tries to be innocent about it.

Q2. Scan any one of the following passages and comment on its prosodic features:
(a) I put my hat upon my head
And walked into the strand
And there I met another man
Whose hat was in his hand

(b) May thou month of rosy beauty
Month when pleasure is a duty
Month of bees and month of flowers
Month of blossom laden bowers

Q3. Write brief notes illustrating your points with the help of suitable examples on *any two* of the following:
(a) Metre (b) Metonymy (c) Simile (d) Symbol

Q4. Identify the strains of classicism and romanticism in Gray's "Elegy written in a country churchyard".

Q5. Explain 'The Daffodils' as a poem about the process of poetic creation.

Q6. Describe the characters of the duke and duchess from your reading of 'My Last Duchess'.

Q7. Examine the poem "The Unknown Citizen" as a comment on modern man.

Q8. Write a critical appreciation of the poem 'Stopping By Woods on a Snowy Evening'.

Q9. Assess Nissim Ezekiel as a poet.

EEG-6: UNDERSTANDING POETRY
December, 2010

Note: Questions 1, 2 and 3 are compulsory. Attempt 3 more from the rest.

Q1. Explain any four of the following passages with reference to the context, supplying brief critical comments where necessary:

(a) Where were ye, Nymmphs, when the remorseless deep Closed o'er the head of your loved Lycidas?

(b) Oh lift me as a wave, a leaf, a cloud!
I fall upon the thorns of life! I bleed!

(c) We find We find also in the sound a thought,
Hearing it by this distant northern sea.

(d) The best lack all conviction, while the worst
Are full of passionate intensity.

(e) Shine here to us, and thou art every where;
This bed thy centre is, these walls, thy spheare.

(f) We slowly drove – He knew no haste
And I had put away
My labour and my leisure too
For his civility –

Q2. Scan any one of the following passages and comment on its prosodic features:

(a) Thy way not mine, O Lord
However dark it be;
Lead me with thine own hand
Choose out the path for me.

(b) Tell me not in mournful numbers
Life is but an empty dream;
For the soul is dead that slumbers,
And the things are not what they seem.

Q3. Write briefly notes illustrating your points with the help of suitable examples on any two of the following:

(a) Rhyme (b) Alliteration (c) Personification (d) Metaphor

Q4. Examine The Rape of the Lock as a mock-epic.

Q5. State briefly the central idea of the poem 'To a Skylark'.

Q6. Comment on the imagery used by Tennyson in 'The Lady of Shalott'.

Q7. Discuss the theme of the poem 'The Lake Isle of Innisfree'.

Q8. Critically evaluate Whitman's "Passage to India".

Q9. What does Jayant Mahapatra put across, in his poem 'A Missing Person'?

EEG-6: UNDERSTANDING POETRY
June, 2011

Note: Answer questions 1 and 2 and 3 more from the remaining ones.

Q1. Explain any four of the following passages with references to the context, supplying brief critical comments where necessary:

(a) Only reapers, reaping early
In among the bearded barley
Hear a song that echoes cheerly
Down to tower'd Camelot

(b) For sudden the worst turns the best to the brave,
The black minute's at end,
And the elements rage, the fiend - voices
that rave,
shall dwindle, shall blend,

(c) A throe of the heart,
Whose pining visions dim, forbidden hopes profound,
No dying cadence nor long sigh can sound,
For all our art.

(d) In her hands she holds
the oil lamp
whose drunken yellow flames
Know where her lonely body hides.

(e) May the poison purify your flesh
of desire, and your spirit of ambition,
they said, and they sat around
on the floor with my mother in the centre,
the peace of understanding on each face.

(f) The walls are cracked and torn
And moistened by the rains,
The tiles have fallen here and there
The windows whine and groan

Q2. Scan any one of the following passages and comment on its prosodic features:

(a) It started as a pilgrimage,
Exalting minds and making all
The burdens light. The second stage
Explored but did not test the call,

The sum beat down to match our rage.

(b) Some are like fields of sunlit corn,
Meet for a bride on her marriage fire;
Or rich with the hue of her heart's desire,
Tinkling, luminous tender, and clear.
Like her bridal laughter and bridal tear.

Q3. Write brief notes on any two of the following:

(a) Elegy (b) Ode (c) Sounet (d) Epic

Q4. How does Milton succeed in introducing classical, Christian and humanist elements into his poem 'Lycidas' framed within the pastoral convention?

Q5. Discuss the theme of the poem 'Ulysses'.

Q6. Describe the theme of the poem 'The Lotus Eaters'.

Q7. Explain what thoughts and feelings are expressed in the poem 'The Lake Isle of Innisfree'.

Q8. Write a note on the poetic devices used in 'Brahma'.

Q9. Explain the notion of the metaphysical 'conceit' based on your reading of the poems of John Donne and Andrew Marvell.

EEG-6: UNDERSTANDING POETRY
December, 2011

Note : Answer questions 1 and 2 and 3 more from the remaining ones.

Q1. Explain any four of the following passages with reference to the contexts, supplying brief critical comments where necessary.

(a) And the stately ships go on
To their haven under the hill;
But O for the touch of a vanished hand,
And the sound of a voice that is still!

Refer to Chapter-4, Q.No.-5

(b) ....all down his cold white side
The crimson torrent rain, dim now and soil'd,
Like the Soil'd tissue of white violets
Left, freshly gather'd, on their native bank,
By children, whom their nurses call with haste
Indoor from the Sun's eye..........

Refer to Chapter-4, Q.No.-15

(c) We returned to our places, these kingdoms,
But no longer at ease here, in the old dispensation,
With an alien people clutching their Gods,
I should be glad of another death.

Refer to June-2007, Q.No.-2(iv)

(d) By what lake's edge or pool
Delight men's eyes when I awake some day
To find they have flown away?

Reference: These lines have been taken from the last stanza of the poem "The Wild Swans At Coole" written by William Butler Yeats. In this poem, W.B. Yeats presents a beautiful description of the grace and enduring splendor of the swans in the lake inside Coole Park where his friend and patron Lady Augusta Gregory lived. At Coole, Yeats is supposed to have found a life of order and of labour where all outward things were mere signatures of an inward life. The poet is the observer in this poem and he places himself against a Time framework in which the passing of nineteen years seems to produce a change in him without in anyway affecting the swans.

Context: In these lines, Yeats gazes fondly at the swans. They are mysterious and beautiful. He questions their future. He wonders where else they will inhabit. He imagines they will fly away from him to show their beauty to other people. As he ages, Yeats feels that he no longer has the respect of nature. These lines become a little enigmatic, but there is terrible sensation of loss, almost as if the swans were passing away from the poet's life to be enjoyed by others- providing perhaps a glance at the fact that youth and experience of love have passed away too.

The poem thus becomes the poet's commentary on his personal happiness generated in him due to the passing of time. Yeats considers here the changes in his own life since his visit some nineteen years ago. The swans form the focus of the poet's projection, and they are the "still point" against which he presents the changes all around.

(e) The Past! the past! the past!
The Past – the dark unfathom'd retrospect!
The teeming gulf – the sleepers and the shadows!
The past – the infinite greatness of the past!

Reference: These lines have been taken from the poem "Passage to India" by Walt Whiteman. First published in 1868, the poem has nine sections. Whitman was greatly impressed by three great engineering achievements: the opening of the Suez Canal (1869), the laying of the transatlantic undersea cable (1866), and the joining of the Union Pacific and Central Pacific railroads at Utah to produce the nation's first transcontinental railway (1869). These events resulted in improved communication and travel, thus making possible a shorter passage to India. But in Whitman's poem, the completion of the physical journey to India is only a prelude to the spiritual pathway to India, the East, and, ultimately, to God.

Context: The poet, in these lines, celebrates his time, singing of "the great achievements of the present," and listing "our modern wonders": the opening of the Suez Canal, the building of the great American railroad, and the laying of the transatlantic cable. Yet these achievements of the present have grown out of the past, "the dark unfathom'd retrospect." If the present is great, the past is greater because, like a projectile, the present is "impell'd by the past." Whiteman came to the conclusion that the historic sequence of events had a spiritual meaning. He wanted to harmonise the past with the present and he was keen on providing that the past was a part of the present. As a mystic poet, he thought that he must give a new faith to inspire the future.

Here Whitman presents the world of physical reality, an antecedent to the world of spiritual reality. The essential idea in emphasising the three engineering marvels is to indicate man's progress in terms of space. The space-time relationship is at the heart of the matter. The present is significant, but it is only an extension of the past and, therefore, its glories can be traced to times before. Man has mastered space, but he must enrich his spiritual heritage by evoking his past. His achievement in space will remain inadequate unless it is matched, or even surpassed, by his achievement in time and his spiritual values.

(f) Of human misery; we
Find also in the sound a thought,
Hearing it by this distant Northern sea

Reference: These lines have been taken from the poem "Dover Beach" written by Matthew Arnold published in 1867 in the collection, New Poems. This poem deals with religion and he is concretely talking about the loss of faith. But it is also about the industrialisation and the changes in the cities (the progress) that were occurring in that period of time (the Victorian age). "Dover Beach" is a poem with the mournful tone of an elegy and the personal intensity of a dramatic monologue. Because the meter and rhyme vary from line to line, the poem is said to be in free verse – that is, it is unencumbered by the strictures of traditional versification.

Context: These lines connect Arnold's sense of sadness in the sea to the ancient Greek playwright Sophocles' tragic sensibility. "Sophocles long ago/Heard it on the Aegean, and it brought/Into his mind the turbid ebb and flow/Of human misery; we/Find also in the sound a thought,/Hearing it by this distant northern sea." This granting roar was probably also heard by Sophocles long ago on the shores of the Aegean sea and it was this that perhaps induced in his mind the sense of the miseries in human life which are reflected in his great tragedies. Just as the sound of the ebb and flow of the waves was able to evoke the feelings of human misery in Sophocles' mind, so also it evokes similar thoughts in the mind of Arnold and his wife who stand much further north, separated from him by time and space. By attributing his own interpretation of the sound of the sea as a metaphor for the relentless nature of human sadness to the ancient Sophocles, Arnold expresses that this sadness, like the tides, is both timeless and inevitable.

Q2. Scan any one of the following passages and comment on its prosodic features:

(a) But when the difference arose
On how to cross a desert patch,
We lost a friend whose stylish prose
Was quite the best of all our batch
A shadow falls on us and grows.

Ans. (i) The rhyme scheme of the lines is ab ab a.

(ii) The poem is in the form of an allegory of the pilgrimage theme with a suggestion of futility.

(iii) Emotive use of language is made.

(b) Some are meet for a maiden's wrist,
Silver and blue as the mountain – mist

Some are flushed like the buds that dream
On the tranquil brow of a woodland stream;
Some are aglow with the bloom that cleaves
To the limpid glory of new – born leaves.

Ans. (i) The rhyme scheme of the lines is aa bb cc.

(ii) The lines encompass a Kaleidoscope of Indian scenes, sights, sounds and experiences transmuted into a fantastic vision of color and rhythm.

(iii) Images and metaphors come out readily in the passage and the poetry is intensely emotional and passionate.

(iv) Description is intermingled with reflection.

Q3. Write brief notes illustrating your points with the help of suitable examples on any two of the following:

(a) Ballad

Refer to Page No.-3 (The Ballad)

(b) Dramatic monologue

Refer to Page No.-5 (The Dramatic Monologue)

(c) Lyric

Refer to Page No.-5 (Lyric)

(d) Myth

Refer to Dec-2006, Q.No.-1(i)

Q4. Write a note on Browning's use of poetic devices in 'Meeting at Night'.

Ans. Refer to Chapter-4, Q.No.-8

In lines 3 and 4, the reflection of the moonlight on the waves is conveyed in the effective image of a head of curly golden hair of someone who has woken up with a start. The poem is almost like a painting with its vivid portrayal of a 'grey' sea, 'black' land and 'yellow' moon. The subdued colors of the first two lines give way to a more vivid image in line 3 and 4 as the pace of the lover's journey is conveyed. Not only does Browning make us see but he also make us smell the "sea-scented beach". He makes us hear the 'sharp scratch' of the lighted match and finally makes us feel the 'two hearts beating'.

Q5. Explain Hardy's poem 'God Forgotten', as a lyric that exemplifies Hardy's philosophy that 'Providence' is indifferent to human suffering.

Ans. 'God Forgotten' presents an ironic picture of God's complete indifference towards man. Presented in a dramatic form, the poet suggests that the human race has been utterly forsaken by its Creator. According to the narrator, he was sent thither by men and the other sons of the earth to find the answers to their cry, so he towered far and stood within the presence of the Lord Most High. God admitted that he created the Earth and the Human Race, but now he has no remembrance of such a place since the whole lot of this world is not fashioned as per his plan. The narrator asked God to forgive him as he dimly recalls that it was God who spoke the word that made it all including the Earth that men live.

The first time that God lost his interest of the world was when his ills were succeeded by the ills of mankind. In fact, he was under the impression that earth had perished leaving behind no signs of its existence. God recalls that earlier he could hear cries for help and favors from the earth but then suddenly human beings seemed to have snapped all ties with him and there was complete silence that remained unbroken till the poet's plea. Haply the earth died of doing what it does best, but the narrator pleaded with God that the earth and everything in it still exist. The people of the world used to ask God for the gift of good till it came with its severance and self entail, then the sudden silence from the side of the world began to ensue and till now it still prevails.

Still all other planets have kept in touch with the God. Their voices reached him speedily and it was rather strange that earth should expect any attention after its utter decadence. In comparison, all other planets were pure and faultless. God's people took upon themselves overmuch in sundering themselves from him. Though it is sad enough to see, yet it is strange that the earth's race should think that the ones whose call frames the daily and shining spheres of flawless stuff must heed their tainted ball. In spite of this, God is moved with sympathy at the plight of human beings. God directs his heavenly messenger to set out immediately and put an end to human problems. Clearly, this did not happen but the narrator still hopes in moments of crises that such divine help will be forthcoming.

The poem's end finds resemblance to Hardy's drama *Dynasts* in which he says: "It lends Its heed/To other worlds, being wearied out with this". "It" here refers to Providence. Hardy is mounting a direct attack on the idea of Providence. According to Christian belief, those who do good deeds are rewarded with heaven. In Hardy's scheme of things there is no such easy assurances. Hardy believes that men may hope and hope, but will not find any relief or sympathy from God.

Q6. Interpret the poem 'Brahma' in terms of Indian thought.

Ans. Refer to Chapter-6, Q.No.-2

Ralph Waldo Emerson's poem, "Brahma" is miraculous in its blend of Eastern and Western thought. In the poem, Emerson assumes the role of Brahma, the Hindu God of creation. Emerson is able to use clever, yet complex paradoxical logic in order to present his philosophy in poetic terms. Throughout the poem, Emerson alludes to Hindu mythology. The knowledge of which he gained through reading the Bhagavad-Gita and other Hindu scriptures. In Ralph Waldo Emerson's poem, "Brahma", the overall theme is the divine relationship and continuity of life and the unity of the universe.

In the first stanza, Emerson expresses the continuity of life. He says that if a killer thinks he has killed another or if the dead think that they are truly well, they do not fully realise his power; for he, Brahma, can create, destroy and re-create. In the end the "red-slayer", or the Hindu God Krishna, and his victim are merged in the unity of Brahma. When Brahma re-creates or "turns again," it is commonly known as the concept of reincarnation. Thus, the continuity of life is expressed through Brahma's eyes.

The ultimate unity of the universe is expressed through the second stanza. Emerson uses such opposites such as shadow and sunlight, good and evil, in order to prove this philosophical belief. In essence, Emerson states that all opposites are reconciled in the ultimate unity of the universe. This is proven as he states that shadow and sunlight are the same as are shame and fame. Thus, when it comes down to it, the universe is built through harmony and not counteracting forces such as good and evil.

In the last stanza, Emerson calls upon the reader to do something. He states, "Find me (Brahma), and turn thy back on heaven, this is a definite allusion to the statement in the eighteenth chapter in the Bhagavad-Gita which says, "Abandoning all religious duties, seek me as thy refuge. I will deliver thee from all sin." In lines before he makes this request, he states that the sacred seven, the highest priests, and the strong gods, the Hindu gods Indra, Agni, and Yama, pray to him in vain and ask for his asylum. Thus, he is saying that praying to him for material goods will not accomplish anything. Thus, the request that he makes is for the readers to join him in the ultimate unity of the universe, also known as the Hindu philosophy of Mukhti.

In Ralph Waldo Emerson's poem, "Brahma", the overall theme is the divine relationship and continuity of life and the unity of the universe. To begin with, this is explained through the concept of re-incarnation, which is expressed in the first stanza. Second, Emerson clarifies it the second stanza in which he states that the universe lives in harmony ad not opposing forces such as good and evil. Lastly, Emerson calls upon the reader to abandon praying for material thoughts or asking him, Brahma, for asylum and join him in the ultimate unity of the universe. In writing "Brahma," Emerson boldly crosses new bounds by assuming the perspective of a God and by cleverly mixing Eastern and Western thought.

Q7. Write a critical appreciation of 'A Psalm of Life'.

Ans. Refer to Chapter-6, Q.No.-11

Henry Wadsworth Longfellow begins his poem "A Psalm of Life" with the same exuberance and enthusiasm that continues through most of the poem. He begs in the first stanza to be told "not in mournful numbers" about life. He states here that life does not abruptly end when one dies; rather, it extends into another after life. Longfellow values this dream of the afterlife immensely and seems to say that life can only be lived truly if one believes that the soul will continue to live long after the body dies. The second stanza continues with the same belief in afterlife that is present in the first.

Longfellow states this clearly when he writes, "And the grave is not its goal." Meaning that, life does not end for people simply because they die; there is always something more to be hopeful and optimistic for. Longfellow begins discussing how humans must live their lives in constant anticipation for the next day under the belief that it will be better than each day before it: "But to act that each to-morrow/Find us farther than today."

In the subsequent stanza, Longfellow asserts that there is never an infinite amount of time to live, but art that is created during one's life can be preserved indefinitely and live on long after its creator dies. In the following stanzas, Longfellow likens living in the world to fighting on a huge field of battle.

He believes that people should lead heroic and courageous lives and not sit idle and remain ineffectual while the world rapidly changes around them: "Be not like dumb, driven cattle! Be a hero in the strife!" His use of the word "strife" is especially interesting, since it clearly acknowledges that life is inherently difficult, is a constant struggle, and will never be easy. Longfellow then encourages everyone to have faith and trust the lord and not to rely on an unknown future to be stable and supportive.

Longfellow concludes the poem by exhorting us to live active, courageous lives. He is urging the reader to strive continuously to accomplish good, useful deeds: these good deeds, it is suggested, give life meaning and purpose. The last word of the poem, "wait," has a few possible meanings; it can mean "to serve" others - in this case, by working or "laboring" diligently; it can mean "to be ready" for someone or some event; or it can mean to be "watchful" - to be on the lookout for good opportunities as well as to be on guard against unexpected events or dangers. The poem ends, then, as it began, with a word of caution and of hope.

Q8. Discuss the presentation of the house in the poem 'My grandmother's House'.

Ans. In "My Grandmother's House", the house is presented with concern and pathos and the poetess expresses her poignant feelings of yearning for this house. She wishes to go back to it.

Kamala Das recalls her ancestral house that was filled with the all-pervading presence of her grandmother. And this is why her grandmother's house is singular: Kamala Das received love there. When the poetess speaks of 'love' in particular she ascertains that it is unconditional and selfless. With the death of the Grandmother, the house ceased being inhabited. It now became an isolated and remote entity, echoed by the phrase 'far away'. The poetess asserts that with the death of her grandmother, silence began to sink in in the house. Kamala Das, at that juncture, was too small to read books, but emotional enough to comprehend the true feeling of love. With the death of the Grandmother, her life that was hitherto filled only with emotions becomes numb. Her veins thus become cold rather than warm. It is as cold of the moon, the moon being an emblem of love. The worms on the books seem like snakes at that moment, in comparison to the size of the little girl; and in keeping with the eeriness of the situation. The poetess also implies that the deserted house is like a desert with reptiles crawling over. The poetess now longs to 'peer' at a house that was once her own. She has to peek through the 'blind eyes' of the windows as the windows are permanently closed. The air is frozen now, as contrasted to when the grandmother was alive-the surroundings were filled with the warmth of empathy. Kamala Das pleads with us to "listen" to the "frozen" air; that is an impossibility. Neither is the air a visual medium, nor can air cause any displacement because it is "frozen".

In wild despair, she longs to bring in an "armful of darkness". Note firstly, that it is not a 'handful' but an armful. Secondly, 'darkness' that generally has negative shades to it, has positive connotations here of a protective shadow. It also reflects the 'coziness' inside the house. This armful of darkness is her essence of nostalgia. With this piece of darkness, she can lie down for hours, like a brooding dog behind the door, lost in contemplation.

The speaker claims that in her quest for love she had now become wayward. The poetess speaks to her husband that she who is now thirsty for genuine love, received at one point in her life, absolute love in the form of her grandmother. Ironically, she addresses her husband as "Darling", and talks of the lack of love in her life in the same breath and tone.

Her pursuit of love has driven her to the doors of strangers to receive love at least in the form of 'a tip'. Previously she was 'proud', as she did not have to compromise on her self-respect. Now she has to move in the maze of male monopolistic chauvinism, and beg for love in the form of change.

The poem emphasises the languishing desire of the poetess for a sentiment peep into her past and resurrect her dreams and desires. With the dereliction of the old house, the windows have become blind. Only the heat of the reunion with the house will melt the ice and the windows will again be restored to old life. The crumbling of the old house and death of the old woman has left an impact on the poetess also. With them crumbles her own life of innocence and the cherished values.

Q9. In the poem 'The Express' the train becomes a symbol of modern industrial civilization. Discuss.

Ans. The Express has been regarded as a typical poem by Stephen Spender glorifying the express train. The train here becomes a symbol of the modern industrial civilization. The glorious march of the train to its destination is vividly captured by the poet, who considers this machine as an object of great beauty. It is interesting to note that the movement of the lines of the poem mimes the majestic journey of the train.

The first three lines of the poem set the train in motion. After the first forceful blowing of the engine's whistle, the movement of the pistons announces the departure of the train, which moves away from the station smoothly and majestically as a queen. There is so much beauty in this machine and feminine qualities are attributed to it.

The next seven lines trace the first stage of the train's movement. A cross section view is also given of the surrounding area through this description. The train passes the houses that humbly crowd outside. It moves past the gasworks and then by the cemetery in which the gravestones have printed the heavy page of death. The train next goes in to the open countryside where she picks up speed and becomes mysterious. She now controls herself perfectly like a stately ship moving on the ocean. In the next four lines, the poet focuses his attention on the various sounds emitted by the train. At first, the Express sings low. Then the sound becomes more loud and ultimately it breaks into a loud madness.

The next six lines describe the joyous rhythm of the train. The Express speeds through the metal track and shows up startling features of the landscape. In the next seven lines, night sets in. The train seems to have moved beyond Edinburgh or Rome and one can only notice a very clear line or phosphorous. The train now moves like a comet through flame. The next eleven lines take us to a very intimate realisation. The passenger and the train are shut together in a darkness where no one can interfere and all identity seems to be lost. The last eight lines presents an extremely sensuous picture when the whole train of romantic associations will be let loose and the passengers will come to realise that the Express, in fact, represents all the women that have ever been.

Thus, the poem admirably captures the various movements, sounds, moods and associations set loose by the Express train. The poem is remarkable for its suggestive expressions and realistic description. The expressions like "black statement of pistons", "heavy page of death, printed by gravestones", and "fingers tangled in their yellow hair" are very thought provoking. The similes add to the richness of the poem. It is not only the train which has been personified. Even the houses crowd outside humbly as if they too were living beings. The poem indeed is a powerfully evocative tribute paid by a man to the machine.

EEG-6: UNDERSTANDING POETRY
June, 2012

Note : Section A is ***compulsory***. Answer any three questions from Section B

SECTION A

Q1. Explain any four of the following passages with reference to the context, supplying brief critical comments where necessary:

(a) Shall I compare thee to a summer's day?
Thou art more lovely and more temperate:
Rough winds do shake the darling buds of May,
And summer's lease hath all too short a date.

Reference: These lines have been taken from the sonnet 18 "Shall I Compare thee to a Summer's Day" written by Shakespeare. This sonnet is addressed to a friend or Fair Youth. The speaker here assumes the twin role of a friend and a poet. It is full of scale immortalisation of art and through art. In this sonnet, the poet sets up the power of time and then introduces the power of his verse as a defence against time. Sonnet 18 is the best known and most well-loved of all 154 sonnets. It is also one of the most straightforward in language and intent. The stability of love and its power to immortalise the poetry and the subject of that poetry is the theme.

Context: The speaker opens the poem with a question addressed to the beloved: "Shall I compare thee to a summer's day?" The next lines are devoted to such a comparison. In line 2, the speaker stipulates what mainly differentiates the young man from the summer's day: he is "more lovely and more temperate." Summer's days tend toward extremes: they are shaken by "rough winds"; in them, the sun ("the eye of heaven") often shines "too hot," or too dim. And summer is fleeting: its date is too short, and it leads to the withering of autumn, as "every fair from fair sometime declines."

This sonnet is certainly the most famous in the sequence of Shakespeare's sonnets. On the surface, the poem is simply a statement of praise about the beauty of the beloved; summer tends to unpleasant extremes of windiness and heat, but the beloved is always mild and temperate. Summer is incidentally personified as the "eye of heaven" with its "gold complexion"; the imagery throughout is simple and unaffected, with the "darling buds of May" giving way to the "eternal summer", which the speaker promises the beloved. The language, too, is comparatively unadorned for the sonnets; it is not heavy with alliteration or assonance, and nearly every line is its own self-contained clause—almost every line ends with some punctuation, which effects a pause.

(b) Two roads converged in a wood, and I
__________ I took the one less travelled by,
And that has made all the difference.

Reference: These lines have been taken from the poem "The Road Not Taken" written by Robert Frost. It was published in 1916 in the volume of poems entitled Mountain Interval. It is one the most popular lyrics of Robert Frost. Frost's imagination set at work by the difficulty of choosing one of the two roads which diverge at a particular point. The problem of making a choice is an important theme in Frost's poetry and it is also the theme of the present poem.

Context: The first stanza states that in a point of the speaker's journey, two roads diverged and he did not know which to take. At the point of divergence, the speaker stood and started observing both the roads. He took the first one and saw it carefully. He inspected the road as far as his eyes permitted him to. After inspecting the first road, he moved on to the second road. He saw that the second road was more grassy and lacked usage. Also the second road appealed to him more than the first road did. However, he felt that both the roads were same. As on both the roads, the leaves which had fallen were unstepped. However, he decided to travel through the second road. The speaker knew that his choice might not lead him to his desired destination and that he might not get a chance to come back. The speaker took a brave decision to choose the road which was not preferred by travelers. In the future the speaker would be able to tell proudly that at a point during his journey he took the road which was less travelled by travelers which has made all the difference in his life. This poem teaches to make right decisions in life. It also states that opportunities once lost are lost forever. We have to face the consequences of choices made by us. This poem also symbolises life in a way.

"The Road Not Taken" is a great lyric which records a personal experience of the poet. But, from the personal and individual, the poet rises to the universal and general. The difficulty of making a choice becomes a universal poem. The poet's experiences becomes symbolic of human experience in all times and countries. Moreover, it was the choice the poet Robert Frost made which determined his destiny and made him a poet different from others. It is thus that even minor decisions have far-reaching consequences. A step once taken or way once chosen can never be retraced.

(c) One short sleep part, we wake eternally And
death shall be no more,
Death thou shalt die

Reference: These lines form part of the Sonnet "Holy Sonnet X" by poet John Donne written between 1601-1610. Also known as "Death Be Not Proud", it is among the most famous and most beloved poems in English literature. Its popularity lies in its message of hope couched in eloquent, quotable language. Donne's theme tells the reader that death has no right to be proud, since human beings do not die but live eternally after "one short sleep." Although some people depict death as mighty and powerful, it is really a lowly slave that depends on luck, accidents, decrees, murder, disease, and war to put men to sleep. But a simple poppy (whose seeds provide a juice to make a narcotic) and various charms (incantations, amulets, spells, etc.) can also induce sleep—and do it better than death can. After a human being's soul leaves the body and enters eternity, it lives on; only death dies. To convey his message, Donne relies primarily on personification, a type of metaphor, which extends through the entire poem. Thus, death becomes a person whom Donne addresses, using the second-person singular.

Context: These final lines sum up the metaphysical paradox of the resurrection of the dead in the Christian tradition: death itself will die because the dead will be resurrected. In arguing that Death should not be "proud" of its ability to kill, Donne points out in the poem that Death is actually the slave of forces beyond its power. Not only that, but Death's supposed victory–the end of a human life–is ultimately a transition from one's temporary, mortal life to waking "eternally" in immortal form. This is why death is more like a "short sleep" than any kind of victory for Death. This couplet caps the argument against Death. Not only is Death the servant of other powers and essentially impotent to truly kill anyone, but also Death is itself destined to die when, as in the Christian tradition, the dead are resurrected to their eternal reward. Here Donne echoes the sentiment of the Apostle Paul in I Corinthians 15:26, where Paul writes that "the final enemy to be destroyed is death." Donne taps into his Christian background to point out that Death has no power and one day will cease to exist.

(d) Along the margin of a bay:
Ten thousand saw I at a glance
Tossing their heads in Sprightly dance.

Reference: These lines have been taken from the poem "Daffodils" by "William Wordsworth".

Context: The poem records an anecdote of Wordsworth's life history when he came upon a bunch of daffodils while walking in Lake District. Daffodils are yellow flowers that are found in plenty in Lake District, a picturesque mountainous region in England. Wordsworth says that Daffodils is not just a poem of simple human sentiments of pleasure and delight on his seeing a bunch of daffodils but this tender and delicate poem has much to offer to the readers in terms of "Knowledge". The poem is remarkable for its accuracy of description, and it also offers an account of the way poetry is created. It illustrates the working of Wordsworth's imagination as it acts on the picture of daffodils given by the senses and turns it into a rich, perennial source of joy and inspiration. He can then recall these images at the time of stress and strain or during periods of loneliness. Daffodils is yet another instance of the overflow of emotions recollected in tranquility.

In the above lines, Wordsworth is remarkable for his accuracy in his presentation of details. The Daffodils need adequate water and shade for their growth. Hence, the poet says that the daffodils are seen in abundance besides the lake and beneath the trees. The poet sees the fluttering and dancing movement of the flowers as they are swayed by the breeze that blows across the lake. The Daffodils are linked with the stars that shine and twinkle on "the milky way". By instituting their comparison with the stars, Wordsworth has made the Daffodils a part of the universal order. The multitudinous flowers tossing their heads in sprightly dance resembles the bright stars in the galaxy. Shinning, twinkling and dancing, the flowers exude joy and life that lift the lonely heart of Wordsworth in to a state of bliss.

In William Wordsworth's "The Daffodils", the daffodils become much more than mere flowers. They are a symbol of natural beauty and, more importantly, symbolise living a life as rich in experience and sensation as would make a life worth living. They represent, in their light-hearted dance, the joy and happiness of living an adoring and fulfilling life, embracing it for every drop of nectar it could so bring. Romanticism, a poetic philosophy that Wordsworth himself engendered, finds much virtue in this meaning; the daffodils reaching out and catching the eye of Wordsworth's narrator, or perhaps Wordsworth himself, and inspiring him so much emotionally, that he was left with little choice than to express them poetically.

(e) Softly, O softly we bear her along,
She hangs like a star in the dew of our song;
She springs like a beam on the brow of the tide,
She falls like a tear from the eyes of a bride.

Refer to June-2007, Q.No.-2(vi)

(f) Away! away! for I will fly to thee,
Not charioted by Bacchus and his pards,
But on the viewless wings of Poesy,

Reference: These lines have been taken from stanza VI of the poem "Ode to a Nightingale" written by "John Keats" in the year 1819. The poet employs the use of apostrophe and is written in the form of an ode. Two voices can be heard in the poem. The first voice pays rich tribute to the song of a nightingale. It speaks of the poet's identification with the bird. The voice at the end is skeptical and it questions whether the poet had genuinely experienced heightened feelings of ecstasy or was it but a subjective half-dream. The dramatic tension in the poem is built around the poet's initial identification with the bird and his later separateness from it.

Context: Stanza VI expresses Keats morbid impulse to die at that very moment of experiencing an intense joy and empathy with nature so that he ceases to experience pain thereafter. The poet says that it is rich to die in his present state of heightened ecstasy. But alongside this death wish comes the still greater painful awareness that death marks not only severance from the pains of life but also from the bird and its sweet song as well.

All this thinking about how depressing the world is makes the poet think about an escape plan. He wants to fly away to join the nightingale in its refuge from the world. But he knows that the bird isn't going to take him. He can't rely on Bacchus, the Greek god of wine, or any of Bacchus's friends ("pards"), which is what he wanted. Instead of wine, he is going to fly on the wings of his own poetry. Poetry's wings are invisible, or "viewless". He is hopeful that poetry will take him to the nightingale's world even though his brain is not so helpful in making the trip. His brain confuses him and slows him down.

The thought of sickness, old age and death makes him seek an alternative to wine in his search for a supporting aid to wing him back the happy sojourn of nightingale. The poet turns to poetic fancy to bridge the division between him and the bird. The creative activity arising out of his appeal to poetic imagination limits himself to a three-line ornate composition, at the end of which Keats is back on the ground again, far away from the nightingale's habitation. Initially he soars high on the wings of poetic fancy to the tree tops where perches the nightingale, but before long he is back on earth where there is no light other than what flickers of the moonlight through the branches and leaves of the trees. Keats speaks of the wings of poesy as invisible, because the flight is too high for a vision of earth to be visible. The poet expects to soar high into the far distant, almost ethereal world of the bird aided by poetry.

(g) And we are here as on a darkling plain
Swept with confused alarms of struggle and flight
Where ignorant armies clash by night.

Reference: These lines have been taken from the last stanza of the poem "Dover Beach" written by Matthew Arnold.

Context: One of Arnold's most celebrated lyrics, the tone of the poem is almost conversational. In the above lines, the poet feels that this world does not contain any basic human values. These have disappeared, along with the light and religion and left humanity in darkness. "We" could just refer to the lyrical self and his love, but it could also be interpreted as the lyrical self-addressing humanity. The pleasant scenery turns into a "darkling plain", where only hostile, frightening sounds of fighting armies can be heard. According to Ian Hamilton, these lines refer to a passage in Thucydides, The Battle of Epipolae, where – in a night encounter – the two sides could not distinguish friend from foe".

The image of the sea is present throughout the poem. But in these lines the poet refers to sea as a darkling plain. The sea is calm at the outset. Slowly a 'granting roar' is discernible, an ebb and flow that turns the poet's thought to meditate on the loss of faith with which humanity was now beset. This loss of religious faith is depicted by the image of the receding tide with its melancholy, long, withdrawing roar. Without religious faith to invest life with some meaning and sense of value, the world is like an anarchic battlefield in the dark where people ignorant of their friends and foes are engaged in a hideous clash.

Q2. Scan one of the following passages and comment on its prosodic aspects:

(a) For oft when on my couch I lie
In vacant or in pensive mood,
They flash upon that inward eye
Which is the bliss of solitude;

Ans. (i) The lines are a part of six-line stanzas with an ab ab rhyme scheme in tetrameters.

(ii) The poet employs the use of simile.

(iii) Archaisms are used in the language of the poem.

(b) It is an ancient Mariner,
And he stoppeth one of three
'By they long grey beard and glittering eye,
Now wherefore stopp'st thou me?

Ans. (i) Rhyme scheme used is ab ab.

(ii) The lines form part of a literary ballad.

(iii) Archaic words and spellings are used to create authentic atmosphere.

Q3. Write brief notes on any two of the following:

(a) Ballad

Refer to Page No.-3 (The Ballad)

(b) Alliteration

Ans. In language, alliteration is the repetition of a particular sound in the first syllables of a series of words or phrases. Alliteration has developed largely through poetry, in which it more narrowly refers to the repetition of a consonant in any syllables that, according to the poem's meter, are stressed, as in James Thomson's verse "Come…dragging the lazy languid Line along". Alliteration is the repetition of initial sounds in neighboring words. In other words, it is the matching or repetition of consonants, or the repeating of the same letter (or sound) at the beginning of words following each other immediately or at short intervals.

(c) Metonymy

Ans. Metonymy is a figure of speech used in rhetoric in which a thing or concept is not called by its own name, but by the name of something intimately associated with that thing or concept. Metonyms can be either real or fictional concepts representing other concepts real or fictional, but they must serve as an effective and widely understood second name for what they represent. Metonymy works by the contiguity (association) between two concepts. It substitutes a word that relates to or suggests an idea for a person or place or thing.

(d) Onomatopoeia

Ans. Onomatopoeia is a word that imitates or suggests the source of the sound that it describes. Onomatopoeia (as an uncountable noun) refers to the property of such words. Common occurrences of onomatopoeias include animal noises, such as "oink" or "meow" or "roar" or "chirp". Onomatopoeias are not the same across all languages; they conform to some extent to the broader linguistic system they are part of. It is a device in which the meaning of a word is suggested by its sound.

(e) Simile

Refer to June 2007, Q.No.-1(a) (Simile)

SECTION B

Answer any three of the following:

Q1. Discuss Shakespearean Sonnets with special reference to the three sonnets you have studied.

Ans. A sonnet is a form of a poem of fourteen lines that follows a strict rhyme scheme and specific structure that originated in Europe, mainly Italy. A Shakespearean, or English, sonnet consists of 14 lines, each line containing ten syllables and written in iambic pentameter, in which a pattern of an unstressed syllable followed by a stressed syllable is repeated five times. The rhyme scheme in a Shakespearean sonnet is *a-b-a-b, c-d-c-d, e-f-e-f, g-g*; the last two lines are a rhyming couplet.

Shakespeare's sonnets are a collection of 154 sonnets, dealing with themes such as the passage of time, love, beauty and mortality, first published in a 1609. The sonnets include a dedication to "Mr. W.H.". The identity of this person remains a mystery and has provoked a great deal of speculation. When analysed as characters, the subjects of the sonnets are usually referred to as the Fair Youth, the Rival Poet, and the Dark Lady. The speaker expresses admiration for the Fair Youth's beauty, and later has an affair with the Dark Lady. It is not known whether the poems and their characters are fiction or autobiographical.

Sonnet 18, often alternately titled *"Shall I compare thee to a summer's day?"*, is one of the best-known of 154 sonnets. Part of the Fair Youth sequence, it is the first of the cycle after the opening sequence now described as the Procreation sonnets. On the surface, the poem is simply a statement of praise about the beauty of the beloved; summer tends to unpleasant extremes of windiness and heat, but the beloved is always mild and temperate. Summer is incidentally personified as the "eye of heaven" with its "gold complexion"; the imagery throughout is simple and unaffected, with the "darling buds of May" giving way to the "eternal summer", which the speaker promises the beloved. The language, too, is comparatively unadorned for the sonnets; it is not heavy with alliteration or assonance, and nearly every line is its own self-contained clause – almost every line ends with some punctuation, which effects a pause. An important theme of the sonnet is the power of the speaker's poem to defy time and last forever, carrying the beauty of the beloved down to future generations. The beloved's "eternal summer" shall not fade precisely because it is embodied in the sonnet: "So long as men can breathe or eyes can see," the speaker writes in the couplet, "So long lives this, and this gives life to thee."

Sonnet 55 is one of the best and most critically acclaimed sonnets of the 154 sonnets. It is a member of the Fair Youth sequence, in which the poet expresses his love towards a young man. Sonnet 55 builds on Horace's theme of poetry outlasting physical monuments to the dead. It asserts the immortality of the poet's sonnets to withstand the forces of decay over time. He manages to demonstrate a superbly confident spirit: "Not marble, nor the gilded monuments/ Of princes, shall outlive this powerful rime." He contrasts his verses' immortality to "unswept stone, besmeared with sluttish time," meaning that the young man will be remembered longer because of the poet's having written about him than if descriptions of his beauty had been chiseled in stone. The next four lines address the same theme of immortality, but now the poet boasts that not only natural forces but human wars and battles cannot blot out his sonnets, which are a "living record" of the youth. In lines 9 through 12, he boldly asserts that death is impotent in the face of his sonnets' immortality: To the youth he says, "Against death and all-oblivious enmity/Shall you pace forth." In fact, he asserts that the young man's name will be remembered until the last survivor on earth perishes. This notion of "the ending doom" is the main point in the concluding couplet. The poet assures the youth that his beauty will remain immortal as long as one single person still lives to read these sonnets, which themselves will be immortal.

Shakespeare begins Sonnet 65 by listing several seemingly vast and unbreakable things which are destroyed by time, then asking what chance beauty has of escaping the same fate. A main theme is that many things are powerful, but nothing remains in this universe forever, especially not a fleeting emotion such as love. Mortality rules over the universe and everything is perishable in this world, so it is only through the timeless art of writing that emotion and beauty can be preserved. Continuing many of the images from Sonnet 64, the poet concludes that nothing withstands time's ravages. The hardest metals and stones, the vast earth and sea – all submit to time "Since brass, nor stone, nor earth, nor boundless sea,/But sad mortality o'er-sways their power." "O fearful meditation!" he cries, where can the young man hide that time won't wreak on him the same "siege of batt'ring days"? But the poet reverses this gloomy trend and once again is reassured that his sonnets will provide the youth immortality – his verse is the only thing that can withstand time's decay. Returning to the power of poetry to bestow eternal life, the poet asserts, "That in black ink my love may still shine bright." He believes that his love verse can preserve the youth's beauty. Ironically, this back-and-forth thinking mirrors the movement of the waves to the shore - an image the poet uses in many of the time-themed sonnets in this sequence.

Since these three sonnets are addressed to a friend, the speaker assumes the twin role of a friend and a poet. The poet contemplates on their close friendship against the inevitable mutability through the afflux of time. In all the three sonnets we notice the skillful use of the couplet to suggest the possibility of art to confer immortality both on itself and on the subject it is concerned with. The poet's friend can be preserved in the verse which will last as long as Time lasts. The three sonnets 18, 55 and 65 are examples of a strong and unified structure built on "a powerful rhyme" and therefore they speak with credible authenticity about the immortality of art.

Q2. What is Metaphysical poetry? Introduce John Donne as a Metaphysical poet.

Ans. Refer to Chapter-2, Q.No.-1

John Donne is the classic representative of metaphysical poetry. His instinct compelled him to bring the whole of experience into his verse and to choose the most direct and natural form of expression by his learned and fantastic mind. He is colloquial, rhetorical, and erudite in all his poems. There is a plenty of passion in this kind of poetry. In the "Anniversary", Donne gives a lofty expression to the love and mutual trust of himself and his wife, his restless mind to seek far-fetched ideas, similitude and images in order to convey to the readers the exact quality of this love and interest.

Metaphysical poetry is inspired by "philosophical conception of universe and the role assigned to the human spirit in the great drama of existence." John Donne and his followers are metaphysical poets in a restricted sense. Donne also represents a clash between the old and new, the world of faith and the world of reason, the clash between the old geographers and Copernicus and his followers.

John Donne has written many songs and sonnets on the subject of love. He does not follow the Petrarchan tradition of love poetry as found in Spenser and Shakespeare. Donne was the first who revolted against this tradition of poetry. He does not flatter his beloved or glorify her. On the contrary, in many of his songs, he shows a cynical contempt for women. His song, "Goe And Catch A Falling Starre" is an example for this connection.

John Donne is also capable of deep feelings. The poems he wrote to celebrate his wedded love are full of such feelings. He says to his wife in the "Anniversary" that all honors and glories, all the princes and their favorites might perish but "only our love hath no decay."

In his early life, John Donne had lived an irregular life but in his middle age he took religion whole-heartedly and entered the church. His divine poems as his religious verse are a brooding thought on the subject of death and a strong faith in resurrection. Donne seems like a representative before God. Unified sensibility which is the combination of thinking and feeling is an important element of metaphysical poetry. John Donne and the metaphysical had a unified sensibility. Their poetry expressed thoughts, feelings and thinking at the same time. Here is a direct apprehension of thought or creation of thought into feeling.

Another characteristic feature of the metaphysical verse is indulgence in "dissimilar images of discovery occult resemblance in things apparently unlike." The metaphysical poetry is full of far-fetched images or often called conceits and allusions and references borrowed from branches of learning. For example, Donne represents himself in "Twickhnam Garden" as an unhappy lover. He wants to be converted himself in a fountain so that he may weep all the time. But his tears would be true tears of love. Metaphysical conceits convey a unified experience. According to Greisens, the hallmark of all metaphysical poetry is passionate feeling and paradoxical concentration is an important quality of metaphysical poetry in general and Donne's poetry in particular. In all his poems, the reader is held to one idea or line of argument.

Intellect and wit blending with emotion and feeling marks metaphysical poetry especially that of Donne. Indeed John Donne represents very well the school of poetry somewhat vaguely called "Metaphysical". He brought the whole of his experience into his poetry. The term metaphysical was applied to the poetry of John Donne and his followers by Dryden. In their poetry, there is a habit of always seeking to express something after something behind, the simple and obvious first sense and suggestion of a subject. According to Johnson, these poets only wanted to display their learning and to say something which had not been said before.

Q3. Evaluate W.B. Yeats as a modernist poet.

Ans. William Butler Yeats was an Irish poet and playwright, and one of the foremost figures of 20th century literature. A pillar of both the Irish and British literary establishments, in his later years he served as an Irish Senator for two terms. Yeats was a driving force behind the Irish Literary Revival and, along with Lady Gregory, Edward Martyn, and others, founded the Abbey Theatre, where he served as its chief during its early years. In 1923, he was awarded the Nobel Prize in Literature as the first Irishman so honoured for what the Nobel Committee described as "inspired poetry, which in a highly artistic form gives expression to the spirit of a whole nation."

Yeats is generally considered one of the twentieth century's key English language poets. He was a Symbolist poet, in that he used allusive imagery and symbolic structures throughout his career. Yeats chose words and assembled them so that, in addition to a particular meaning, they suggest other abstract thoughts that may seem more significant and resonant. His use of symbols is usually something physical that is both itself and a suggestion of other, perhaps immaterial, timeless qualities. Unlike other modernists who experimented with free verse, Yeats was a master of the traditional forms. The impact of modernism on his work can be seen in the increasing abandonment of the more conventionally poetic diction of his early work in favour of the more austere language and more direct approach to his themes that increasingly characterises the poetry and plays of his middle period, comprising the volumes *In the Seven Woods*, *Responsibilities* and *The Green Helmet*. His later poetry and plays are written in a more personal vein, and the works written in the last twenty years of his life include mention of his son and daughter, as well as meditations on the experience of growing old.

While Yeats' early poetry drew heavily on Irish myth and folklore, his later work was engaged with more contemporary issues, and his style underwent a dramatic transformation. His work can be divided into three general periods. The early poems are lushly pre-Raphaelite in tone, self-consciously ornate, and, at times, according to unsympathetic critics, stilted. Yeats began by writing epic poems such as *The Isle of Statues and The Wanderings of Oisin*. His other early poems are lyrics on the themes of love or mystical and esoteric subjects. Yeats' middle period saw him abandon the pre-Raphaelite character of his early work and attempt to turn himself into a Landor-style social ironist.

Critics who admire his middle work might characterise it as supple, muscular in its rhythms, and sometimes harshly modernist, while others find these poems barren and weak in imaginative power. Yeats' later work found new imaginative inspiration in the mystical system he began to work out for himself under the influence of spiritualism. In many ways, this poetry is a return to the vision of his earlier work. The opposition between the worldly-minded man of the sword and the spiritually minded man of God, the theme of *The Wanderings of Oisin*, is reproduced in *A Dialogue between Self and Soul*.

Some critics claim that Yeats spanned the transition from the nineteenth century into twentieth-century modernism in poetry much as Pablo Picasso did in painting while others question whether Yeats really has much in common with modernists of the Ezra Pound and T. S. Eliot variety. Modernists read the well-known poem *The Second Coming* as a dirge for the decline of European civilization in the mode of Eliot, but later critics have pointed out that this poem is an expression of Yeats' apocalyptic mystical theories, and thus the expression of a mind shaped by the 1890s. His most important collections of poetry started with *The Green Helmet* (1910) and *Responsibilities* (1914). In imagery, Yeats' poetry became sparer, more powerful as he grew older. *The Tower* (1928), *The Winding Stair* (1929), and *New Poems* (1938) contained some of the most potent images in twentieth-century poetry.

Yeats' mystical inclinations, informed by Hindu theosophical beliefs and the occult, provided much of the basis of his late poetry, which some critics have judged as lacking in intellectual credibility. The metaphysics of Yeats' late works must be read in relation to his system of esoteric fundamentals in *A Vision* (1925).

Q4. Write a critical appreciation of Shelleyan thought with special reference to the poem. 'Ode to the West Wind'.

Ans. Shelleyan thought uses the medium of human perception. Shelley was influenced by Plato who claimed that material world around us provides dull suggestions of a world of ideal forms which lies beyond our sense perceptions. One cause of suffering for human beings is that they are afraid of death. But Shelley considers death to be delightful and the beginning of immortal life. As against that men is torn by regrets for past and fears for the future; even the sincerest of our delight has a touch of sadness in it and our most touching songs are those that sing the tragedies of life.

"Ode to the West Wind" is a lyric poem that addresses the west wind as a powerful force and asks it to scatter the poet's words throughout the world. The poet desires the irresistible power of the wind to scatter the words he has written about his ideals and causes, one of which was opposition to Britain's monarchical government as a form of tyranny. Believing firmly in democracy and individual rights, he supported movements to reform government. In 1819, England's nobility feared that working-class citizens–besieged by economic problems, including high food prices–would imitate the rebels of the French Revolution and attempt to overthrow the established order. On August 16, agitators attracted tens of thousands of people to a rally in St. Peter's Field, Manchester, to urge parliamentary reform and to protest laws designed to inflate the cost of corn and wheat. Nervous public officials mismanaged the unarmed crowd and ended up killing 11 protesters and injuring more than 500 others. In reaction to this incident, Shelley wrote *The Masque of Anarchy* in the fall of 1819 to urge further nonviolent action against the government. However, this work was not published during his lifetime. However, "Ode to the West Wind," also written in the fall of 1819, was published a year later. The poem obliquely refers to his desire to spread his reformist ideas when it says, "Scatter, as from an unextinguish'd hearth/Ashes and sparks, my words among mankind!"

In the poem, the speaker invokes the "wild west wind" of autumn, which scatters the dead leaves and spreads seeds so that they may be nurtured by the spring, and asks that the wind, a "destroyer and preserver," hear him. The speaker calls the wind the "dirge/Of the dying year," and describes how it stirs up violent storms, and again implores it to hear him. The speaker says that the wind stirs the Mediterranean from "his summer dreams," and cleaves the Atlantic into choppy chasms, making the "sapless foliage" of the ocean tremble, and asks for a third time that it hear him.

The speaker says that if he were a dead leaf that the wind could bear, or a cloud it could carry, or a wave it could push, or even if he were, as a boy, "the comrade" of the wind's "wandering over heaven," then he would never have needed to pray to the wind and invoke its powers. He pleads with the wind to lift him "as a wave, a leaf, a cloud!"– for though he is like the wind at heart, untamable and proud – he is now chained and bowed with the weight of his hours upon the earth.

The speaker asks the wind to "make me thy lyre," to be his own Spirit, and to drive his thoughts across the universe, "like withered leaves, to quicken a new birth." He asks the wind, by the incantation of this verse, to scatter his words among mankind, to be the "trumpet of a prophecy." Speaking both in regard to the season and in regard to the effect upon mankind that he hopes his words to have, the speaker asks: "If winter comes, can spring be far behind?"

This poem is a highly controlled text about the role of the poet as the agent of political and moral change. This was a subject which Shelley wrote a great deal about, especially around 1819.

Q5. Jayanta Mahapatra's contemplative vision is reflected in his poems. Discuss.

Ans. Jayanta Mahapatra is one of the most esteemed names in the domain of contemporary Indo-Anglican poetry. He is usually regarded as a post-modern experimental poet. An important aspect of the new poetry or modernist poetry has been a constant encounter with the personal and immediate perception in relation to the outer reality or the external world. Jayanta Mahapatra emerges as a poet of human conditions and grows into one of the finest contemporary Indo-Anglican poets. Mahapatra is a poet of quiet but ironic reflection of life's bitter-sweet memories, happenings and revelations.

Mahapatra's style of obsessive writing and hopeless search in the meaning of human condition is an important characteristic of post modernism. The basic problem that haunts the poems of Mahapatra is the relationship of the self with the other, the distance felt by the consciousness between being aware and what one is aware of. In Mahapatra's poetry such feelings are intensified as he questions the existence of the self, the other often takes the form of local society and especially Hindu culture, ritual and spirituality, symbols and past from which he had been alienated by his grandfather's conversion to Christianity and his own English education.

Mahapatra observed his environment and listened quietly and sensitively to his inner feelings, the sources of his poetry brought momentary perception of relationships and fleeting images of contrast. It was difficult, obscure poetry of meditation recording reality as an unknowable flux. It more often deconstructed what was perceived. It was poetry of inner spaces, of psychology, of contradiction and renewed feelings of depression, guilt, desire, lust and attention. Many of his poems seemed sealed against interpretation.

It seemed from his writings that he has evolved his poetic style largely on his own as an intellectual act. The words used by Mahapatra become concepts and symbols. He had used symbols from his environment to articulate an inner space of feelings. In fact, the titles of his poems are indicative of how the external world especially the Indian landscape and seasons became the starting point of his imagination.

Mahapatra's poems record a distance between himself and the customs of his surroundings. In his poems there are the sounds of temple bells, the prayers of priests, the funeral pyres, the uncomplaining acceptance of the past, representing a possible reality or a mentality to which he did not belong. The listening and waiting were in fact result of consciousness of the rational mind which is aware of its individualisation and difference. His poems keep returning to the desires to overcome such alienation through passive attention in the hope that some renewal will definitely occur.

It can be said that Jayanta Mahapatra's world is filled with personal pain, guilt, remorse, hunger, desire and moments of renewal, his environment is filled with symbols of beliefs by the ordinary lives of the people of Cuttack, the temples, the Hindu festivals and the monuments. The poems are varied attempts to bridge an epistemological, phenomenological gap to know, to be part of, to enclose and to experience with the world and other whether it is a woman, temple stone or a Hindu priest.

Q6. Tennyson strikes a balance between melancholy and a sense of living life actively in the poem 'Ulysses'. Discuss.

Ans. Ulysses is a poem in blank verse by the Victorian poet Alfred Lord Tennyson (1809–1892), written in 1833 and published in 1842 in Tennyson's well-received second volume of poetry. An oft-quoted poem, it is popularly used to illustrate the dramatic monologue form. Ulysses describes, to an unspecified audience, his discontent and restlessness upon returning to his kingdom, Ithaca, after his far-ranging travels. Facing old age, Ulysses yearns to explore again, despite his reunion with his wife Penelope and son Telemachus.

The speaker's language is unadorned and forceful, and it expresses Ulysses' conflicting moods as he searches for continuity between his past and future. There is often a marked contrast between the sentiment of Ulysses' words and the sounds that express them. For example, the poem's insistent iambic pentameter is often interrupted by spondees (metrical feet consisting of two long syllables), which slow down the movement of the poem; the laboring language casts into doubt the reliability of Ulysses' sentiments.

W. W. Robson writes that the poem brings in together the two conflicting sides of Tennyson - the "responsible social being" and the "melancholic poet". Though they come together in the text of the poem, they do not recognise each other. Furthermore, Tennyson wrote Ulysses after the death of his Cambridge friend, the poet Arthur Henry Hallam, who was extremely dear to him. As per the Victorian critic Linda Hughes, the "emotional gulf between the state of his domestic affairs and the loss of his special friendship informs the reading of Ulysses – particularly its treatment of domesticity." His urge to overcome the emotions and manage his huge household posed as a challenge to him. The idea of his protagonist transcending an age in such a circumstance was symbolic of him defying his own circumstances. Hence, he utilises such a myth to mirror his anxieties at the moment. Tennyson states, "There is more about myself in Ulysses, which was written under the sense of loss and that all had gone by, but that still life must be fought out to the end. It was more written with the feeling of his loss upon me than many poems in In Memoriam."

Ulysses' desire to travel does not simply represent a desire for adventure. According to RB Martin, it gives the "feeling about the need of going forward and braving the struggle of life". Ulysses represents the human desire for striving beyond human limits to achieve something noble and great. Human beings must not simply live and die a mundane life but must try to achieve something great before death.

Having returned to his kingdom Ithaca after an action-packed journey and eventful past, Ulysses finds little pleasure in a 'still hearth'. The metaphor is employed to comment on his own condition. Like a fireplace, it no longer carries the flame in it, only the ashes of a once fiery lifestyle. The phrase "barren crags" points to the island of Ithaca in the kingdom of Ulysses: a limestone ridge seventeen miles long and four miles broad at its widest, singular for its ruggedness and barrenness, and considered unhealthy for cultivation. It serves to reflect on the crude state of affairs in the king's life and the sterility that prevails. Penelope was 'fifty' at the time, and did not match his passion for adventure and quest for exploration. On the other hand, Ulysses aspires to live life to the fullest, to the lees. Here, 'lees' implies the residual part of the drink that lies at the bottom of the glass. This is evident in the lines, "I will drink/Life to the lees" to "The wine of life is drawn and the mere lees is left this vault to brag of."

EEG-6: UNDERSTANDING POETRY
December, 2012

Note: Section A is ***compulsory***. Answer any three questions from Section B

SECTION A

Q1. Explain any four of the following passages with reference to the context, supplying brief critical comments where necessary:

(a) I cannot rest from travel: I will drink Life to
the lees: all times I have enjoyed Greatly,
have suffered greatly, both with those That
loved me and alone,

(b) Turning and turning in the widening gyre.
The falcon cannot hear the falconer;
Things fall apart; the centre cannot hold.

(c) Exult O shores, and ring O bells!
But I with mournful tread.
Walk the deck my captain lies,
Fallen cold and dead.

(d) The trumpet of a prophecy! O Wind, If
winter comes, can spring be far behind

(e) She's all States, and all Princes I, Nothing
el'se is.

(f) My mother only said
Thank God the scorpion picked on me and
spared my children.

(g) Here rests his head upon the lap of Earth
A youth, to Fortune, and to Fame unknown;
Fair Science frown'd on his humble birth,
And Melancholy mark'd him for her own.

Q2. Scan one of the following passages and comment on its prosodic aspects:

(a) Know then thyself, presume not God to Scan,
The proper study of mankind is man.

(b) Time doth transfixe the flourish set on youth,
And delves the parallels in beauties brow,
Feeds on the rarities of nature's truth, And
nothing stands but for his sieth to mow.

Q3. Write brief notes on any two of the following:

(a) Petrarchan Sonnet **(b) Heroic Metre**

(c) Metaphor **(d) Assonance**
(e) Dramatic Monologue

SECTION B

Answer any three questions:

Q1. What is pastoral elegy? How does Milton succeed in blending the pastoral, Christian and personal elements in 'Lycidas'?

Q2. State the features of a mock – epic poem and discuss Alexander Pope as a successful practitioner of the same.

Q3. Attempt a critique of Lord Byron as a romantic poet.

Q4. Evaluate the "Journey of the Magi" as a Christian poem.

Q5. Critically appreciate the poem 'Stopping by woods on a Snowy Evening'.

Q6. Kamala Das's poetry is concerned with both the worlds – external and internal. Discuss.

EEG-6: UNDERSTANDING POETRY
June, 2013

Note : Section A is ***compulsory***. Answer any three questions from Section B

SECTION A

Q1. Explain any four of the following passages with reference to the context, supplying brief critical comments where necessary:

(a) Oh fearful meditation! where alack, Shall Time's best jewel from Time's Chest lie hid? Or what strong hand can hold his Swift foot back? Or who his shoil of beauty can forbid?

(b) Goe tell Court huntsmen, that the king will ride
Call Country ants to harvest offices;
Love, all alike, no season knowes nor clyme,
Nor, houres, days, months, which are the rags of time

(c) Scatter, as from an unexitinguished
hearth Ashes and sharks, my words among mankind!
Be through my lips to unawakened earth
The trumpet of a prophecy.

(d) That I could think there trembled through
his happy good – night air
Some blessed hope, where of he knew
And I was unaware.

(e) We returned to our places, these Kingdoms,
But no longer at ease here, in the old dispensation
With an alien people clutching their gods, I
should be glad of another death.

(f) Nor you alone Ye facts of modern science,
But myths and fables of old, Asia's, Africa's fabler,
The far – darting beans of the spirit, the unloos'd dreams;
The deep diving bibles and legends.

(g) I who have lost,
My way and beg now at strangers' doors to
Receive love, at least in small change?

Q2. Scan any one of the following passages and comment on its prosodic features:

(a) He must not float upon his watery bier
Unwept and welter to the parching wind
Without the meed of some melodious tear.

(b) Touch her not scornfully
Think of her mournfully
Gently and humanly
Not of the remains of her
Now is pure womanly

Q3. Write brief notes on any two of the following:

(a) Personification	**(b) Metonymy**
(c) Lyric	**(d) Petrarclan Sonnet**

SECTION B

Answer any three questions:

Q4. How does Shakespeare celebrate the power of imagination in his sonnets?

Q5. Comment upon the New – classical and Romantic elements in Gray's Elegy written in a country Churchyard".

Q6. Discuss Byron's treatment of nature.

Q7. Critically examine Browning's attitude of optimism.

Q8. Discuss the theme of "The Second Coming".

Q9. Comment on Poe's use of, poetic devices in "The Raven."

Q10. Give your estimate of Ramanujan as a poet.

EEG-6: UNDERSTANDING POETRY
December, 2013

Note : Answer questions 1 and 2 and 3 more from the remaining once.

Q1. Explain any four of the following passages with reference to the context, supplying brief critical comments where necessary:

(a) I come to pluck your berries harsh and
crude, And with forced fingers rude.
shatter your leaves before the mellowing
year.

(b) Full many a gem of purest ray serene the
dark unfathom'd of ocean bear:
Full many a flower is born to blust unseen,
And waste its sweetness on the desert air.

(c) About, about, in real and rout The
death-fires danced at night;
The Water, like a witch's oils,
Burnt green and blue and white.

(d) Yes! in the sea of life enisled
With echoing straits between us thrown,
Dotting the shoreless watery wild.
We mortal millions live alone.

(e) And our teachers report that he never
interfered with their education.
Was he free? Was he happy? The question
absurd:
Had anything been wrong we should
certainly have heard.

(f) Since then - its Centuries - and yet Feels
shorter than the Day
I first surmised the Horses' Heads Were
toward Eternity.

(g) In her hands are holds
The oil lamp
Whose drunken yellow flames
know where her lonely body hides.

Q2. I can one of the following passage and comment on its procedure features:

(a) They way not mine O lord
However dark it be;
Lead me with there own hand
choose out the path for me.

(b) **Tell me not in meaningful numbers**
Life is but an empty dream;
For the soul is dead that Humbles,
And things are not what they seem.

Q3. Write short notes on any two of the following:

(a) **metaphor**
(b) **synecdoche**
(c) **dramatic monologue**
(d) **pastoral elegy**

Q4. Discuss the theme of 'On His Blindness' by John Milton.

Q5. Why should death not be proud? Discuss their question with reference to Holy Sonnel X by John Donne.

Q6. How does nature influence man according to William Wordsworth?

Q7. Describe the personality of The Lady of shalott as it emerges from the lines you have read.

Q8. What are the salient features of modern poetry as understood by you?

Q9. Discuss the theme of 'The Road Not Taken by Robert Frost.

Q10. Write an essay on the role of memory in the poetry of Kamaladas.

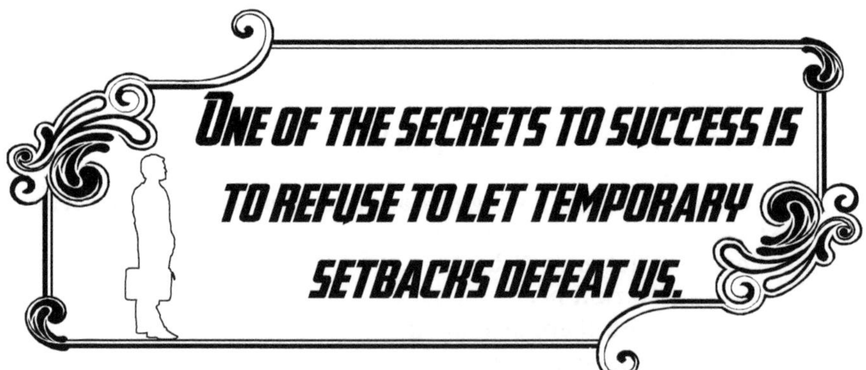

EEG-6: UNDERSTANDING POETRY
June, 2014

Note : Questions 1 and 2 are ***compulsory***. Answer any three of the remaining questions.

Q1. Explain any four of the following passages with reference to the context, supplying brief critical comments where necessary:

(a) Oh! None, unless this miracle
have might -
That in black ink my love may
still shine bright.

(b) I cannot rest from travel: I will drink
Life to the lees: all times I have enjoy'd
Greatly, have suffered greatly, both with
those
That loved me, and alone;

(c) And we are here as on a darkling
plain Swept with confused alarms of
struggle and flight,
Where ignorant armies clash by night.

(d) Wild spirit, which art moving everywhere;
Destroyer and preserver; hear, oh, hear!

(e) The peasants came like swarms of flies and
buzzed the name of God a hundred times
to paralyse the evil one.

(f) Lightly, O lightly we glide and we sing,
We bear her along like a pearl on a string.

Q2. Scan any one of the following passages and comment on its prosodic features:

(a) I wandered lonely as a cloud
That floats on high o'er vales and hills,
When all at once I saw a crowd,
A host of golden daffodils;

(b) Merrily, merrily shall I live now
Under the blossom that hangs on the bough.

Q3. Write brief notes on any two of the following:

(a) The Ballad
(b) The Lyric
(c) The Dramatic Monologue
(d) The English Sonnet

Q4. Discuss how shelley presents the West Wind both as Destroyer and Preserver in the poem 'Ode to the West Wind'.

Q5. What is the theme of the poem 'The Road Not Taken'? Discuss.

Q6. Discuss the development of the thought in 'Ode to a Nightingale'.

Q7. Attempt a critical appreciation of the poem 'Ulysses'.

Q8. How does the poem 'The Bangle Sellers' throw light on Sarojini Naidu's conception of Indian women? Discuss.

Q9. What idea does Jayanta Mahapatra put across in his poem 'A Missing Person'?

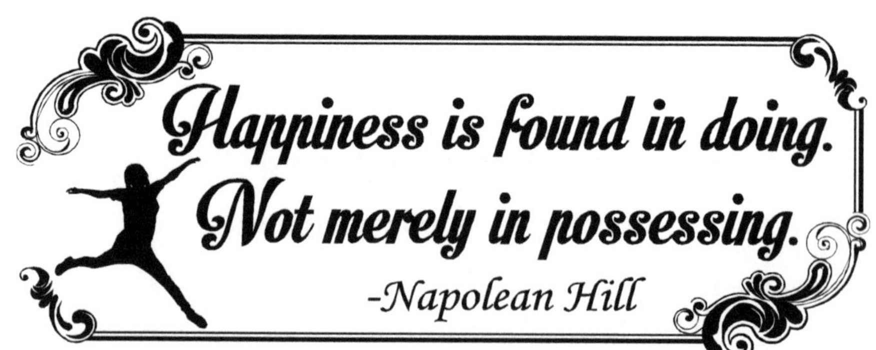

EEG-6: UNDERSTANDING POETRY
December, 2014

Note : Questions 1 and 2 and 3 are ***compulsory***. Answer any three of the remaining questions.

Q1. Explain any four of the following passages with reference to the context, supplying brief critical comments where necessary:

(a) The Trumpet of a prophecy! O Wind,
If Winter comes, can Spring be far behind?

(b) ... his state
Is Kingly; thousands at his bidding speed
And post o'er land and ocean without rest:
They also serve who only stand and wait.

(c) O heart! O heart! If she'd but turn her head,
You'd know the folly of being comforted.

(d) The woods are lovely dark and deep
But I have promises to keep
And miles to go before I sleep
And miles to go before I sleep.

(e) Let not Ambition mock their useful toil,
Their homely joys, and destiny obscure;
Nor Grandeur hear with a disdainful smile
The short and simple annals of the Poor.

(f) 'A cold coming we had of it,
Just the worst time of the year
For a journey, and such a long journey:
The ways deep and the weather sharp,
The very dead of winter.'

Q2. Scan any one of the following passages and comment on its prosodic features:

(a) Tell me not in mournful numbers
"Life is but an empty dream!"
For the soul is dead that slumbers,
And thing are not what they seem.

(b) No longer mourn for me when I am dead
Than you shall hear the surly, sullen bell
Give warning to the world that I am fled
From this vile world, with vilest worms to dwell.

Q3. Write brief notes on any two of the following:

(a) The Heroic Couplet

(b) The Shakespearean Sonnet

(c) Simile

(d) Metonymy

Q4. Discuss the theme of the sonnet 'Shall I Compare Thee to a Summer's Day'.

Q5. Discuss John Donne as a metaphysical poet.

Q6. How does the poet depict rural India in the poem 'Night of the Scorpion?'

Q7. Critically comment on the use of imagery in 'To a Skylark'.

Q8. Who do you think is the speaker in the poem 'The Unknown Citisen'? What impression do you gather about him/her?

Q9. Discuss Milton's 'Lycidas' as a pastoral elegy.

EEG-6: UNDERSTANDING POETRY
June, 2015

Note : Questions 1, 2 and 3 are ***compulsory***. Answer any three from the remaining questions.

Q1. Explain any four of the following passages with reference to the context, and supply brief critical comments of your own:

**(a) She' is all States, and all Princes, I,
Nothing else is.
Princes doe but plays us; compar'd to this,
All honor's mimique; All wealth alchimie.**

**(b) Here rests his head upon the lap of Earth
A Youth, to Fortune and to Fame unknown;
Fair Science frown'd not on his humble birth,
And Melancholy mark'd him for her own.**

**(c) He came to his sceptre young; he leaves it old;
Look to the state in which he found his realm,
And left it; and his annals too behold,
How to a minion first he gave the helm;**

**(d) Death closes all: but something ere the end,
Some work of noble note, may yet be done,
Not unbecoming men that strove with Gods.**

**(e) But now they drift on the still water,
Mysterious, beautiful;
Among what rushes will they build,
By what lake's edge or pool
Delight men's eyes when I awake some day
To find they have flown away?**

**(f) Two road converged in a wood, and I—
I took the one less travelled by,
And that has made all the difference.**

**(g) The snake-shrine is dark with weeds
And all the snake-gods in the shrine
Have lichen on their hoods.**

Q2. Scan any one of the following passages and comment on its prosodic features:

**(a) Tell me not, in mournful numbers,
Life is but an empty dream!**

For the soul is dead that slumbers,
And things are not what they seem.
(b) The Assyrian came down like a wolf on the fold,
And his cohorts were gleaming in purple and gold;

Q3. Write short notes on any two of the following:
(a) Lyric
(b) Synecdoche
(c) The Spenserian Stanza
(d) Sprung Rhythm
(e) Catalectic

Q4. Evaluate 'Lycidas' as a pastoral elegy.

Q5. Comment on the neo-classical elements in the poetry of Alexander Pope.

Q6. Wordsworth half creates and half perceives things that go into his poetry. Do you agree? Give reasons for your answer.

Q7. Critically appreciate *either* "The Darkling Thrush" *or* "Nightingales".

Q8. Attempt a critique of the poetry of *either* Walt Whitman *or* Ralph Waldo Emerson.

Q9. Compare and contrast Sarojini Naidu and Kamala Das as Indian-English poets.

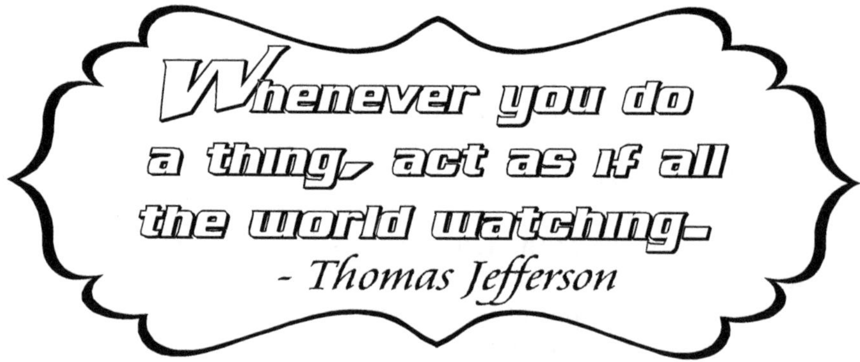

EEG-6: UNDERSTANDING POETRY
December, 2015

Note : Answer questions no 1, 2 and 3. Answer three more questions from the remaining ones.

Q1. Explain any four of the following passages with reference to their contexts supplying brief critical comments where necessary:

(a) O fearful meditation! where, alack,
Shall Time's best jewel from Time's
chest lie hid?
Or what strong hand can hold his swift
foot back?
Or who his spoil of beauty can forbid?

(b) One speaks the Glory of the British Queen,
And one describes a charming Indian Screen;
A third interprets motions, looks, and eyes;
At ev'ry word a reputation dies.

(c) Thou wast not born for death, immortal Bird!
No hungry generations tread three down;
The voice I hear this passing night was heard
In ancient days by emperor and clown;

(d) So little cause for carolings
Of such ecstatic sound
Was written on terrestrial things
Afar or nigh around,

(e) There was a Birth, certainly,
We had evidence and no doubt I have seen
birth and death,
But had thought they were different;
this Birth was
Hard and bitter agony for us,
like Death, our death.

(f) Towers of fables immortal fashion'd
from mortal dreams!
You too I welcome and fully the
same as the rest!
You too with joy I sing.

(g) O Bird of Time, say where do you learn
The changing measures you sing?

Q2. Scan any *one* of the following passages and comment on its prosodic features:

(a) Confusion, shame, remorse, despair,
At once his bosom swell;
The damps of death bedewed his brow;
He shook, he groaned, he fell.

(b) I am monarch of all I survey;
My right there is none to dispute;
From the centre all round to the sea
I am lord of the fowl and the brute.

Q3. Write brief notes on any *two* of the following:

(a) Petrarchan Sonnet
(b) Metaphor
(c) Metonymy
(d) Eye rhyme
(e) Enjambment

Q4. Comment on Shakespeare as a sonneteer. Cite suitable examples from his sonnets in support of your points.

Q5. Characterize Thomas Gray as a transition poet.

Q6. Critically appreciate *either* 'Roll on, Thou Deep and Dark Blue Ocean' or 'To a Skylark'.

Q7. Do you agree with the view that Browning speaks in two voices in 'My Last Duchess'? Which are those?

Q8. Evaluate *either* Edger Allan Poe or Robert Frost as a poet.

Q9. Bring out the Indian elements in the poetry of A.K. Ramanujan and Jayant Mahapatra.

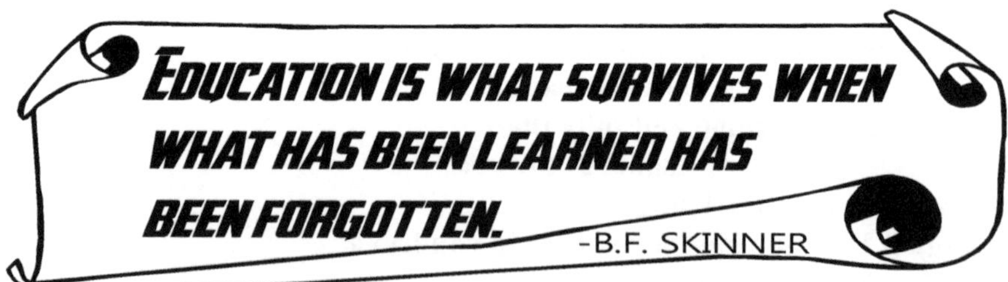

EEG-6: UNDERSTANDING POETRY
June, 2016

Note : (i) Questions 1, 2 and 3 are compulsory. (ii) Answer any three of the remaining questions.

Q1. Explain any four of the following passages with reference to their contexts, supplying brief critical observations where necessary:

(a) Oh fearful meditation ! Where alack,
Shall Time's best jewel from Time's chest lie hid?
Or what strong hand can hold his swift foot back?
Or who his spoil of beauty can forbid?

(b) Their name, their years, spelt by the unlettei'd Muse,
The place of fame and elegy supply:
And many a holy text around she strews
That teach the rustic movalist to die.

(c) He died! his death made no great stir on earth;
His burial made some pomp; there was profusion
Of velvet, gilding, brass, and no great death.
Of aught but tears-save those shed by collusion.

(d) We returned to our places, these Kingdoms,
But no longer at ease here, in the old dispensation,
With an alien people clutching their gods,
I should be glad of another death.

(e) Here captain ! dear father!
The arm beneath your head!
It is some dream that on the deck,
You've fallen cold and dead.

(f) The good wife
lies in my bed
through the long afternoon;
dreaming still, unexhausted
by the deep roar of funeral pyres.

Q2. Scan one of the following passages and comment on its prosodic features:

(a) May thou month of rosy beauty,
Month when pleasure is a duty,
Month of bees and month of flowers,
Month of blossom laden bowers.

(b) With ravished ears
The monarch hears
Assumes the God
Affects to nod
And seems to shake the spheres.

Q3. Write brief notes on any two of the following:
(a) Blank verse
(b) Assonance
(c) Symbol
(d) Lyric

Q4. Critically appreciate one of the following poems:
(a) To a skylark
(b) The unknown citizen
(c) The Road not Taken
(d) Looking for a cousin on a swing

Q5. Discuss the salient features on mock-heroic poetry and illustrate your points with examples from The Rape of the Lock.

Q6. Assess S.T. Coleridge as a Romantic poet.

Q7. Comment on the use of irony by Indian English poets.

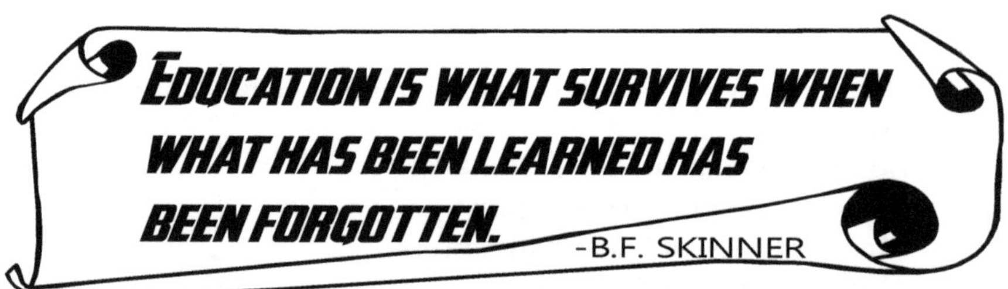

EEG-6: UNDERSTANDING POETRY
December, 2016

Note : Questions 1,2 and 3 are compulsory. Answer any three of the remaining questions.

Q1. Explain any four of the following passages with reference to their contexts, supplying brief critical comments where necessary:

(a) Yet once more, O ye laurels, and once more
Ye myrtles brown, with ivy never sear,
I come to pluck your berries harsh and crude,
And with forced fingers rude
Shatter your leaves before the mellowing year.

(b) The skilful nymph reviews her force with care;
`Let Spades be trumps !' she said, and trumps they were.

(c) Though the sad heart of Ruth, when sick for home,
She stood in tears amid the alien corn;
The same that oft-times hath
Charm'd magic casements, opening on the foam
Of perilous seas, in faery lands forlorn.

(d) One equal temper of heroic hearts,
Made weak by time and fate, but strong in will
To strive, to seek, to find, and not to yield.

(e) We paused before a House that seemed
A Swelling on the Ground
The Roof was scarcely visible —
The Cornice — in the Ground —

(f) The trip had darkened every face,
Our deeds were neither great nor rare.
Home is where we have to gather grace.

Q2. Scan one of the following passages and comment on its prosodic features:

(a) Thy way not mine O Lord
However dark it be;
Lead me by thine own hand
Choose out the path for me.

(b) On a mountain stretched beneath a hoary willow
Lay a shepherd swain and viewed the rolling billow.

Q3. Write brief notes on any two of the following:

(a) Metaphor

(b) Feminine rhyme

(c) Apostrophe

(d) Ode

Q4. Critically appreciate one of the following poems:

(a) The Daffodils

(b) The Darkling Thrush

(c) Hamatreya

(d) Palanquin Bearers

Write an essay on Metaphysical Poetry with special reference to John Donne's poems.

Q6. Comment on Matthew Arnold's use of epic similes in Sohrab and Rustum.

Q7. Write an essay on W.B. Yeats as a poet.

EEG-6: UNDERSTANDING POETRY
June, 2017

Note : Questions no. 1, 2 and 3 are compulsory. Answer any three parts from question no. 4.

Q1. Explain any four of the following passages with reference to their contexts, supplying brief critical comments where necessary:

(a) So long as men can breathe, or eyes can see,
So long lives this, and this gives life to thee.

(b) Where were ye, Nymphs, when the remorseless deep
Closed o'er the head of your loved Lycidas ?

(c) She's all states, and all Princes, I, Nothing else is.

(d) Close by those meads, for ever crown'd with flowers,
Where Thames with pride surveys his rising towers,
There stands a structure of majestic frame,
Which from the neighb'ring Hampton takes its name.

(e) The trumpet of a prophecy ! O Wind,
If Winter comes, can Spring be far behind ?

(f) The sea is calm tonight,
The tide is full, the moon lies fair
Upon the straits; on the French coast the light
Gleams and is gone; the cliffs of England stand,
Glimmering and vast, out in the tranquil bay.

(g) Softly, O softly we bear her along,
She hangs like a star in the dew of our song;
She springs like a beam on the brow of the tide,
She falls like a tear from the eyes of a bride.

Q2. Scan any one of the following passages and comment on its prosodic features:

(a) We noticed nothing as we went,
A straggling crowd of little hope,
Ignoring what the thunder meant,
Deprived of common needs like soap.
Some were broken, some merely bent.

(b) Trust no Future, howe'er pleasant !
Let the dead Past bury its dead !
Act, — act in the living Present !
Heart within, and God o'erhead !

Q3. Write brief notes on any two of the following:

(a) Elegy

(b) Metaphor

(c) Caesura

(d) Feminine Rhyme

(e) Apostrophe

Q4. Answer any three of the following:

(a) Give a detailed analysis of the characteristic features of a pastoral elegy, with special reference to the poetry of John Milton.

(b) Metaphysical poetry is characterized by its intellectual content, passionate feelings, learned but startling imagery. Discuss.

(c) Critically comment on the sensuous imagery and poetic craftsmanship of John Keats.

(d) Characterize the pictorial qualities of Alfred Lord Tennyson's verse, with special reference to "The Lady of Shallot".

(e) Interpret the poetry of Ralph Waldo Emerson in terms of his Indian thought, with special reference to "Brahma".

(f) Bring out the autobiographical qualities in the poetry of Jayanta Mahapatra. Is recollection a mode of redemption for Mahapatra?

EEG-6: UNDERSTANDING POETRY
December, 2017

Note : Questions no. 1, 2 and 3 are compulsory and answer any three from the remaining questions.

Q1. Explain any four of the following passages with reference to their contexts, supplying brief critical comments where necessary:

(a) Surely some revelation is at hand;
Surely the Second Coming is at hand.

(b) Were we led all the way for
Birth or Death? There was a Birth, certainly,
We had evidence and no doubt. I had seen birth and death,
But had thought they were different; this Birth was
Hard and bitter agony for us, like Death, our death.

(c) The curfew tolls the knell of parting day,
The lowing herd wind slowly o'er the lea,
The ploughman homeward plods his weary way,
And leaves the world to darkness and to me.

(d) After twenty hours it lost its sting.
My mother only said
Thank God the scorpion picked on me and spared my children.

(e) My heart aches, and a drowsy numbness pains
My sense, as though of hemlock I had drunk,
Or emptied some dull opiate to the drains
One minute past, and Lethe-wards had sunk:
'Tis not through envy of thy happy lot,
But being to happy in thine happiness.

(f) Fear death? — to feel the fog in my throat, The mist in my face,
When the snows begin, and the blasts denote I am nearing the place.

(g) He gives his harness bells a shake
To ask if there is some mistake.
The only other sound's the sweep
Of easy wind and downy flake.

Q2. Scan any one of the following passages and comment on its prosodic features:

(a) One more unfortunate
Weary of breath
Rashly importunate

Gone to her death!
(b) The ice was here, the ice was there,
The ice was all around:
It cracked and growled, and roared and howled,
Like noises" in a swound!

Q3. Write brief notes on any two of the following:
(a) Spenserian Sonnet
(b} The Dramatic Monologue
(c) Myth
(d) Metonymy
(e) Onomatopoeia

Q4. Critically appreciate any one of the following poems:
(a) The Sunne Rising
(b) Roll on, thou deep and dark blue Ocean
(c) Dover Beach
(d) A Psalm of Life

Q5. Assess the importance of any one of the following poets to their age:
(a) John Milton
(b) Thomas Gray
(c) Walt Whitman
(d) Nissim Ezekiel

Q6. Assess the contribution of the Victorian poets to their age.

Q7. Comment on the Indian influence on nineteenth century American poetry with special reference to the poems prescribed for you.

EEG-6: UNDERSTANDING POETRY
June, 2018

Note : Questions no. 1, 2 and 3 are compulsory. Answer any two from questions no. 4, 5, 6 and 7.

Q1. Explain any three of the following passages with reference to their contexts, supplying brief critical comments where necessary:

(a) For we were nursed upon the selfsame hill,
Fed the same flock, by fountain, shade, and rill.
Together both, ere the high lawns appear'd
Under the opening eye-lids of the morn,

(b) Here thou, great Anna ! whom three realms obey,
Dost sometimes counsel take — and sometimes tea,

(c) For I have learned
To look on nature, not as in the hour
Of thoughtless youth; but hearing oftentimes
The still, sad music of humanity,
Nor harsh nor grating, though of ample power
To chasten and subdue.

(d) And thou, who didst the stars and sunbeams know,
Self-schooled, self-scanned, self-honoured, self-secure
Didst tread the earth unguessed at — Better so !

(e) O heart ! O heart ! if she'd but turn her head,
You'd know the folly of being comforted.

Q2. Read closely and scan one of the following passages and comment on the use of metre and rhyme in it.

(a) Was this the face that launch'd a thousand ships,
And burnt the topless towers of Ilium?

(b) Tell me not, in mournful numbers,
"Life is but an empty. dream" !
For the soul is dead that slumbers,
And things are not what they seem

Q3. Write brief notes on any two of the following:

(a) Rhythm
(b) Rhyme Royal
(c) Verse Paragraph
(d) Consonance

(e) Epanadiplosis

Q4. Critically appreciate any one of the following poems:
(a) Nightingales
(b) On This Island
(c) Because I Could Not Stop for Death
(d) Night of the Scorpion

Q5. Attempt a critique of Romanticism in English poetry with special reference to the poems prescribed in your course.

Q6. Compare and contrast W.B. Yeats and T.S. Eliot as modern poets.

Q7. Evaluate either Ralph Waldo Emerson or Walt Whitman as American poets.

EEG-6: UNDERSTANDING POETRY
December, 2018

Note : Answer questions no. 1, 2 and 3 and any two of the remaining questions.

Q1. Explain any three of the following passages with reference to the context, supplying brief critical comments where necessary:

(a) When I consider how my light is spent
Ere half my days, in this dark world and wide,
And that one talent which is death to hide
Lodged me useless, though my soul more bent.

(b) Belinda now, whom thirst of fame invites,
Burns to encounter two adventurous knights,
At Ombre singly to decide their doom;
And swells her breast with conquests yet to come.

(c) Drive my dead thoughts over the universe
Like withered leaves to quicken a new birth!

(d) Sir, 't was not
Her husband's presence only,
called that spot
Of joy into the Duchess' cheek:

(e) We returned to our places, these Kingdoms,
But no longer at ease here,
in the old dispensation,
With an alien people clutching their gods.
I should be glad of another death.

Q2. Read closely and scan one of the following passages and comment on the use of metre and rhyme in it.

(a) With ravished ears,
The monarch hears;
Assumes the God
Affects to nod,
And seems to shake the spheres.

(b) Take her up tenderly,
Lift her with care;
Fashion'd so slenderly,
Young, and so fair!

Q3. Write brief notes on any two of the following:
(a) Cadence
(b) Ottava Rima
(c) Terza Rima
(d) Assonance
(e) Epanaphora

Q4. Write critical appreciation of any one of the following poems:
(a) 'Roll on, Thou Deep and Dark Blue Ocean'
(b) The Unknown Citizen
(c) Stopping by Woods on a Snowy Evening
(d) The Bird of Time

Q5. Would you consider the great Victorian poets as closely following the principles of Romanticism? Give reasons in support of your answer.

Q6. Account for the greatness of Shakespeare's poetry.

Q7. Consider A.K. Ramanujan and Jayant Mahapatra as representative voices of Indian experience.

EEG-6: UNDERSTANDING POETRY
June, 2019

Note : Attempt five questions in all. Section A is compulsory. Attempt any three questions from Section B.

SECTION A

Q1. Write brief notes on any two of the following:

(a) The Shakespearean Sonnet

(b) Ballad

(c) Onomatopoeia

(d) Simile

(e) Epanalepsis

Q2. Explain any three of the following passages with reference to their context and supply brief critical comments where necessary:

(a) The hungry Sheep look up, and are not fed,
But swoln with wind and the rank mist they draw,
Rot inwardly, and foul contagion spread:

(b) No farther seek his merits to disclose,
Or draw his frailties from their dread abode,
(There they alike in trembling hope repose)
The bosom of his father and his God.

(c) I have owed to them,
In hours of weariness, sensations sweet,
Felt in the blood, and felt along the heart;
And passing even into my purer mind
With tranquil restoration:

(d) She had
A heart — how shall I say? — too soon made glad,
Too easily impressed; she liked whate'er
She looked on, and her looks went . everywhere.

(e) There was a Birth, certainly
We had evidence and no doubt. I had seen birth and death,
But had thought they were different; this Birth was
Hard and bitter agony for us, like Death, our death.

SECTION B

Q3. What is a metaphysical conceit? Examine Donne's use of conceit in the poems prescribed in your syllabus.

Q4. Critically appreciate any one of the following poems:

(a) Tintern Abbey

(b) George the Third

(c) Ulysses

(d) The Second Coming

Q5. Evaluate the poetry of either Emerson or Whitman with special reference to the poems prescribed for you.

Q6. Compare and contrast A.K. Ramanujan and Jayant Mahapatra as Indian English poets in the light of their themes and styles.

EEG-6: UNDERSTANDING POETRY
December, 2019

Note : (i) Answer questions 1 and 2 and any three of the remaining questions.
(ii) Attempt five questions in all. Section A is compulsory. Attempt any three questions front Section B.

SECTION A
(Compulsory)

Q1. Write brief notes on any two of the following.
(a) The heroic couplet
(b) Elegy
(c) Alliteration
(d) Metaphor
(e) Epanaphora

Q2. Explain any three of the following passages with reference to their contexts and supply brief critical comments where necessary.

(a) Not marble, nor the gilded monuments
Of princes, shall outlive this powerful rhyme;
But you shall shine more bright in these contents
Than unswept stone, besmear'd with sluttish time.

(b) She stood in tears amid the alien corn;
The same that oft-times hath
Charmed magic casements, opening on the foam
Of peri lous seas, in faery lands forlorn

(c) And thou, who didst the stars and sunbeams know,
Self-schooled, self-scanned, self-honoured, self-secure,
Didst tread on earth unguessed at. - Better so!

(d) I have looked upon those brilliant creatures,
And now my heart is sore.
All's changed since I, hearing at twilight,
The first time on this shore

(e) My mother only said Thank God the scorpion picked
on me and spared my children.

SECTION B

Attempt any three of the following questions.

Q3. Compare and contrast Eliot and Yeats as modern poets in the light of the themes and poetic techniques used by both, with special reference to the poems prescribed.

Q4. Critically appreciate one of the following poems.

(a) The Sunne Rising

(b) To a Skylark

(c) Dover Beach

(d) The Unknown Citizen

Q5. Examine Robert Frost as a New England poet.

Q6. Evaluate the poetry of either Sarojini Naidu or Kamala Das with reference to their themes.

EEG-6: UNDERSTANDING POETRY
June, 2020

Note: Question Nos. 1 and 2 are compulsory. Answer any three of the remaining questions.

SECTION A
(Compulsory)

Explain any four of the following passages with reference to the context, supplying brief critical comments : 10 each

**(a) Shall I compare thee to a summer's day ?
Thou art more lovely and more temperate :
Rough words do shake the darling buds of May,
And summer's lease hath all too short a date.**

**(b) She stood in tears amid the alien corn;
The same that oft-times hath
Charmed magic casements, opening on the foam
Of peri lous seas, in faery lands forlorn**

**(c) And thou, who didst the stars and sunbeams know,
Self-schooled, self-scanned, self-honoured, self-secure,
Didst tread on earth unguessed at. - Better so!**

**(d) I have looked upon those brilliant creatures,
And now my heart is sore.
All's changed since I, hearing at twilight,
The first time on this shore**

(e) My mother only said Thank God the scorpion picked on me and spared my children.

SECTION B

Attempt any three of the following questions.

Q3. Compare and contrast Eliot and Yeats as modern poets in the light of the themes and poetic techniques used by both, with special reference to the poems prescribed.

Q4. Critically appreciate one of the following poems.

(a) The Sunne Rising

(b) To a Skylark

(c) Dover Beach
(d) The Unknown Citizen

Q5. Examine Robert Frost as a New England poet.

Q6. Evaluate the poetry of either Sarojini Naidu or Kamala Das with reference to their themes.

Feedback is the breakfast of Champions.

Ken Blanchard

You can Help other students.
"Inform any error or mistake in this book."

We and Universe
will reward you for Your Kind act.

Email at : feedback@gullybaba.com
or
WhatsApp on 9350849407

www.ingramcontent.com/pod-product-compliance
Ingram Content Group UK Ltd.
Pitfield, Milton Keynes, MK11 3LW, UK
UKHW022002190726
13853UKWH00004B/1688

9 789381 638828